Better Homes and Gardens®

budget-friendly meals

WILEY

John Wiley & Sons, Inc

This book is printed on acid-free paper. ♾

Published by John Wiley & Sons, Inc., Hoboken, New Jersey
Published simultaneously in Canada

For general information on our other products and services or for technical support, please contact our Customer Care Department within the United States at (800) 762–2974, outside the United States at (317) 572–3993 or fax (317) 572–4002.

Wiley also publishes its books in a variety of electronic formats. Some content that appears in print may not be available in electronic books. For more information about Wiley products, visit our web site at www.wiley.com.

Library of Congress Cataloging-in-Publication Data is available upon request.

ISBN: 978-0470-54028-2

Printed in the United States of America

10 9 8 7 6 5 4 3 2 1

Cover photo: Beef Fajitas, page 130

Meredith Corporation

Editors: Jan Miller; Lisa Kingsley, Waterbury Publications, Inc.

Contributing Editor: Tricia Laning, Lois White, Waterbury Publications, Inc.

John Wiley & Sons, Inc.

Publisher: Natalie Chapman

Associate Publisher: Jessica Goodman

Executive Editor: Anne Ficklen

Editor: Adam Kowit

Editorial Assistant: Cecily McAndrews

Production Director: Diana Cisek

Manufacturing Manager: Tom Hyland

Design Director: Ken Carlson, Waterbury Publications, Inc.

Associate Design Director: Doug Samuelson, Waterbury Publications, Inc.

Senior Designer: Chad Jewell, Waterbury Publications, Inc.

Production Assistant: Mindy Samuelson, Waterbury Publications, Inc.

Better Homes and Gardens® Test Kitchen

Our seal assures you that every recipe in *Budget-Friendly Meals* has been tested in the Better Homes and Gardens® Test Kitchen. This means that each recipe is practical and reliable and meets our high standards of taste appeal. We guarantee your satisfaction with this book for as long as you own it.

56

Your family is going to LOVE dinner tonight!

When creating recipes for this book, we listened to what families say about the way they live and cook. In e-mail messages, focus groups, and surveys, they say that household budgets are tighter than ever—and that they're busier than ever, with little time to prepare weeknight meals. But time together is precious, and they aren't ready to give up on family dinner and reserve a corner table at the nearest fast food outlet. That's more expensive and less healthful than eating at home.

We know you want to feed your family well and still stay on budget. The recipes in this book call for inexpensive ingredients and create great flavor out of very few of them. Stir-fries, casseroles, soups, sandwiches, main-dish salads—no matter how you prefer to cook, we have easy, delicious recipes to suit your style. If you're a fan of the slow cooker, see "Slow & Simple," beginning on page 126, for recipes for main dishes, soups, sandwiches, and more. For some families, any time of year is grilling season; you can check out our selections "From the Grill," beginning on page 102.

You'll also find side dish and dessert recipes to complete your menu. And speaking of menus, watch throughout this book for boxes of ideas for accompaniments to make the meal. The page opposite has more suggestions.

So choose a recipe, buy the ingredients on your way home, prepare a great meal tonight, and get ready for compliments.

—the editors

{contents}

Cranberry-Glazed
Pork Roast

meaty main dishes

With beef, pork, or lamb as your starting point, you're assured hearty, satisfying eating. Whether you're planning a special-occasion dinner or a weeknight family meal, look here for a recipe that's exactly what you want.

Cranberry-Glazed Pork Roast

Prep: 15 minutes   *Roast:* 1½ hours   *Stand:* 15 minutes
Makes 8 to 10 servings

- ¼ teaspoon salt
- ¼ teaspoon ground black pepper
- ½ teaspoon ground sage
- 1 2½- to 3-pound boneless pork top loin roast (single loin)
- 1 16-ounce can whole or jellied cranberry sauce
- ½ teaspoon finely shredded orange peel
- ⅓ cup orange juice

1. Preheat oven to 325°F. For rub, in a small bowl, stir together salt, pepper, and ¼ teaspoon of the sage. Sprinkle rub evenly over all sides of pork roast; rub in mixture with your fingers. Place roast on rack in a shallow roasting pan. Roast, uncovered, for 1 hour.

2. For sauce, in a medium saucepan, stir together cranberry sauce, orange peel, orange juice, and the remaining ¼ teaspoon sage. Bring to boiling; reduce heat. Simmer, uncovered, about 10 minutes or until mixture has thickened slightly.

3. Spoon about ¼ cup of the sauce over meat. Roast, uncovered, for 30 to 45 minutes more or until done (155°F). Remove from oven. Cover meat loosely with foil; let stand for 15 minutes before slicing. (The temperature of the meat will rise 5°F during standing.) Reheat remaining sauce. Serve warm sauce with meat.

Per Serving: 290 cal., 7 g fat (2 g sat. fat), 77 mg chol., 132 mg sodium, 23 g carbo., 1 g fiber, 31 g pro.

Country Chops and Peppers

Any color of sweet pepper looks appetizing and tastes great with pork chops. If you have more than one kind on hand, feel free to mix them.
Start to Finish: 20 minutes
Makes 4 servings

- 4 pork loin chops, cut ¾ inch thick
   Seasoned salt
   Ground black pepper
   Nonstick cooking spray
- 1 medium sweet pepper, cut into strips
- 1 tablespoon butter
- ⅓ cup Worcestershire sauce for chicken or 2 tablespoons Worcestershire sauce and ¼ cup water

1. Trim fat from chops. Sprinkle chops on both sides with seasoned salt and pepper. Lightly coat a large skillet with cooking spray. Heat skillet over medium-high heat. Add chops and cook for 5 minutes. Turn chops; top with sweet pepper strips. Cover and cook for 5 to 7 minutes more or until chops are done (160°F) and sweet pepper strips are crisp-tender. Remove chops and sweet pepper strips from skillet; keep warm.

2. For sauce, add butter and Worcestershire sauce to hot skillet. Cook over medium heat until mixture thickens slightly, stirring to loosen any brown bits in bottom of skillet. Pour sauce over chops and sweet pepper strips.

Per Serving: 282 cal., 11 g fat (5 g sat. fat), 101 mg chol., 282 mg sodium, 6 g carbo., 1 g fiber, 38 g pro.

Soy and Sesame Pork

To toast sesame seeds, spread them in a single layer in a shallow baking pan and bake in a 350°F oven about 5 minutes or until light golden brown. Watch carefully and stir once or twice so they don't burn.

Prep: 5 minutes   *Marinate:* 4 hours   *Roast:* 20 minutes
Makes 4 servings

1	1-pound pork tenderloin
¼	cup reduced-sodium soy sauce
1	tablespoon ketchup
¼	teaspoon garlic powder
2	to 3 tablespoons sesame seeds, toasted

1. Trim fat from pork. Place pork in a large resealable plastic bag set in a shallow dish. For marinade, in a small bowl, combine soy sauce, ketchup, and garlic powder. Pour marinade over pork. Seal bag; turn to coat pork. Marinate in the refrigerator for 4 to 24 hours, turning bag occasionally.

2. Preheat oven to 425°F. Drain pork, discarding marinade. Place pork on a rack in a shallow roasting pan. Roast for 20 to 30 minutes or until done (160°F). Sprinkle sesame seeds on a piece of foil; carefully roll pork in sesame seeds.

Per Serving: 162 cal., 5 g fat (1 g sat. fat), 73 mg chol., 357 mg sodium, 2 g carbo., 1 g fiber, 25 g pro.

Bacon-Cheese Burgers

The cheese and bacon you usually find on top are stuffed inside these double-decker burgers.

Prep: 15 minutes   *Broil:* 11 minutes
Makes 4 servings

1¼	pounds lean ground beef
8	thin slices Colby and Monterey Jack cheese or cheddar cheese (4 ounces)
4	slices bacon, crisp-cooked and crumbled
4	hamburger buns, split and toasted
¼	cup dairy sour cream onion dip

1. Preheat broiler. Shape the ground beef into eight ¼-inch-thick patties. Place one cheese slice on top of each of four of the patties; sprinkle with crumbled bacon. Place remaining four patties on top of the bacon-and-cheese-topped patties. Seal edges well.

2. Place patties on the unheated rack of a broiler pan. Broil 3 to 4 inches from the heat for 10 to 12 minutes or until done (160°F), turning patties once halfway through cooking. Place remaining four cheese slices on top of patties. Broil for 1 minute more.

3. Meanwhile, spread cut sides of toasted buns with the onion dip. Serve burgers on prepared buns.

Per Serving: 636 cal., 36 g fat (17 g sat. fat), 119 mg chol., 778 mg sodium, 23 g carbo., 1 g fiber, 41 g pro.

Quick Skillet Lasagna

Talk about quick. The most time-consuming part of this recipe is boiling the water for the pasta. After that, a hearty lasagna comes together in minutes.

Start to Finish: 30 minutes
Makes 6 servings

3	cups (6 ounces) dried mafalda (mini lasagna) noodles
12	ounces lean ground beef or bulk pork sausage
1	26- to 27¾-ounce jar tomato-base pasta sauce
1½	cups shredded mozzarella cheese (6 ounces)
¼	cup grated Parmesan cheese (1 ounce)

1. Cook pasta according to package directions; drain.

2. Meanwhile, in a large nonstick skillet, cook meat until brown; drain off fat. Set meat aside. Wipe skillet with paper towel.

3. Spread half of the cooked pasta in the skillet. Cover with half of the sauce. Spoon cooked meat over sauce. Sprinkle with 1 cup of the mozzarella cheese. Top with remaining pasta and sauce. Sprinkle remaining mozzarella cheese and the Parmesan cheese over top.

4. Cover and cook over medium heat for 5 to 7 minutes or until heated through and cheese melts. Remove skillet from heat and let stand, covered, for 1 minute.

Per Serving: 389 cal., 16 g fat (6 g sat. fat), 55 mg chol., 1,045 mg sodium, 30 g carbo., 2 g fiber, 25 g pro.

MAKE IT A MENU
Quick Skillet Lasagna, tossed greens salad with Italian dressing, Easy Apple Crisp (page 190)

Quick Skillet Lasagna

Most lasagnas require considerable time to assemble and bake, but this one cooks *on top of the stove*. Serve it right from the *skillet in which it was cooked*.

Upside-Down Pizza Casserole

Sausage-Cavatelli Skillet

Start to Finish: 30 minutes
Makes 4 servings

   8 ounces dried cavatelli pasta (1¾ cups)
   1 pound bulk Italian sausage or ground beef
   ¾ cup chopped green sweet pepper (1 medium)
       (optional)
   1 20-ounce jar pasta sauce with mushrooms
   1 cup shredded mozzarella cheese (4 ounces)

1. Cook cavatelli according to package directions.
Drain well.

2. Meanwhile, in a large skillet, cook sausage and,
if desired, sweet pepper over medium heat until
sausage is brown. Drain off fat. Stir in pasta sauce;
cook about 2 minutes or until heated through. Stir in
the drained cavatelli. Sprinkle with cheese. Cover
and cook about 2 minutes more or until cheese melts.
*Per Serving: 700 cal., 31 g fat (15 g sat. fat), 96 mg chol.,
1,513 mg sodium, 60 g carbo., 4 g fiber, 33 g pro.*

Upside-Down Pizza Casserole

*Refrigerated biscuits top the ground beef mixture
in this "pizza."*
Prep: 20 minutes   *Bake:* 15 minutes
Makes 10 small or 5 large servings

   1½ pounds lean ground beef
    1 15-ounce can Italian-style tomato sauce
   1½ cups shredded mozzarella cheese (6 ounces)
    1 10-ounce package refrigerated biscuits
        (10 biscuits)

1. Preheat oven to 400°F. In a large skillet, cook
ground beef over medium heat until brown. Drain
off fat. Stir in tomato sauce; heat through. Transfer
beef mixture to a 2-quart rectangular baking dish
or 10-inch deep-dish pie plate. Sprinkle with cheese.
Flatten each biscuit with your hands; arrange the
biscuits on top of cheese.

2. Bake, uncovered, about 15 minutes or until biscuits
are golden.
*Per Small Serving: 321 cal., 20 g fat (8 g sat. fat), 58 mg chol.,
551 mg sodium, 15 g carbo., 1 g fiber, 17 g pro.*

GROUND MEAT
When purchasing ground meat, check the label
for a "sell by" date. The package should be
tightly wrapped and without holes. Store it in your
refrigerator's coldest section for up to 2 days.
Freeze for longer storage; use within 4 months.
Thaw frozen ground meat in the refrigerator and
cook as soon as possible.

Pork Skillet with Sauerkraut and Apples

Start to Finish: 25 minutes

Makes 4 servings

- 1   12- to 16-ounce pork tenderloin
- 1   tablespoon olive oil
- 1   14.5-ounce can sauerkraut, rinsed and well drained
- 1   large apple, cored and thinly sliced
- ¼   cup apple juice

1. Trim fat from pork. Cut pork crosswise into 12 slices. Place one slice, cut side down, between two pieces of plastic wrap. Using a flat side of a meat mallet, pound pork from center to edges to ½-inch thickness. Repeat with remaining pork slices.

2. In a 12-inch nonstick skillet, heat oil over medium-high heat. Add pork; cook for 6 to 8 minutes or until slightly pink in the center (160°F), turning once halfway through cooking. Reduce heat to medium if oil starts to spatter. Transfer pork to a serving platter; cover to keep warm.

3. Add sauerkraut, apple slices, and apple juice to hot skillet. Cover and cook over medium heat for 4 to 6 minutes or just until apple slices are tender, stirring occasionally. Serve apple mixture with pork.

Per Serving: 200 cal., 8 g fat (2 g sat. fat), 47 mg chol., 695 mg sodium, 12 g carbo., 4 g fiber, 21 g pro.

Prosciutto-Wrapped Beef

Prosciutto may seem a little pricey, but because it's so thinly sliced and intensely flavored, a little goes a long way and makes a simple dish special.

Prep: 15 minutes   *Broil:* 12 minutes

Makes 4 servings

- 1   ounce sliced prosciutto, chopped
- 1   small carrot, shredded
- 1   green onion, sliced
- 4   beef tenderloin steaks, cut 1 inch thick
- 4   thin slices prosciutto

1. Preheat broiler. For stuffing, combine chopped prosciutto, carrot, and green onion. Cut a horizontal pocket in each steak by cutting from one side almost to, but not through, the other side. Fill pockets with stuffing. Cut the sliced prosciutto into 1-inch-wide strips; wrap prosciutto strips around each steak. Secure with wooden toothpicks.

2. Place steaks on the unheated rack of a broiler pan. Broil 3 to 4 inches from the heat until desired doneness, turning once. Allow 12 to 14 minutes for medium rare (145°F) and 15 to 18 minutes for medium (160°F).

Per Serving: 296 cal., 13 g fat (5 g sat. fat), 115 mg chol., 516 mg sodium, 1 g carbo., 0 g fiber, 40 g pro.

> **MAKE IT A MENU**
> Prosciutto-Wrapped Beef, Mixed Green Salad with Pears (page 163), buttered whole wheat rolls, Ginger Peach Freeze (page 190)

Italian Pizza Burgers

Don't rely on the internal color of a burger to determine doneness. A beef, veal, lamb, or pork patty cooked to 160°F is safe regardless of color. Insert an instant-read thermometer into the side of the patty to a depth of 2 to 3 inches.

Prep: 15 minutes   *Broil:* 11 minutes

Makes 4 servings

- 4   3¾-ounce purchased refrigerated uncooked hamburger patties*
- 4   ¾-inch-thick slices sourdough bread
- 1   cup purchased mushroom pasta sauce
- 1   cup shredded provolone or mozzarella cheese (4 ounces)
- 2   tablespoons thinly sliced fresh basil

1. Preheat broiler. Place the hamburger patties on the unheated rack of a broiler pan. Broil 3 to 4 inches from heat for 10 to 12 minutes or until done (160°F), turning once halfway through broiling. Add the bread slices to broiler pan for the last 2 to 3 minutes of broiling; turn once to toast evenly.

2. Meanwhile, in a medium saucepan, heat the pasta sauce over medium heat until bubbly, stirring occasionally. Place patties on bread slices. Spoon pasta sauce over patties; sprinkle with cheese. Place on the rack of the broiler pan. Broil for 1 to 2 minutes more or until cheese melts. Top with basil.

*Note: If refrigerated uncooked hamburger patties are not available, shape 1 pound ground beef into four ½-inch-thick patties.

Per Serving: 504 cal., 30 g fat (13 g sat. fat), 96 mg chol., 815 mg sodium, 27 g carbo., 2 g fiber, 30 g pro.

Jamaican Pork
Stir-Fry

Dijon Pork Salad

Prep: 10 minutes   *Roast:* 20 minutes
Makes 4 servings

1	1-pound pork tenderloin
	Salt and ground black pepper
2/3	cup bottled Dijon-lime salad dressing or oil and vinegar salad dressing
8	cups torn mixed salad greens
2	ounces Gouda or white cheddar cheese, cut into bite-size strips
12	cherry tomatoes, quartered

1. Preheat oven to 425°F. Trim fat from pork. Place pork on a rack in a shallow roasting pan. Sprinkle with salt and pepper. Brush pork with 2 tablespoons of the salad dressing. Roast, uncovered, for 20 to 30 minutes or until done (160°F).

Jamaican Pork Stir-Fry

Start to Finish: 20 minutes
Makes 4 servings

1	tablespoon cooking oil
1	16-ounce package frozen sweet pepper and onion stir-fry vegetables
12	ounces pork strips for stir-frying
2	to 3 teaspoons Jamaican jerk seasoning
1/2	cup bottled plum sauce
	Soy sauce (optional)
	Peanuts (optional)
	Hot cooked rice

1. In a wok or large skillet, heat oil over medium-high heat. Add frozen vegetables; cook and stir for 5 to 7 minutes or until vegetables are crisp-tender. Remove vegetables from wok.

2. Toss pork with jerk seasoning; add to wok. Add more oil if necessary. Cook and stir for 2 to 5 minutes or until pork is no longer pink.

3. Add plum sauce to wok; return vegetables. Gently toss to coat; heat through. If desired, season with soy sauce and sprinkle with peanuts. Serve over rice.
Per Serving: 357 cal., 9 g fat (2 g sat. fat), 54 mg chol., 405 mg sodium, 45 g carbo., 2 g fiber, 22 g pro.

2. Meanwhile, arrange salad greens on four salad plates. Top with cheese and tomatoes. Thinly slice pork; arrange pork slices on salads. Serve with remaining salad dressing.
Per Serving: 336 cal., 24 g fat (5 g sat. fat), 71 mg chol., 535 mg sodium, 5 g carbo., 2 g fiber, 23 g pro.

Steak with Creamy Onion Sauce

Sweet onion varieties include Vidalia, Maui, and Walla Walla. This steakhouse favorite is a snap to prepare at home—and is much less expensive than a meal out.

Prep: 10 minutes   *Broil:* 17 minutes
Makes 4 servings

1	medium sweet onion, thinly sliced
4	6-ounce beef ribeye steaks, cut 1 inch thick
1	tablespoon Mediterranean seasoning blend or lemon-pepper seasoning
1	8-ounce carton dairy sour cream
2	tablespoons drained capers

1. Preheat broiler. Place onion slices in a single layer on the rack of an unheated broiler pan. Broil 3 to 4 inches from heat for 5 minutes; turn onions. Meanwhile, sprinkle steaks with 1½ teaspoons of the seasoning blend. Place steaks on the broiler pan rack with onions. Broil steaks and onions about 5 minutes or until onions are browned. Remove onions to a cutting board. Continue to broil steaks until desired doneness, turning once. Allow 7 to 9 minutes more for medium rare (145°F) or 10 to 13 minutes more for medium (160°F).

2. Meanwhile, for sauce, coarsely chop onions. In a small saucepan, combine onion, sour cream, capers, and remaining 1½ teaspoons seasoning blend. Cook over medium-low heat until heated through (do not boil).

3. Transfer steaks to serving plates. Spoon sauce over steaks.
Per Serving: 398 cal., 22 g fat (11 g sat. fat), 106 mg chol., 472 mg sodium, 4 g carbo., 0 g fiber, 39 g pro.

MAKE IT A MENU
Jamaican Pork Stir-Fry, hot cooked rice, Peach-Blueberry Crisp (page 178)

Oven-Fried
Pork Chops

Peppered Tenderloins

Start to Finish: 15 minutes
Makes 4 servings

4	beef tenderloin steaks, cut 1 inch thick
1	teaspoon coarsely ground black pepper
1	tablespoon butter or margarine
1	ounce Asiago cheese, shaved
¼	cup beef broth

1. Rub steaks with pepper. In a large skillet, melt butter over medium-high heat. Add steaks. Reduce heat to medium; cook for 10 to 13 minutes or until desired doneness (145°F for medium rare or 160°F for medium), turning once. Transfer steaks to a platter, reserving drippings. Top steaks with cheese; keep warm.

2. Add beef broth to skillet. Cook and stir until bubbly to loosen any browned bits in skillet. Pour over steaks.
Per Serving: 294 cal., 18 g fat (8 g sat. fat), 103 mg chol., 225 mg sodium, 1 g carbo., 0 g fiber, 31 g pro.

Oven-Fried Pork Chops

Prep: 10 minutes   *Bake:* 20 minutes
Makes 4 servings

1	egg
2	tablespoons milk
1	cup packaged corn bread stuffing mix
4	pork loin chops, cut ½ inch thick (1 to 1½ pounds total)
1	20-ounce package frozen roasted russet potato pieces

1. Preheat oven to 425°F. In a shallow dish, beat egg with a fork; stir in milk. Place dry stuffing mix in another shallow dish. Trim fat from chops. Dip chops into egg mixture. Coat both sides with stuffing mix. Arrange pork chops in a single layer on one side of a 15×10×1-inch baking pan. Add potato pieces to the other side of pan, mounding potatoes as needed to fit.

2. Bake, uncovered, about 20 minutes or until pork is done (160°F) and potatoes are light brown and crisp, turning pork and stirring potatoes once.
Per Serving: 443 cal., 17 g fat (4 g sat. fat), 88 mg chol., 1,251 mg sodium, 51 g carbo., 2 g fiber, 20 g pro.

MAKE IT A MENU
Oven-Fried Pork Chops, green beans with garlic butter, Angel Food Cake with Lemon Cream and Berries (page 190)

Ham and Asparagus Pasta

Start to Finish: 20 minutes

Makes 4 servings

- 4 cups dried bow tie, rotini, or other medium-size pasta
- 1 10-ounce package frozen cut asparagus or broccoli
- 8 ounces sliced cooked ham, cut into thin strips
- 1 8-ounce tub cream cheese spread with chives and onion
- ⅓ cup milk

1. Cook pasta according to package directions, adding the frozen asparagus for the last 5 minutes and the ham the last 1 minute of the cooking time. Drain and return to the pan.

2. In a medium bowl, whisk together cream cheese and milk until smooth; add to the pasta mixture in the pan. Stir gently over medium heat until heated through. Add additional milk, if necessary, to reach desired consistency. Serve immediately.

Per Serving: 459 cal., 24 g fat (15 g sat. fat), 89 mg chol., 1,001 mg sodium, 38 g carbo., 3 g fiber, 19 g pro.

Pork Loin with Vegetables

If you don't have apricot preserves, you can make this succulent pork dish with peach or pineapple preserves.

Prep: 15 minutes   *Roast:* 35 minutes   *Stand:* 15 minutes

Makes 4 servings

- 12 ounces packaged, peeled baby carrots (2½ cups)
- 12 ounces small new potatoes, quartered
- 1 12- to 16-ounce pork tenderloin
- ⅔ cup apricot preserves
- ¼ cup white wine vinegar or white vinegar

1. Preheat oven to 425°F. In a medium saucepan, cook the carrots and potatoes in small amount of boiling water for 4 minutes; drain. Meanwhile, place the tenderloin in a 13×9×2-inch baking pan. Arrange carrots and potatoes around meat. Roast, uncovered, for 20 minutes.

2. In a small bowl, stir together the preserves and vinegar; brush some of the mixture over meat. Drizzle remaining preserves mixture over vegetables; toss to coat. Roast, uncovered, about 15 minutes more or until center of meat registers 155°F. Stir vegetables.

3. Loosely cover meat and vegetables and let stand for 15 minutes. (Temperature of meat will rise 5°F to 10°F.) Transfer meat to a platter; slice meat. Using a slotted spoon, transfer vegetables to the platter. Drizzle pan juices over meat and vegetables.

Per Serving: 365 cal., 2 g fat (1 g sat. fat), 50 mg chol., 84 mg sodium, 62 g carbo., 5 g fiber, 23 g pro.

MAKE IT A MENU
Basil-Garlic Sirloin Roast, roasted potatoes, Mixed Greens Salad with Pears, (page 163), Chocolate Ricotta Mousse (page 184)

Basil-Garlic Sirloin Roast

Though sirloin is a little more expensive than other cuts of meat, it makes terrific leftovers.

Prep: 15 minutes   *Roast:* 50 minutes   *Stand:* 10 minutes

Makes 10 to 12 servings

- 1 3- to 3½-pound boneless beef sirloin roast, cut 1¾ inches thick
- ¼ teaspoon salt
- ¼ teaspoon ground black pepper
- 2 cups lightly packed fresh basil leaves, snipped
- 8 to 10 cloves garlic, minced, or 2 tablespoons bottled minced garlic
- 2 teaspoons olive oil

1. Preheat oven to 425°F. Make five or six 5-inch-long slits along the top of the roast, cutting almost through it. Sprinkle roast with salt and pepper. In a small bowl, combine basil and garlic; stuff into slits in roast. Tie roast with clean heavy-duty string to hold slits closed. Drizzle roast with olive oil.

2. Place meat on a rack in a shallow roasting pan. Insert a meat thermometer into center of meat. Roast for 15 minutes. Reduce oven temperature to 350°F. Roast for 35 to 45 minutes more or until desired doneness (160°F for medium). Loosely cover and let stand 10 minutes before slicing.

Per Serving: 255 cal., 13 g fat (5 g sat. fat), 91 mg chol., 121 mg sodium, 1 g carbo., 0 g fiber, 31 g pro.

Hot Italian Beef Salad

Start to Finish: 20 minutes
Makes 4 servings

- 12 ounces beef flank steak or beef top round steak, cut 1 inch thick
- 6 cups torn mixed salad greens
- 3 teaspoons olive oil or salad oil
- 1 medium red or green sweet pepper, cut into bite-size strips
- ½ cup bottled Italian salad dressing or red wine vinegar and oil salad dressing
  Coarsely ground black pepper

1. Trim fat from steak. Cut steak into thin, bite-size strips. Arrange salad greens on four salad plates; set aside.

2. In a large skillet, heat 2 teaspoons of the oil over medium-high heat; add sweet pepper to skillet. Cook and stir for 1 to 2 minutes or until nearly crisp-tender.

3. Add the remaining 1 teaspoon oil to the skillet; add steak strips. Cook and stir for 2 to 3 minutes or until desired doneness. Add salad dressing to skillet. Cook and stir until heated through.

4. Spoon beef mixture over the salad greens. Sprinkle with pepper.

Per Serving: 317 cal., 24 g fat (5 g sat. fat), 34 mg chol., 284 mg sodium, 7 g carbo., 2 g fiber, 20 g pro.

Maple-Pecan-Glazed Pork Chops

Start to Finish: 15 minutes
Makes 4 servings

- 4 boneless pork loin chops, cut ¾ inch thick (about 1 pound)
  Salt and ground black pepper
- 4 tablespoons butter or margarine, softened
- 2 tablespoons pure maple syrup or maple-flavored syrup
- ⅓ cup chopped pecans, toasted

1. Trim fat from chops. Sprinkle chops with salt and pepper. In a 12-inch skillet, melt 1 tablespoon of the butter over medium-high heat. Add chops; cook for 8 to 12 minutes or until done (160°F), turning once. Transfer chops to a serving platter.

2. Meanwhile, in a small bowl, combine the remaining 3 tablespoons butter and the maple syrup. Spread maple syrup mixture evenly over the cooked chops and let stand about 1 minute or until melted. Sprinkle with toasted pecans.

Per Serving: 333 cal., 23 g fat (10 g sat. fat), 98 mg chol., 310 mg sodium, 8 g carbo., 1 g fiber, 23 g pro.

Stroganoff-Sauced Beef Roast

Start to Finish: 30 minutes
Makes 3 or 4 servings

- 1 16-ounce package refrigerated cooked beef pot roast with gravy
- 2 cups fresh shiitake, cremini, or button mushrooms
- ½ cup dairy sour cream French onion-flavor dip
- 2 cups hot cooked noodles

1. Transfer beef with gravy to a large skillet (leave meat whole). Remove stems from shiitake mushrooms; halve or quarter mushrooms. Add mushrooms to skillet. Cover and cook over medium-low heat about 15 minutes or until heated through, stirring mushrooms once and turning roast over halfway through cooking time.

2. Using a wooden spoon, break meat into bite-size pieces. Stir onion dip into meat mixture; heat through (do not boil). Stir in hot cooked noodles.

Per Serving: 488 cal., 17 g fat (9 g sat. fat), 115 mg chol., 771 mg sodium, 48 g carbo., 3 g fiber, 38 g pro.

Dress up a package of *ready-to-go beef pot roast* with a quick mushroom-studded sour cream dip and toss it all with hot noodles. Now that's *comfort food*.

Stroganoff-Sauced Beef Roast

Beef Steaks with Blue Cheese and Walnuts

Blue cheese and steak are a popular restaurant combination, but it's incredibly easy to make at home. Use the rest of the blue cheese in a salad with sliced apple or pear.

Start to Finish: 20 minutes

Makes 4 servings

4	beef tenderloin steaks, cut 1 inch thick
½	teaspoon garlic salt
	Nonstick cooking spray
⅓	cup dairy sour cream
3	tablespoons crumbled blue cheese
3	tablespoons chopped walnuts, toasted

1. Sprinkle both sides of steaks with garlic salt. Lightly coat a large skillet with cooking spray. Heat skillet over medium-high heat. Add steaks. Reduce heat to medium and cook for 10 to 13 minutes or until desired doneness (145°F for medium rare or 160°F for medium), turning steaks halfway through cooking. Transfer steaks to a serving platter.

2. Meanwhile, in a small bowl, stir together sour cream and blue cheese; spoon on top of steaks. Sprinkle with walnuts.

Per Serving: 264 cal., 17 g fat (6 g sat. fat), 81 mg chol., 255 mg sodium, 2 g carbo., 0 g fiber, 26 g pro.

Beef and Noodle Casserole

Prep: 15 minutes   *Bake:* 30 minutes   *Stand:* 5 minutes

Makes 4 servings

1	pound lean ground beef
½	cup milk
½	of an 8-ounce tub cream cheese spread with chives and onion (½ cup)
½	cup shredded carrot (1 medium)
1	4.6-ounce package vermicelli with garlic and olive oil or one 4.8-ounce package angel hair pasta with herbs
1½	cups boiling water

1. Preheat oven to 350°F. Grease a 1½-quart casserole; set aside. In a large skillet, cook ground beef until brown. Drain off fat.

2. Meanwhile, in prepared casserole, gradually whisk milk into cream cheese until smooth. Stir in carrot and seasoning packet from pasta. Stir in browned meat.

Break pasta from pasta mix into 1-inch pieces; stir into meat mixture.

3. Slowly pour boiling water over meat mixture. Bake, covered, for 30 to 35 minutes or until noodles are tender, stirring twice. Let stand, covered, for 5 minutes. Stir before serving.

Per Serving: 463 cal., 25 g fat (13 g sat. fat), 101 mg chol., 619 mg sodium, 28 g carbo., 2 g fiber, 28 g pro.

MAKE IT A MENU
Mexican Beef and Tortillas with fresh tomato salsa, Fruit and Broccoli Salad (page 166), Shortcut Malted Chocolate Cake (page 177)

Mexican Beef and Tortillas

Put a package of refrigerated beef pot roast in your grocery cart. It's ready to heat and serve right from the package, plus it works in easy fix-ups like this one.

Start to Finish: 20 minutes

Makes 4 servings

8	6-inch corn tortillas
1	17-ounce package refrigerated beef pot roast with juices
1	14.5-ounce can diced tomatoes with green chiles, undrained
1	green sweet pepper, cut into strips
1	lime, cut into wedges
	Dairy sour cream (optional)
	Fresh cilantro sprigs (optional)

1. Wrap tortillas in microwave-safe paper towels. Microwave on 100% power (high) for 45 to 60 seconds or until warm. Cover; set aside.

2. Microwave beef according to package directions. Meanwhile, place undrained tomatoes in small saucepan; heat through.

3. Remove meat, reserving juices. Cut into slices. Serve on warmed tortillas with tomatoes and green pepper strips. Drizzle with reserved juices. Pass lime wedges and, if desired, sour cream and cilantro.

Per Serving: 319 cal., 10 g fat (5 g sat. fat), 64 mg chol., 857 mg sodium, 34 g carbo., 5 g fiber, 27 g pro.

Mexican Beef
and Tortillas

Steak and Bake

By turning around the proportions of the classic steak and potato dinner we've made this delicious meal inexpensive enough for a weeknight.

Prep: 20 minutes   *Broil:* 15 minutes   *Stand:* 5 minutes
Makes 4 servings

 4   medium baking potatoes
12   to 16 ounces boneless beef sirloin steak, cut 1 inch thick
 2   cups fresh baby spinach
¾   cup bottled blue cheese salad dressing
 1   small red onion, cut in thin wedges

1. Wash potatoes; pierce with fork. Arrange potatoes on a microwave-safe plate in spoke formation, leaving 1 inch between potatoes. Microwave on high (100% power), uncovered, for 14 to 18 minutes or until tender. (Or bake potatoes in a 425°F oven for 40 to 60 minutes.) Let stand for 5 minutes.

2. Meanwhile, preheat broiler. Trim fat from steak. Place meat on the unheated rack of a broiler pan. Broil 3 to 4 inches from heat until desired doneness. Allow 15 to 17 minutes for medium rare (145°F) or 20 to 22 minutes for medium (160°F), turning once halfway through broiling. Transfer meat to cutting board; let stand for 5 minutes.

3. To serve, roll each potato gently under your hand. Cut an "X" in top of potato. Press in and up on ends of potato. Cut steak into bite-size strips. Top potatoes with beef strips and spinach; drizzle with dressing. Top with onion wedges.

Grill Method: Prepare steak as above. For a charcoal grill, grill meat on the rack of an uncovered grill directly over medium coals for 18 to 22 minutes for medium doneness (160°F), turning once. (For a gas grill, preheat grill. Reduce heat to medium. Place meat on grill rack over heat. Cover and grill as above.) Remove from grill. Serve as above.

Per Serving: 580 cal., 35 g fat (9 g sat. fat), 65 mg chol., 577 mg sodium, 35 g carbo., 4 g fiber, 32 g pro.

Thai Beef Stir-Fry

Start to Finish: 15 minutes
Makes 4 servings

 4   ounces dried rice noodles
 2   tablespoons cooking oil
 1   16-ounce package frozen sweet pepper and onion stir-fry vegetables
12   ounces beef strips for stir-frying
½   cup bottled Thai peanut stir-fry sauce

1. Prepare the noodles according to package directions. Drain and set aside.

2. In a large skillet, heat 1 tablespoon of the oil over medium-high heat. Add the stir-fry vegetables; cook and stir for 2 to 3 minutes or until tender. Drain; place stir-fry vegetables in a bowl.

3. In the same skillet, stir-fry beef strips in remaining 1 tablespoon hot oil for 2 to 3 minutes or until desired doneness. Return vegetables to skillet; add sauce. Stir to combine; heat through. Serve over noodles.

Per Serving: 404 cal., 16 g fat (4 g sat. fat), 50 mg chol., 597 mg sodium, 39 g carbo., 3 g fiber, 23 g pro.

Smoked Pork Chop Skillet

Start to Finish: 25 minutes
Makes 4 servings

 4   cooked smoked pork chops, cut ¾ inch thick
 1   16-ounce package frozen French-style green beans
¼   cup water
1½   teaspoons snipped fresh sage or ½ teaspoon dried leaf sage, crushed
½   cup balsamic vinegar

1. Preheat a large nonstick skillet over medium heat. Add pork chops; cook for 3 to 5 minutes on each side or until lightly browned. Remove from skillet; keep warm. Add beans, water, and sage to skillet; return chops to skillet. Cover and cook over medium heat for 5 minutes.

2. Meanwhile, in a small saucepan, boil balsamic vinegar gently about 5 minutes or until reduced to ¼ cup. Brush chops with vinegar; drizzle remaining vinegar over the bean mixture.

Per Serving: 257 cal., 14 g fat (5 g sat. fat), 47 mg chol., 749 mg sodium, 18 g carbo., 3 g fiber, 17 g pro.

Mu Shu–Style Pork Roll-Ups

Asian flavor meets Mexican tortillas—the result is a satisfying supper that's ready in minutes.

Start to Finish: 20 minutes
Makes 4 servings

- 4   10-inch flour tortillas
- 1   teaspoon toasted sesame oil
- 12   ounces pork strips for stir-frying
- 2   cups frozen stir-fry vegetables (any combination)
- ¼   cup bottled plum or hoisin sauce

1. Preheat oven to 350°F. Wrap tortillas tightly in foil. Heat in preheated oven for 10 minutes to soften. (Or wrap tortillas in white, microwave-safe paper towels; microwave on 100% power [high] for 15 to 30 seconds or until tortillas are softened.)

2. Meanwhile, in a large skillet, heat sesame oil over medium-high heat. Add pork strips; stir-fry for 2 to 3 minutes or until no longer pink. Add stir-fry vegetables. Cook and stir for 3 to 4 minutes or until vegetables are crisp-tender.

3. Spread each tortilla with 1 tablespoon of the plum sauce; place one-fourth of the meat mixture just below the center of each tortilla. Fold the bottom edge of each tortilla up and over the filling. Fold in the sides until they meet; roll up over the filling.

Per Serving: 302 cal., 8 g fat (2 g sat. fat), 53 mg chol., 311 mg sodium, 34 g carbo., 2 g fiber, 22 g pro.

Pork and Green Beans

Cashews are the perfect finishing touch, adding a pleasantly nutty taste to the pork and green beans.

Start to Finish: 35 minutes
Makes 4 servings

- 1   tablespoon toasted sesame oil
- 2   cloves garlic, minced, or 1 teaspoon bottled minced garlic
- 16   ounces fresh green beans, trimmed
    Salt and ground black pepper
- 2   tablespoons cashews, coarsely chopped
- 1   16-ounce pork tenderloin

1. In a 12-inch skillet, heat oil over medium-high heat. Add the garlic; cook and stir for 15 seconds. Add green beans. Cover and cook for 10 to 12 minutes or until beans are crisp-tender, stirring occasionally. Season

to taste with salt and pepper. Transfer beans to a serving platter and sprinkle with cashews. Keep warm.

2. Meanwhile, cut tenderloin crosswise into eight slices. Place one slice, cut side down, between two pieces of plastic wrap. Using the flat side of a meat mallet, pound meat to ¼- to ½-inch thickness. Repeat with remaining slices. Sprinkle lightly with salt and pepper.

3. Add pork slices to the skillet. Cook, uncovered, over medium-high heat for 4 to 6 minutes or until pork is slightly pink in the center (160°F), turning once halfway through cooking. Serve pork with green beans.

Per Serving: 248 cal., 12 g fat (3 g sat. fat), 62 mg chol., 203 mg sodium, 9 g carbo., 4 g fiber, 27 g pro.

Maple Pork and Apples

Start to Finish: 20 minutes
Makes 4 servings

- 4   pork loin chops, cut ½ inch thick (about 1¾ pounds)
    Salt and ground black pepper
- 2   tablespoons butter or margarine
- 12   baby carrots with tops, halved lengthwise
- 1   medium apple, sliced crosswise and seeds removed
- ⅓   cup pure maple syrup

1. Sprinkle chops with salt and pepper. In a large skillet, melt butter over medium heat; add chops. Cook for 2 minutes, turning once. Reduce heat to medium-low. Add carrots, apples, and maple syrup. Cover and simmer about 8 minutes or until chops are done (160°F).

2. Using a slotted spoon, transfer chops, carrots, and apple slices to a platter. Bring syrup mixture to boiling. Boil gently, uncovered, for 1 to 2 minutes or until thickened. Pour over chops.

Per Serving: 451 cal., 19 g fat (8 g sat. fat), 124 mg chol., 447 mg sodium, 25 g carbo., 1 g fiber, 44 g pro.

MAKE IT A MENU
Maple Pork and Apples, Honey and Poppy Seed Biscuits (page 163), Banana Split Trifles (page 178)

Maple Pork
and Apples

When checking the *doneness of pork chops*,
you'll get a more accurate reading by inserting an
instant-read thermometer into the edge of the chops.

One-Pot Spaghetti

One-Pot Spaghetti

Cooking the pasta in the tomato sauce rather than on its own saves on cleanup.

Start to Finish: 40 minutes
Makes 4 servings

8	ounces lean ground beef or bulk pork sausage
1	cup sliced fresh mushrooms or one 4-ounce can (drained weight) sliced mushrooms, drained
½	cup chopped onion (1 medium)
1	clove garlic, minced
1	14-ounce can chicken broth or beef broth
1¾	cups water
1	6-ounce can tomato paste
1	teaspoon dried Italian seasoning, crushed
¼	teaspoon ground black pepper
6	ounces dried spaghetti, broken
¼	cup grated Parmesan cheese

1. In a large saucepan, cook ground beef, fresh mushrooms (if using), onion, and garlic over medium-high heat until meat is brown and onion is tender. Drain off fat.

2. Stir in drained canned mushrooms (if using), broth, the water, tomato paste, Italian seasoning, and pepper. Bring to boiling.

3. Add broken spaghetti, a little at a time, stirring constantly. Return to boiling; reduce heat. Boil gently, uncovered, for 17 to 20 minutes or until spaghetti is tender and sauce is desired consistency, stirring frequently. Sprinkle each serving with cheese.

Per Serving: 394 cal., 15 g total fat (6 g sat. fat), 39 mg chol., 926 mg sodium, 44 g carbo., 4 g fiber, 22 g pro.

GARLIC OPTIONS

The following amounts of garlic are equivalent and can be substituted for each other in most recipes: One minced fresh garlic clove equals 1/2 teaspoon of bottled minced garlic, 1/2 teaspoon of garlic power, or 1/2 teaspoon of bottled, dried minced garlic.

Easy Shepherd's Pie

In a time crunch? Substitute refrigerated mashed potatoes for the topper of this family-pleasing dish.

Prep: 30 minutes *Bake:* 25 minutes

Makes 8 servings

- 2   pounds lean ground beef
- ¼   cup all-purpose flour
- 1   envelope (½ of a 2.2-ounce package) onion soup mix
- 1   10.75-ounce can condensed cream of mushroom soup
- 1   8-ounce carton dairy sour cream
- ¾   cup water
- 1   tablespoon ketchup
- 1½ cups water
- ¼   cup butter or margarine
- ½   teaspoon salt
- 2   cups packaged instant mashed potato flakes
- ½   cup milk
- 2   eggs, lightly beaten
- 1   cup all-purpose flour
- 2   teaspoons baking powder

1. Preheat oven to 425°F. In a very large skillet, cook ground beef over medium-high heat until brown. Drain off fat. Stir in the ¼ cup flour and the dry soup mix. Stir in mushroom soup, sour cream, the ¾ cup water, and the ketchup. Cook until heated through, stirring occasionally.

2. Meanwhile, in a medium saucepan, combine the 1½ cups water, the butter, and salt. Bring to boiling; remove from heat. Stir in potato flakes and milk. Stir in eggs, the 1 cup flour, and the baking powder.

3. Transfer meat mixture to an ungreased 3-quart rectangular baking dish. Spoon potato mixture in mounds on top of meat mixture. Bake, uncovered, about 25 minutes or until potatoes are golden brown.

Per Serving: 465 cal., 24 g total fat (11 g sat. fat), 143 mg chol., 911 mg sodium, 32 g carbo., 1 g fiber, 30 g pro.

Norwegian Meatballs

Serve the mushroom-sauced meatballs over rice or buttered noodles.

Prep: 20 minutes *Bake:* 30 minutes

Makes 5 or 6 servings

- 2   eggs, lightly beaten
- ½   cup milk
- ⅔   cup crushed saltine crackers (about 18 crackers)
- ⅓   cup finely chopped onion (1 small)
- ½   teaspoon celery salt
- ½   teaspoon ground nutmeg
- ½   teaspoon ground black pepper
- 2   pounds lean ground beef
- 1   10.75-ounce can condensed cream of mushroom soup
- ¾   cup milk

1. Preheat oven to 350°F. Grease a 3-quart rectangular baking dish; set aside.

2. In a large bowl, combine eggs and the ½ cup milk. Stir in crackers, onion, celery salt, ¼ teaspoon of the nutmeg, and the pepper. Add ground beef; mix well. Shape meat mixture into 20 meatballs. Arrange meatballs in the prepared baking dish. Bake about 30 minutes or until meatballs are done (160°F).

3. For sauce, in a medium saucepan, combine soup, the ¾ cup milk, and the remaining ¼ teaspoon nutmeg. Cook and stir over medium heat until heated through.

4. To serve, transfer meatballs to a serving bowl. Spoon sauce over meatballs.

Per Serving: 469 cal., 26 g total fat (10 g sat. fat), 204 mg chol., 842 mg sodium, 17 g carbo., 1 g fiber, 39 g pro.

Cheeseburger and Fries Casserole

Prep: 15 minutes *Bake:* 45 minutes
Makes 8 to 10 servings

- 2   pounds lean ground beef
- 1   10.75-ounce can condensed golden mushroom soup
- 1   10.75-ounce can condensed cheddar cheese soup
- 1   20-ounce package frozen french-fried crinkle-cut potatoes
  Toppings such as ketchup, pickles, mustard, and/or chopped tomato (optional)

1. Preheat oven to 350°F. In a large skillet cook beef, half at a time, over medium-high heat until brown. Transfer to an ungreased 3-quart baking dish.

2. In a medium bowl, combine mushroom soup and cheese soup; spread over meat. Sprinkle with potatoes.

3. Bake, uncovered, for 45 to 55 minutes or until potatoes are golden brown. Serve with toppings.
Per Serving: 348 cal., 18 g total fat (6 g sat. fat), 78 mg chol., 654 mg sodium, 24 g carbo., 2 g fiber, 24 g pro.

Cajun Fried Pork with Pineapple Sauce

Start to Finish: 25 minutes
Makes 4 servings

- ⅓   cup pineapple preserves
- 1   teaspoon Dijon-style mustard
- 1   teaspoon soy sauce
- 4   boneless pork loin chops, cut 1 inch thick
- ⅓   cup half-and-half or light cream
- ⅔   cup all-purpose flour
- 1   tablespoon Cajun seasoning
- ¼   teaspoon ground black pepper
- 2   tablespoons cooking oil

1. In a small bowl, combine preserves, mustard, and soy sauce. Place each chop between 2 pieces of plastic wrap. Pound with flat side of meat mallet to ½-inch thickness. Remove plastic wrap.

2. Pour half-and-half into a shallow dish. In another dish, combine flour, Cajun seasoning, and pepper. Dip meat in half-and-half, then in flour, turning to coat.

3. In a 12-inch skillet, heat oil over medium-high heat. Add meat; reduce heat to medium. Cook, uncovered, for 6 to 8 minutes or until meat is slightly pink in center (160°F), turning once. Serve with preserves mixture.
Per Serving: 373 cal., 16 g total fat (5 g sat. fat), 60 mg chol., 325 mg sodium, 37 g carbo., 1 g fiber, 19 g pro.

Meatball Lasagna

Use purchased frozen meatballs in this quick-to-assemble family favorite.
Prep: 25 minutes *Bake:* 45 minutes *Stand:* 15 minutes
Makes 8 servings

- 9   dried lasagna noodles
- ½   of a 15-ounce carton ricotta cheese
- 1½   cups shredded mozzarella cheese (6 ounces)
- ¼   cup grated Parmesan cheese
- 1   16-ounce package (32) frozen cooked Italian-style meatballs, thawed
- 1   26- or 28-ounce jar tomato pasta sauce

1. Preheat oven to 375°F. Cook lasagna noodles according to package directions; drain. Rinse with cold water; drain again. Place noodles in a single layer on a piece of foil; set aside.

2. Meanwhile, for filling, in a small bowl, stir together ricotta cheese, 1 cup of the mozzarella cheese, and the Parmesan cheese; set aside. In a medium bowl, stir together meatballs and about 1 cup of the pasta sauce.

3. To assemble, spread about ½ cup of the remaining pasta sauce over the bottom of an ungreased 2-quart square baking dish. Layer 3 of the cooked noodles in the dish, trimming or overlapping as necessary to fit. Spoon meatball mixture over noodles. Layer 3 more noodles over meatball mixture. Spread half of the remaining pasta sauce and all of the ricotta mixture over noodles. Top with the remaining 3 noodles and the remaining pasta sauce.

4. Bake, covered, for 35 minutes. Sprinkle with the remaining ½ cup mozzarella cheese. Bake, uncovered, about 10 minutes more or until heated through. Let stand for 15 to 20 minutes before serving.
Per Serving: 410 cal., 21 g total fat (11 g sat. fat), 66 mg chol., 897 mg sodium, 31 g carbo., 4 g fiber, 23 g pro.

Meatball
Lasagna

This meaty, cheesy *lasagna tastes rich*
but won't break the bank. Just six inexpensive ingredients
feed a crowd for just a few dollars.

Chili Macaroni

Chili Macaroni

Wagon wheel macaroni provides a fun presentation and green beans replace the kidney beans in this skillet meal.
Prep: 15 minutes *Cook:* 15 minutes
Makes 4 servings

12	ounces lean ground beef or uncooked ground turkey
½	cup chopped onion (1 medium)
1	14.5-ounce can diced tomatoes and green chiles, undrained
1¼	cups tomato juice
2	teaspoons chili powder
½	teaspoon garlic salt
1	cup dried wagon wheel or elbow macaroni
1	cup frozen cut green beans
1	cup shredded cheddar cheese or taco cheese blend (4 ounces) (optional)
	Tortilla chips (optional)

1. In a very large skillet, cook ground beef and onion over medium-high heat until meat is brown and onion is tender. Drain off fat. Stir in undrained tomatoes, tomato juice, chili powder, and garlic salt. Bring to boiling.

2. Stir in macaroni and green beans. Return to boiling; reduce heat. Simmer, covered, about 15 minutes or until macaroni and beans are tender.

3. If desired, top each serving with cheese and tortilla chips.

Per Serving: 443 cal., 20 g total fat (9 g sat. fat), 83 mg chol., 881 mg sodium, 37 g carbo., 5 g fiber, 29 g pro.

CHEESE BLEND
You can make your own taco cheese blend by combining equal parts shredded Colby Jack and cheddar. Or, you can substitute shredded Mexican cheese blend for the taco cheese.

These hearty, comforting casseroles are one - pot meals. They make cleanup a snap so you have time to enjoy your evening.

Ham and Cheese Macaroni

Jazz up this all-time favorite by adding ham, broccoli, and sweet red pepper.
Prep: 30 minutes *Bake:* 45 minutes
Makes 6 servings

1½ cups dried elbow macaroni
3   cups broccoli florets
1½ cups coarsely chopped red sweet pepper
     (2 medium)
1½ cups cubed cooked ham
1½ cups milk
4½ teaspoons cornstarch
¼   teaspoon ground black pepper
1½ cups cubed American cheese (6 ounces)
1   cup soft bread crumbs
1   tablespoon butter or margarine, melted

1. Preheat oven to 350°F. Cook macaroni according to package directions, adding broccoli and sweet pepper during the last 2 minutes of cooking; drain. Transfer macaroni mixture to an ungreased 3-quart casserole. Stir in ham; set aside.

2. For sauce, in a small saucepan, stir together milk, cornstarch, and black pepper. Cook and stir over medium heat until thickened and bubbly. Add cheese, stirring until cheese melts. Add sauce to macaroni mixture; stir gently to combine. In a small bowl, combine bread crumbs and melted butter; toss gently to coat. Sprinkle over casserole.

3. Bake, uncovered, about 45 minutes or until bubbly and bread crumbs are light brown.
Per Serving: 373 cal., 16 g total fat (9 g sat. fat), 58 mg chol., 1,036 mg sodium, 35 g carbo., 3 g fiber, 22 g pro.

Zucchini Pork Chop Supper

Layers of herb-seasoned croutons, cream-sauced zucchini, and juicy pork chops create a tasty one-dish meal.
Prep: 30 minutes *Bake:* 50 minutes
Makes 6 servings

1   14-ounce package herb-seasoned stuffing
     croutons
¼   cup butter or margarine, melted
4   cups coarsely chopped zucchini
1   10.75-ounce can condensed cream of celery
     soup
1   8-ounce carton light dairy sour cream
¾   cup milk
½   cup shredded carrot (1 medium)
1   tablespoon snipped fresh parsley or
     1 teaspoon dried parsley flakes
¼   to ½ teaspoon ground black pepper
6   bone-in pork loin chops, cut ¾ inch thick

1. Preheat oven to 350°F. Grease a 3-quart rectangular baking dish; set aside. In a large bowl, combine 7½ cups of the croutons and the melted butter; toss gently to coat. Spread half of the buttered croutons in the prepared baking dish.

2. In another large bowl, combine zucchini, soup, sour cream, ½ cup of the milk, the carrot, parsley, and pepper. Spoon evenly over croutons in dish. Sprinkle with remaining buttered croutons.

3. Pour remaining ¼ cup milk into a shallow dish. Coarsely crush the remaining croutons; place in another shallow dish. Trim fat from chops. Dip chops into milk, then into crushed croutons, turning to coat. Place chops on top of layers in baking dish. Sprinkle with any remaining crushed croutons.

4. Bake, uncovered, for 50 to 60 minutes or until chops are slightly pink in center and juices run clear (160°F).
Per Serving: 639 cal., 24 g total fat (10 g sat. fat), 130 mg chol., 1,417 mg sodium, 57 g carbo., 4 g fiber, 46 g pro.

Fast Chicken
and Rice

quick chicken

Busy cooks have come to rely on chicken because it's quick-cooking, inexpensive, and incredibly versatile. Team it with convenient packaged and canned products, and you'll have a sure winner to bring to your table.

Fast Chicken and Rice

High heat and thin pieces of chicken speed the cooking time. Use your favorite bottled stir-fry sauce for flavor.
Start to Finish: 10 minutes
Makes 4 servings

- ½ cup frozen peas
- 1 8.8-ounce pouch cooked brown or white rice
- 1 tablespoon cooking oil
- 1 pound chicken breast tenders, halved crosswise
- ¼ cup bottled stir-fry sauce
  Packaged oven-roasted sliced almonds

1. Stir peas into rice pouch. Heat in microwave according to package directions.

2. Meanwhile, in a large skillet, heat oil over medium-high heat. Add chicken to skillet; cook and stir for 2 to 3 minutes or until chicken is no longer pink. Stir rice mixture into skillet. Stir in stir-fry sauce; heat through. Sprinkle with almonds.
Per Serving: 311 cal., 9 g fat (1 g sat. fat), 66 mg chol., 453 mg sodium, 25 g carbo., 2 g fiber, 31 g pro.

Stuffed Chicken Breasts

For extra zip, make the easy stuffing with a flavored feta cheese.
Prep: 25 minutes   Cook: 12 minutes
Makes 4 servings

- 4 skinless, boneless chicken breast halves
- 4 ounces crumbled feta cheese with peppercorns, feta cheese with garlic and herb, or plain feta cheese (1 cup)
- ½ of a 7-ounce jar roasted red sweet peppers, drained and cut into strips (½ cup)
- 1 tablespoon olive oil
- ¼ cup chicken broth

1. Place each chicken breast half between two pieces of plastic wrap. Pound lightly with the flat side of a meat mallet to ¼-inch thickness. Remove plastic wrap.

2. Sprinkle each chicken breast half with cheese. Place sweet pepper strips in the center of each breast half. Fold narrow ends over filling; fold in sides. Roll up each breast half from a short side. Secure with wooden toothpicks.

3. In a medium nonstick skillet, heat oil over medium-high heat. Add chicken; cook about 5 minutes, turning to brown evenly. Add chicken broth. Bring to boiling; reduce heat. Simmer, covered, for 7 to 8 minutes or until chicken is no longer pink (170°F). To serve, spoon pan juices over chicken.
Per Serving: 265 cal., 11 g fat (5 g sat. fat), 107 mg chol., 449 mg sodium, 2 g carbo., 0 g fiber, 37 g pro.

Pepper and Peach Fajita Chicken

Start to Finish: 20 minutes

Makes 4 servings

- 4 skinless, boneless chicken breast halves
- 1½ teaspoons fajita seasoning
- 2 tablespoons olive oil or butter
- 1½ cups sweet pepper strips
- 1 medium fresh peach or nectarine, cut into thin slices, or 1 cup frozen peach slices, thawed

1. Sprinkle both sides of chicken breast halves with fajita seasoning. In a large skillet, heat 1 tablespoon of the oil over medium-high heat. Add chicken to skillet; cook for 8 to 10 minutes or until chicken is no longer pink (170°F), turning once. Transfer chicken to a serving platter; keep warm.

2. Add remaining oil to skillet; add sweet pepper strips. Cook and stir about 3 minutes or until crisp-tender. Gently stir in peach slices. Cook and stir for 1 to 2 minutes more or until heated through. Spoon over chicken.

Per Serving: 243 cal., 9 g fat (1 g sat. fat), 82 mg chol., 150 mg sodium, 7 g carbo., 2 g fiber, 33 g pro.

Honey-Glazed Chicken

Get double the kick from the honey-mustard mixture by using it as a marinade for the chicken and as the dressing for the greens or pasta.

Prep: 15 minutes   *Marinate:* 2 hours   *Bake:* 20 minutes

Makes 4 servings

- 1½ pounds skinless, boneless chicken breast halves
- ½ cup honey
- 3 tablespoons lemon juice
- 1 tablespoon reduced-sodium soy sauce
- 1 tablespoon spicy brown mustard
  Torn mixed salad greens or hot cooked pasta (optional)

1. Place chicken breast halves in a resealable plastic bag set in a shallow bowl. For marinade, in a small bowl, whisk together honey, lemon juice, soy sauce, and mustard. Set aside ¼ cup of the marinade. Pour remaining marinade over chicken in the bag. Seal bag; turn to coat chicken. Marinate in the refrigerator for 2 to 4 hours.

2. Preheat the oven to 400°F. Remove chicken from bag, reserving marinade. Place the chicken in a shallow baking pan.

3. Bake chicken, uncovered, about 20 minutes or until no longer pink (170°F), turning once and basting with some of the remaining marinade halfway through baking time. Discard any leftover marinade. Thinly slice chicken. If desired, serve chicken on greens or pasta. Drizzle the ¼ cup reserved marinade over chicken.

Per Serving: 325 cal., 2 g fat (1 g sat. fat), 99 mg chol., 299 mg sodium, 36 g carbo., 0 g fiber, 40 g pro.

MAKE IT A MENU
Mexican Chicken Casserole, fresh pineapple spears, caramel custard

Mexican Chicken Casserole

Prep: 15 minutes   *Bake:* 15 minutes

Makes 4 servings

- 1 15-ounce can black beans, rinsed and drained
- ½ cup chunky salsa
- ½ teaspoon ground cumin
- 1 2- to 2¼-pound deli-roasted chicken
- ¼ cup shredded Monterey Jack cheese with jalapeño peppers (1 ounce)
  Dairy sour cream (optional)

1. Preheat oven to 350°F. In a small bowl, stir together beans, ¼ cup of the salsa, and the cumin. Divide bean mixture among four individual au gratin dishes or casseroles; set aside.

2. Cut chicken into quarters. Place one piece on bean mixture in each dish. Spoon remaining ¼ cup salsa evenly over chicken pieces. Sprinkle evenly with cheese.

3. Bake for 15 to 20 minutes or until heated through. If desired, serve with sour cream.

Per Serving: 468 cal., 23 g fat (7 g sat. fat), 140 mg chol., 596 mg sodium, 16 g carbo., 5 g fiber, 50 g pro.

Mexican Chicken Casserole

A roasted chicken purchased from the deli tops the list of convenient chicken products. For this *super-easy casserole*, we jazzed it up with Mexican flavors: *salsa, cumin, and pepper cheese*.

Fast Chicken Fettuccine

Asian Chicken and Vegetables

Pop this easy chicken dish in the oven and relax; the one-pan meal means simple cleanup too.

Prep: 10 minutes   *Bake:* 40 minutes

Makes 4 servings

- 8   chicken drumsticks and/or thighs, skinned (about 2 pounds total)
- 1   tablespoon cooking oil
- 1½ teaspoons five-spice powder
- ⅓   cup bottled plum sauce or sweet-and-sour sauce
- 1   14-ounce package frozen baby whole potatoes, broccoli, carrots, baby corn, and red pepper mix or one 16-ounce package frozen stir-fry vegetables (any combination)

1. Preheat oven to 400°F. Arrange the chicken pieces in a 13×9×2-inch baking pan, making sure pieces do not touch. Brush chicken pieces with cooking oil; sprinkle with 1 teaspoon of the five-spice powder. Bake, uncovered, for 25 minutes.

2. Meanwhile, in a large bowl, combine plum sauce and the remaining ½ teaspoon five-spice powder. Add frozen vegetables; toss to coat.

3. Move chicken pieces to one side of the baking pan. Add vegetable mixture to the other side of the pan. Bake for 15 to 20 minutes more or until chicken is no longer pink (180°F), stirring vegetables once during baking. Using a slotted spoon, transfer chicken and vegetables to a serving platter.

Per Serving: 277 cal., 9 g fat (2 g sat. fat), 98 mg chol., 124 mg sodium, 21 g carbo., 2 g fiber, 30 g pro.

Fast Chicken Fettuccine

Start to Finish: 20 minutes

Makes 4 servings

- 1   9-ounce package refrigerated fettuccine
- ¼   cup oil-packed dried tomato strips or pieces
- 1   large zucchini or yellow summer squash, halved lengthwise and sliced (about 2 cups)
- 8   ounces chicken breast strips for stir-frying
- ½   cup finely shredded Parmesan, Romano, or Asiago cheese (2 ounces)
      Freshly ground black pepper

1. Use kitchen scissors to cut pasta in half. Cook pasta in lightly salted boiling water according to package directions; drain. Return pasta to hot pan.

2. Meanwhile, drain dried tomato, reserving 2 tablespoons oil from jar; set aside.

3. In a large skillet, heat 1 tablespoon reserved oil over medium-high heat. Add zucchini; cook and stir for 2 to 3 minutes or until crisp-tender. Remove from skillet. Add remaining reserved oil to skillet. Add chicken; cook and stir for 2 to 3 minutes or until no longer pink. Add zucchini, chicken, and tomato to cooked pasta; toss gently to combine. Sprinkle individual servings with cheese and season to taste with pepper.

Per Serving: 381 cal., 14 g fat (1 g sat. fat), 40 mg chol., 334 mg sodium, 40 g carbo., 3 g fiber, 24 g pro.

Chicken Tortilla Bake

Prep: 15 minutes   *Bake:* 45 minutes

Makes 8 servings

- 2   10.75-ounce cans reduced-sodium condensed cream of chicken soup
- 1   10-ounce can diced tomatoes with green chiles, undrained
- 12 6- or 7-inch corn tortillas, cut into thin bite-size strips
- 3   cups cubed cooked chicken (1 pound)
- 1   cup shredded taco cheese (4 ounces)

1. Preheat oven to 350°F. In a medium bowl, combine soup and undrained tomatoes; set aside.

2. Sprinkle one-third of the tortilla strips in the bottom of an ungreased 3-quart rectangular baking dish. Layer half of the chicken over tortilla strips; spoon half of the soup mixture over chicken. Repeat layers. Sprinkle with remaining tortilla strips.

3. Bake, covered, about 40 minutes or until bubbly around edges and center is hot. Uncover and sprinkle with cheese. Bake, uncovered, about 5 minutes more or until cheese melts.

Per Serving: 291 cal., 10 g fat (4 g sat. fat), 64 mg chol., 658 mg sodium, 28 g carbo., 2 g fiber, 22 g pro.

Cheesy Corn and Chicken Turnovers

Prep: 25 minutes   *Bake:* 15 minutes
Makes 4 servings

- 2   cups chopped cooked chicken
- 1   11-ounce can whole kernel corn with sweet peppers, drained
- 1   10.75-ounce can condensed cream of chicken and herbs soup
- 1   cup shredded cheddar cheese (4 ounces)
- 1   15-ounce package rolled refrigerated unbaked piecrust (2 crusts)

1. Preheat oven to 400°F. In a medium bowl, combine chicken, corn, soup, and cheese. Unfold piecrusts according to package directions.

2. On a lightly floured surface, roll each piecrust into a 13-inch circle; cut into quarters. Spoon about ½ cup chicken mixture along one straight side of each triangle, about ¾ inch from edge. Brush edges with water. Fold other straight side of triangle over filling. Seal edges with a fork. Prick triangle several times with a fork. Repeat with remaining pastry and filling. Place wedges on a large greased baking sheet.

3. Bake about 15 minutes or until wedges are golden brown. Serve hot.
Per Serving: 862 cal., 47 g fat (21 g sat. fat), 118 mg chol., 1,625 mg sodium, 73 g carbo., 3 g fiber, 33 g pro.

Thai Chicken Pasta

Start to Finish: 20 minutes
Makes 4 servings

- 8   ounces dried angel hair pasta
- 3   cups cooked chicken cut into strips
- 1   14-ounce can unsweetened coconut milk
- 1   teaspoon Thai seasoning
- ¼   cup roasted peanuts

1. Cook the pasta according to package directions; drain well. Return pasta to pan; keep warm.

2. Meanwhile, in a large skillet combine chicken strips, coconut milk, and Thai seasoning. Cook and gently stir until heated through. Pour chicken mixture over pasta in pan. Toss to coat. Sprinkle with peanuts.
Per Serving: 644 cal., 31 g fat (19 g sat. fat), 93 mg chol., 236 mg sodium, 47 g carbo., 2 g fiber, 42 g pro.

Chicken and Biscuit Kabobs

Chicken and biscuits on a stick are just plain fun. Microwaving the frozen chicken for a minute allows the skewer to be inserted easily.
Start to Finish: 20 minutes
Makes 4 servings

- ½   of a 13.5-ounce package frozen cooked, breaded chicken breast chunks (12)
- 1   4.5-ounce package refrigerated buttermilk or country biscuits (6)
- 1   medium zucchini and/or yellow summer squash, cut into 3×¾-inch strips
- ⅓   cup butter, melted*
- 3   tablespoons honey*

1. Preheat oven to 400°F. Arrange chicken chunks in a single layer on a microwave-safe plate. Microwave, uncovered, on 100% power (high) for 1 minute (chicken will not be heated through).

2. Use kitchen scissors to snip each biscuit in half. On each of four metal or wooden skewers, alternately thread chicken pieces, biscuit halves, and zucchini, leaving ¼ inch between pieces. Place on an ungreased baking sheet. Bake for 10 minutes or until biscuits are golden brown and chicken is heated through.

3. Meanwhile, whisk together melted butter and honey. Drizzle some over kabobs. Pass remainder for dipping.
*Test Kitchen Tip: You can substitute ½ cup honey butter for the melted butter and honey. Place in a microwave-safe bowl and microwave, uncovered, on 100% power (high) for 35 to 45 seconds or until melted.
Per Serving: 376 cal., 22 g fat (9 g sat. fat), 57 mg chol., 649 mg sodium, 37 g carbo., 1 g fiber, 10 g pro.

FOOD ON A STICK

Food cooked and served on a stick is the next best thing to eating with your fingers. Place foods with similar cooking times on the same skewer so some foods are not overcooked by the time the others are done. Always leave about ¼ inch between pieces so the heat can circulate and foods will cook more evenly.

Chicken and Biscuit Kabobs

Herb-Rubbed Roaster

Herb-Rubbed Roaster

Get this bird ready for the oven the night before you plan to serve it. The next day all you have to do is pile potatoes around the chicken and bake it.

Prep: 20 minutes   *Marinate:* 2 hours   *Roast:* 1¼ hours
Stand: 10 minutes
Makes 6 servings

1	3½- to 4-pound whole broiler-fryer chicken
¼	cup olive oil
2	tablespoons herbes de Provence
1	teaspoon salt or smoked salt
1	teaspoon crushed red pepper
¾	teaspoon coarsely ground black pepper
1½	pounds tiny yellow and purple potatoes and/or fingerling potatoes, halved

1. Remove the neck and giblets from chicken. Rinse chicken; pat dry with paper towels. Skewer neck skin to back; tie legs to tail with 100-percent-cotton string. Twist wings under back. Brush chicken with 2 tablespoons of the olive oil.

2. In a small bowl, stir together herbes de Provence, salt, crushed red pepper, and coarsely ground pepper. Rub 2 tablespoons of the herb mixture onto the bird. Cover the remaining herb mixture; set aside. Place chicken in a large resealable plastic bag. Seal bag and place in the refrigerator for 2 to 24 hours.

3. Preheat oven to 375°F. Remove chicken from bag. Place chicken, breast side up, on a rack in a shallow roasting pan. Insert a meat thermometer into center of an inside thigh muscle, not touching bone.

4. In a large bowl, combine the remaining 2 tablespoons oil and reserved herb mixture. Add the potatoes and toss to combine. Arrange potatoes around the chicken. Roast, uncovered, for 1¼ to 1¾ hours or until drumsticks move easily in their sockets and meat thermometer registers 180°F. Remove chicken from oven. Loosely cover and let stand for 10 minutes.

5. To serve, carve the chicken and place on a large platter. Arrange the potatoes around the chicken.
Per Serving: 543 cal., 35 g fat (9 g sat. fat), 134 mg chol., 492 mg sodium, 18 g carbo., 3 g fiber, 37 g pro.

MAKE IT A MENU
Herb-Rubbed Roaster with potatoes, Orange-Asparagus Salad (page 170), peach sorbet

Tuscan Chicken

Prep: 5 minutes   *Cook:* 45 minutes
Makes 4 servings

- 2   tablespoons olive oil
- 2   to 2½ pounds meaty chicken pieces (breast halves, thighs, and drumsticks)
- 1¼   teaspoons pesto seasoning or dried Italian seasoning, crushed
- ½   cup whole pitted Kalamata olives
- ½   cup white wine or chicken broth

1. In a 12-inch skillet, heat oil over medium heat. Add chicken to skillet; cook for 15 minutes, turning to brown evenly. Reduce heat. Drain off excess oil in skillet. Sprinkle pesto seasoning evenly over chicken. Add olives to skillet. Pour wine over all.

2. Cook, covered, for 25 minutes. Uncover; cook for 5 to 10 minutes more or until chicken is no longer pink (170°F for breasts; 180°F for thighs and drumsticks).
Per Serving: 334 cal., 18 g fat (4 g sat. fat), 104 mg chol., 280 mg sodium, 2 g carbo., 1 g fiber, 34 g pro.

Zesty Chicken with Black Beans and Rice

Start to Finish: 30 minutes
Makes 4 servings

- 2   tablespoons cooking oil
- 1   pound skinless, boneless chicken breast halves, cut into 2-inch pieces
- 1   6- to 7.4-ounce package Spanish rice mix
- 1¾   cups water
- 1   15-ounce can black beans, rinsed and drained
- 1   14.5-ounce can diced tomatoes, undrained Sour cream, sliced green onions, and lime wedges (optional)

1. In a 12-inch skillet, heat 1 tablespoon of the oil over medium-high heat. Add chicken pieces; cook in hot oil until chicken is lightly browned. Remove chicken from skillet with a slotted spoon and keep warm.

2. Add rice mix (reserve seasoning packet) and remaining 1 tablespoon oil to skillet; cook and stir for 2 minutes over medium heat. Stir in seasoning packet from rice mix, the water, beans, and undrained tomatoes; add chicken. Bring to boiling; reduce heat. Cover and simmer for 15 to 20 minutes or until rice is tender and chicken is no longer pink. Remove from heat and let stand, covered, for 5 minutes.

3. If desired, serve with sour cream, green onions, and lime wedges.
Per Serving: 424 cal., 9 g fat (2 g sat. fat), 66 mg chol., 1,080 mg sodium, 52 g carbo., 6 g fiber, 37 g pro.

Hoisin-Sauced Cornish Hens

Thick, dark hoisin sauce is sweet, spicy, and salty, making it a good base for Asian sauces. It adds a richly glazed look as well as flavor.
Prep: 15 minutes   *Roast:* 1¼ hours
Makes 4 servings

- 2   1¼- to 1½-pound Cornish game hens, halved lengthwise
       Salt
- ½   cup bottled hoisin sauce
- ¼   cup raspberry or red wine vinegar
- ¼   cup orange juice
- 1   to 2 teaspoons red chili paste

1. Preheat oven to 375°F. Sprinkle hens with salt. Place hens, breast sides up, on a rack in a shallow roasting pan. Cover loosely with foil. Roast for 30 minutes.

2. Meanwhile, in a small bowl, stir together hoisin sauce, vinegar, orange juice, and red chili paste. Brush some of the hoisin sauce mixture over hens.

3. Roast, uncovered, for 45 to 60 minutes more or until chicken is no longer pink (180°F), brushing occasionally with the remaining hoisin sauce mixture.
Per Serving: 371 cal., 23 g fat (5 g sat. fat), 120 mg chol., 2,223 mg sodium, 6 g carbo., 0 g fiber, 38 g pro.

Thai Chicken in Lettuce Cups

A sprinkle of chopped peanuts adds crunch to the spicy chicken strips and onion nestled in lettuce leaves. The spiciness of this dish depends on the brand of Thai dressing used.

Start to Finish: 20 minutes

Makes 4 servings

- 12 ounces chicken breast tenders
- ¼ cup bottled Thai ginger salad dressing and marinade
- ½ cup thinly sliced red onion
- 4 Boston or Bibb lettuce cups
- 3 tablespoons coarsely chopped dry-roasted peanuts

1. In a medium bowl, combine chicken and dressing; toss to coat. Let stand at room temperature for 10 minutes.

2. Heat a large nonstick skillet over medium-high heat for 2 minutes; add undrained chicken mixture and onion. Cook and stir for 3 to 5 minutes or until chicken is no longer pink and onion is tender.

3. Divide chicken mixture among lettuce cups. Sprinkle with peanuts.

Per Serving: 156 cal., 5 g fat (1 g sat. fat), 49 mg chol., 392 mg sodium, 6 g carbo., 0 g fiber, 22 g pro.

Lemon Chicken with Garlic and Rosemary

Prep: 15 minutes *Bake:* 35 minutes

Makes 6 servings

- 1 tablespoon snipped fresh rosemary or 1 teaspoon dried rosemary, crushed
- 1 teaspoon salt
- 1 teaspoon coarsely ground black pepper
- 2½ to 3 pounds meaty chicken pieces (breast halves, thighs, and drumsticks)
- 1 medium lemon
- 2 tablespoons olive oil
- 2 cloves garlic, minced, or 1 teaspoon bottled minced garlic

1. Preheat oven to 425°F. In a small bowl, combine rosemary, salt, and pepper. Using your fingers, rub rosemary mixture onto both sides of chicken pieces. Place chicken pieces, bone sides up, in a lightly greased 13×9×2-inch baking pan.

2. Finely shred 1 teaspoon peel from the lemon. Cut lemon in half; squeeze lemon to get 1 tablespoon juice. In a small bowl, combine lemon peel, lemon juice, oil, and garlic; drizzle over chicken pieces.

3. Bake chicken for 20 minutes. Turn chicken pieces bone sides down; spoon pan juices over chicken. Bake for 15 to 20 minutes more or until chicken is no longer pink (170°F for breasts; 180°F for thighs and drumsticks).

Per Serving: 257 cal., 15 g fat (4 g sat. fat), 86 mg chol., 464 mg sodium, 1 g carbo., 0 g fiber, 28 g pro.

Basil-Tomato Chicken Skillet

When using nonstick cooking spray to trim the fat in a recipe, always spray the pan before heating it.

Start to Finish: 20 minutes

Makes 4 servings

- 1 to 1¼ pounds chicken breast tenderloins Nonstick cooking spray
- ⅛ teaspoon salt
- ⅛ teaspoon ground black pepper
- 1 14.5-ounce can no-salt-added diced tomatoes, drained
- ¼ cup snipped fresh basil
- 1 9- to 10-ounce package prewashed spinach
- 2 tablespoons finely shredded Parmesan cheese

1. Cut any large chicken tenderloins in half lengthwise. Coat an unheated 12-inch skillet with nonstick cooking spray.

2. Cook and stir chicken in hot skillet about 5 minutes or until no longer pink. Sprinkle with salt and pepper.

3. Add tomatoes and basil; heat through. Remove from heat. Add spinach; toss until wilted. Divide among four plates. Sprinkle with Parmesan cheese.

Per Serving: 170 cal., 2 g fat (1 g sat. fat), 68 mg chol., 265 mg sodium, 7 g carbo., 3 g fiber, 30 g pro.

MAKE IT A MENU
Basil-Tomato Chicken Skillet, garlic bread, Banana Split Trifles (page 178)

Basil-Tomato
Chicken Skillet

Pan-Roasted Chicken with Shallots

Pan-Roasted Chicken with Shallots

So simple but so delicious, this bistro-style dish is great for a special-occasion dinner.

Start to Finish: 20 minutes
Makes 4 servings

8	shallots or 1 large onion
4	skinless, boneless chicken breast halves Salt and ground black pepper
1	tablespoon olive oil
1	medium zucchini, halved lengthwise and cut into ¼-inch slices
¼	cup snipped fresh parsley

1. Peel shallots; halve small shallots and quarter large shallots. (If using onion, cut into thin wedges.) You should have 1 cup shallots or onion wedges; set aside. Sprinkle chicken lightly with salt and pepper. In a large skillet, heat oil over medium-high heat. Reduce heat to medium. Add chicken; cook for 2 minutes.

2. Turn chicken. Add shallots to skillet. Sprinkle shallots lightly with additional salt and pepper. Cook for 8 to 10 minutes more or until chicken is no longer pink (170°F), stirring shallots frequently and turning chicken, if necessary, to brown evenly. If necessary, add additional oil to prevent sticking. Reduce heat to medium-low if chicken or shallots brown too quickly.

3. Transfer chicken and shallots to a serving platter. Cover to keep warm. Add zucchini to skillet. Cook and stir for 3 to 5 minutes or until crisp-tender. Add to platter with chicken. Sprinkle with parsley.

Per Serving: 193 cal., 5 g fat (1 g sat. fat), 66 mg chol., 231 mg sodium, 9 g carbo., 1 g fiber, 28 g pro.

SHALLOTS

Shallots are upmarket onions, formed with cloves in heads like garlic, but they taste like mild onions. Fresh shallots are available only in the spring, but dried ones are sold year-round. Choose dry shallots that are plump and firm, and store them in a cool, dry place for up to 1 month. Use them as you would onions.

Chicken Veronique

This version of the classic chicken and grape dish replaces the cream sauce with one of butter and sherry vinegar. If your grapes have seeds, use the tip of a spoon to remove them from the halved grapes.

Start to Finish: 20 minutes

Makes 4 servings

4	skinless, boneless chicken breast halves
¼	teaspoon salt
¼	teaspoon ground black pepper
4	tablespoons butter
1	cup seedless red grapes, halved
3	tablespoons sherry vinegar or red wine vinegar
¼	teaspoon dried thyme, crushed

1. Sprinkle chicken with salt and pepper. In a large skillet, melt 2 tablespoons of the butter over medium-high heat. Add chicken to skillet; cook in the hot butter over medium-high heat for 8 to 10 minutes or until no longer pink (170°F), turning once. Transfer to a serving platter; keep warm.

2. For sauce, add the remaining 2 tablespoons butter, grapes, vinegar, and thyme to hot skillet. Cook and stir until slightly thickened, loosening any brown bits in skillet. Serve sauce over chicken.

Per Serving: 301 cal., 15 g fat (8 g sat. fat), 115 mg chol., 348 mg sodium, 7 g carbo., 0 g fiber, 33 g pro.

Polenta with Turkey Sausage Florentine

Start to Finish: 25 minutes

Makes 2 servings

½	of a 16-ounce tube refrigerated cooked Italian herb, mushroom, or plain polenta
1	9- or 10-ounce package frozen creamed spinach
8	ounces bulk turkey sausage
2	tablespoons pine nuts or sliced almonds, toasted

1. Cut polenta in half crosswise, then cut each portion in half diagonally; set aside. Cook creamed spinach according to package directions.

2. Meanwhile, in a medium skillet, cook sausage over medium-high heat until brown. Remove sausage, reserving drippings in skillet. (If there are no drippings, add a little olive oil to the skillet.)

3. Add polenta slices to reserved drippings. Cook over medium heat about 6 minutes or until lightly browned, turning once. Transfer polenta to a serving platter.

4. Stir cooked sausage into creamed spinach; heat through. Spoon spinach mixture next to polenta. Sprinkle with toasted nuts.

Per Serving: 487 cal., 26 g fat (6 g sat. fat), 102 mg chol., 1,454 mg sodium, 32 g carbo., 6 g fiber, 29 g pro.

Parmesan-Sesame-Crusted Turkey

Start to Finish: 20 minutes

Makes 4 servings

½	cup finely shredded Parmesan cheese
¼	cup sesame seeds
1	egg, lightly beaten
4	turkey breast slices, ½ inch thick
¼	teaspoon salt
¼	teaspoon ground black pepper
1	tablespoon olive oil or cooking oil

1. In a shallow dish or pie plate, combine Parmesan cheese and sesame seeds. Place egg in another shallow dish or pie plate. Dip turkey slices into egg; coat with Parmesan cheese mixture. Sprinkle turkey slices with salt and pepper.

2. In a large skillet, heat oil over medium-high heat. Add turkey; cook turkey in hot oil for 8 to 10 minutes or until turkey is no longer pink (170°F), turning once.

Per Serving: 498 cal., 28 g fat (13 g sat. fat), 171 mg chol., 1,336 mg sodium, 3 g carbo., 1 g fiber, 57 g pro.

Turkey Supper Salad

Start to Finish: 15 minutes

Makes 4 servings

4	cups packaged torn mixed greens
2	cups sliced mushrooms
8	ounces smoked turkey, cut into bite-size strips
¾	cup mild Cheddar cheese cubes
¼	cup bottled light Caesar or Italian salad dressing

1. In a very large salad bowl, combine greens, mushrooms, turkey, and cheese. Drizzle with dressing and toss to coat. Serve immediately.

Per Serving: 212 cal., 13 g fat (6 g sat. fat), 57 mg chol., 1,017 mg sodium, 5 g carbo., 1 g fiber, 20 g pro.

Mediterranean Cheese-Stuffed Chicken

Prep: 20 minutes   *Cook:* 25 minutes
Makes 4 servings

- **4** skinless, boneless chicken breast halves
  Salt and ground black pepper
- **4** oil-packed dried tomatoes, drained and cut into thin strips
- **2** ounces mascarpone cheese or crumbled feta cheese
- **4** teaspoons snipped fresh oregano, basil, tarragon, or parsley or ½ teaspoon dried oregano, basil, tarragon, or parsley, crushed
- **2** tablespoons olive oil

1. Place each chicken breast half between two pieces of plastic wrap. Pound lightly with the flat side of a meat mallet to ¼-inch thickness. Remove plastic wrap. Sprinkle chicken with salt and pepper. On each chicken breast half, layer tomato strips, cheese, and herb. Fold narrow ends over filling; fold in sides. Roll up each breast half from a short side. Secure with wooden toothpicks.

2. In a medium skillet, heat oil over medium-low heat. Add chicken; cook about 25 minutes or until chicken is no longer pink (170°F), turning to brown evenly.
Per Serving: 257 cal., 17 g fat (6 g sat. fat), 77 mg chol., 114 mg sodium, 2 g carbo., 0 g fiber, 25 g pro.

Fresh Garlic and Pecan Chicken

Prep: 30 minutes   *Roast:* 1¼ hours   *Stand:* 10 minutes
Makes 4 servings

- **1** 3- to 3½-pound whole broiler-fryer chicken
- **6** cloves garlic, thinly sliced
- **⅔** cup finely chopped pecans
- **¼** cup butter or margarine, melted
- **1** tablespoon snipped fresh thyme or
  1 teaspoon dried thyme, crushed
- **½** teaspoon ground black pepper
- **¼** teaspoon salt

1. Preheat oven to 375°F. Rinse inside of chicken; pat dry. Skewer neck skin of chicken to back; tie legs to tail with 100-percent-cotton string. Twist wing tips under back. Using a small, sharp knife, make numerous slits about 1 inch wide and ½ inch deep in the breast portions of the chicken. Stuff garlic into slits.

2. In a small bowl, combine pecans, melted butter, thyme, pepper, and salt. Pat mixture onto top of chicken.

3. Place chicken, breast side up, on a rack in a shallow roasting pan. Insert a meat thermometer into center of an inside thigh muscle. Do not allow thermometer bulb to touch bone.

4. Roast, uncovered, for 1¼ to 1½ hours or until drumsticks move easily in their sockets and thermometer registers 180°F. (If necessary, cover chicken loosely with foil for the last 10 to 15 minutes of roasting to prevent pecans from overbrowning.) Remove chicken from oven. Cover and let stand for 10 minutes before carving. Spoon any pecans from roasting pan over each serving.
Per Serving: 725 cal., 59 g fat (18 g sat. fat), 205 mg chol., 400 mg sodium, 4 g carbo., 2 g fiber, 45 g pro.

Chicken Quesadillas

Start to Finish: 25 minutes
Makes 4 servings

- Nonstick cooking spray
- **1** cup sliced fresh mushrooms
- **1** 2- to 2¼-pound deli-roasted chicken
- **4** 8- to 10-inch flour tortillas
  Fresh spinach leaves
- **2** cups shredded Monterey Jack cheese (8 ounces)
  Salsa, guacamole, and sour cream (optional)

1. Coat a small nonstick skillet with cooking spray. Add mushrooms to skillet; cook over medium-high heat until tender. Remove skillet from heat; set aside.

2. Remove meat from chicken (discard skin and bones). Chop meat; reserve 2 cups. (Cover and chill or freeze remaining chicken for another use.) Spoon reserved chicken evenly on one half of each tortilla. Top with spinach and mushrooms. Sprinkle cheese evenly over mushrooms. Fold tortillas in half.

3. Preheat a griddle over medium heat. Cook quesadillas on hot griddle until browned on both sides and cheese melts. If desired, serve with salsa, guacamole, and sour cream.
Per Serving: 472 cal., 28 g fat (15 g sat. fat), 120 mg chol., 513 mg sodium, 18 g carbo., 2 g fiber, 37 g pro.

Chicken Quesadillas

Warm from the griddle and *stuffed with melted cheese*, quesadillas make an easy snack or appetizer. Add chopped cooked chicken and a few more ingredients to the filling and you'll have an *irresistible main dish*.

Tortellini, Chicken, and Cheese

Chicken with Cranberry-Olive Couscous

Start to Finish: 15 minutes
Makes 4 servings

- 1 cup uncooked quick-cooking couscous
- ¼ cup dried cranberries
- 3 tablespoons sliced pitted Kalamata olives
- 2 6-ounce packages refrigerated grilled chicken breast strips
- 1 tablespoon snipped fresh mint
  Salt and ground black pepper

1. Prepare couscous according to package directions, adding cranberries and olives with the couscous. Fluff with a fork. Stir in chicken breast strips. Sprinkle with fresh mint. Season to taste with salt and pepper.
Per Serving: 337 cal., 4 g fat (1 g sat. fat), 60 mg chol., 1,011 mg sodium, 43 g carbo., 3 g fiber, 28 g pro.

Tortellini, Chicken, and Cheese

Start to Finish: 20 minutes
Makes 4 servings

- 1 9-ounce package refrigerated cheese tortellini
- 1 cup frozen peas, corn, or pea pods
- 1 8-ounce tub cream cheese spread with garden vegetables or chives and onion
- ½ cup milk
- 1 9-ounce package frozen chopped cooked chicken breast

1. In a large saucepan, cook tortellini according to package directions. Place frozen vegetables in colander. Drain hot pasta over vegetables to thaw; return pasta-vegetable mixture to pan.

2. Meanwhile, for sauce, in a small saucepan, combine cream cheese and milk; heat and stir until cheese melts. Heat chicken according to package directions.

3. Stir cheese sauce into the cooked pasta-vegetable mixture. Cook and gently stir until heated through. Spoon into individual bowls. Top with chicken.
Per Serving: 505 cal., 26 g fat (15 g sat. fat), 130 mg chol., 525 mg sodium, 32 g carbo., 2 g fiber, 32 g pro.

Turkey-Potato Bake

If you grew up loving saucy, delicious poultry-and-cheese casseroles but now find them too rich and heavy, this light, modern version should comfort you.

Prep: 15 minutes   *Bake:* 30 minutes   *Stand:* 10 minutes
Makes 4 servings

- 2¼ cups water
- 1 4.5- to 5-ounce package dry julienne potato mix
- 2 cups chopped cooked turkey or chicken breast
- 1 cup shredded cheddar cheese (4 ounces)
- 1 teaspoon dried parsley flakes
- ⅔ cup milk

1. Preheat oven to 400°F. In a medium saucepan, bring the water to boiling. Meanwhile, in a 2-quart square baking dish combine dry potatoes and sauce mix from potato mix. Stir in turkey, ½ cup of the cheese, and the parsley flakes. Stir in the boiling water and the milk.

2. Bake, uncovered, for 30 to 35 minutes or until potatoes are tender. Sprinkle with the remaining ½ cup cheese. Let stand for 10 minutes before serving (mixture will thicken on standing).
Per Serving: 370 cal., 15 g fat (8 g sat. fat), 87 mg chol., 1,050 mg sodium, 27 g carbo., 1 g fiber, 32 g pro.

Warm Chicken and Wilted Greens

Don't let the greens stay on the heat too long. For best texture, they should be wilted, not cooked through.
Start to Finish: 25 minutes
Makes 4 servings

- 2 cups frozen sweet pepper and onion stir-fry vegetables
- 1 9-ounce package frozen chopped cooked chicken breast, thawed
- ¼ cup bottled sesame salad dressing
- 6 cups fresh baby spinach and/or torn leaf lettuce

1. In a 12-inch skillet, prepare frozen stir-fry vegetables according to package directions. Stir in chicken and salad dressing; heat through. Add spinach. Toss mixture in skillet for 30 to 60 seconds or until spinach is just wilted.
Per Serving: 153 cal., 6 g fat (1 g sat. fat), 34 mg chol., 309 mg sodium, 8 g carbo., 2 g fiber, 17 g pro.

Turkey-Pesto
Pot Pie

Bacon-Wrapped Turkey Mignons

Cook the bacon until brown but not crisp to make it pliable enough to wrap around the turkey mignons.

Prep: 25 minutes   *Bake:* 30 minutes
Makes 6 servings

- 6 slices bacon
- 2 turkey breast steaks
  Salt and ground black pepper
- ¼ cup bottled honey-mustard dipping sauce

1. In a large skillet, cook bacon slices over medium heat until lightly browned but still limp, turning once. Drain the bacon on paper towels and cool until easy to handle.

2. Preheat oven to 400°F. Season turkey steaks with salt and pepper. Cut both steaks crosswise into four pieces. Press the two end pieces of each steak together to form one piece (you should have six "mignons"). Wrap one slice of partially cooked bacon around each mignon; secure with wooden toothpicks. Place mignons in a 13×9×2-inch baking pan.

3. Bake for 30 to 40 minutes or until turkey is no longer pink (170°F), brushing with dipping sauce the last 15 minutes of baking.

Per Serving: 239 cal., 7 g fat (2 g sat. fat), 109 mg chol., 401 mg sodium, 2 g carbo., 0 g fiber, 39 g pro.

Turkey-Pesto Pot Pie

Prep: 15 minutes   *Bake:* 15 minutes
Makes 6 servings

- 1 12-ounce jar turkey gravy
- ⅓ cup purchased basil or dried tomato pesto
- 3 cups cubed cooked turkey (about 1 pound)
- 1 16-ounce package frozen peas and carrots
- 1 11-ounce package refrigerated breadsticks (12)
  Grated Parmesan cheese (optional)
  Dried basil (optional)

1. Preheat oven to 375°F. In a large saucepan, combine turkey gravy and pesto; stir in turkey and vegetables. Bring to boiling, stirring frequently. Divide turkey mixture evenly among six 8-ounce casseroles.

2. Unroll and separate breadsticks. Arrange one breadstick on top of each casserole, curling into a spiral to fit. Set remaining breadsticks aside. If desired, sprinkle casseroles with Parmesan cheese and basil.

3. Bake casseroles about 15 minutes or until breadsticks are golden. Bake remaining breadsticks according to package directions.

Per Serving: 365 cal., 16 g fat (5 g sat. fat), 52 mg chol., 964 mg sodium, 36 g carbo., 4 g fiber, 20 g pro.

Lemon-Dill Butter Chicken and Cucumbers

Cook the cucumber until it begins to soften but still has a bit of crispness. If you like, seed the cucumber before chopping it.

Prep: 10 minutes   *Broil:* 12 minutes
Makes 4 servings

- 4 skinless, boneless chicken breast halves
- 1 medium lemon
- 3 tablespoons butter
- ½ teaspoon dried dill
- ¼ teaspoon salt
- ¼ teaspoon ground black pepper
- 1½ cups coarsely chopped cucumber
  or zucchini

1. Preheat broiler. Place chicken on the unheated rack of a broiler pan. Broil 4 to 5 inches from heat for 12 to 15 minutes or until no longer pink (170°F), turning once halfway through broiling.

2. Meanwhile, finely shred ½ teaspoon peel from the lemon. Cut lemon in half; squeeze lemon to get 2 tablespoons juice.

3. In a small skillet, melt butter over medium heat. Stir in lemon peel, lemon juice, dill, salt, and pepper. Add cucumber. Cook and stir over medium heat for 3 to 4 minutes or until cucumber is just tender. Spoon sauce over chicken.

Per Serving: 244 cal., 11 g fat (6 g sat. fat), 107 mg chol., 477 mg sodium, 2 g carbo., 0 g fiber, 33 g pro.

MAKE IT A MENU
Turkey-Pesto Pot Pie, molded cranberry-raspberry salad, chocolate sundaes

Easy Chicken and Dumplings

Easy Chicken and Dumplings

Prep: 25 minutes *Cook:* 15 minutes
Makes 4 to 6 servings

1	2- to 2½-pound purchased roasted chicken
1	16-ounce package frozen mixed vegetables
1	10.75-ounce can reduced-fat and reduced-sodium condensed cream of chicken soup
1¼	cups reduced-sodium chicken broth or water
½	teaspoon dried Italian seasoning, crushed
⅛	teaspoon ground black pepper
1	11.5-ounce package (8) refrigerated corn bread twists

1. Remove meat from chicken, discarding skin and bones. Chop or shred chicken. In a large saucepan, stir together chicken, frozen vegetables, soup, broth, Italian seasoning, and pepper. Bring to boiling; reduce heat. Simmer, covered, about 15 minutes or until vegetables are tender.

2. Meanwhile, cut corn bread twists along perforations. Twist 2 twists together; place on an ungreased baking sheet. Repeat with the remaining twists. Bake according to package directions.

3. Serve chicken mixture with corn bread.

Per Serving: 650 cal., 30 g total fat (8 g sat. fat), 107 mg chol., 1399 mg sodium, 57 g carbo., 5 g fiber, 42 g pro.

Transform a ready-to-eat *deli-roasted chicken* into a hearty meal simply by adding frozen veggies and *condensed soup.*

Chicken Paprikash

In this traditional Hungarian dish, chicken bakes on top of vegetables and noodles flavored with bacon and paprika. The tangy sour cream gravy adds richness and extraordinary flavor.

Prep: 30 minutes *Bake:* 35 minutes
Makes 6 servings

4	cups dried medium noodles
3	slices bacon, chopped
1	cup chopped onion (1 large)
1	cup chopped carrot (2 medium)
1	cup chopped celery (2 stalks)
1	teaspoon paprika
½	teaspoon finely shredded lemon peel
¼	teaspoon salt
⅛	teaspoon ground black pepper
1	8-ounce carton dairy sour cream
⅓	cup all-purpose flour
1¾	cups milk
6	skinless, boneless chicken breast halves (about 2 pounds total)
	Paprika
	Salt and ground black pepper

1. Preheat oven to 375°F. Cook noodles according to package directions; drain. Meanwhile, in a very large skillet, cook bacon over medium heat until crisp. Using a slotted spoon, remove bacon and drain on paper towels, reserving drippings in skillet. Add onion, carrot, and celery to the reserved drippings; cook for 5 minutes, stirring occasionally. Stir in the 1 teaspoon paprika, the lemon peel, the ¼ teaspoon salt, and the ⅛ teaspoon pepper.

2. In a medium bowl, combine sour cream and flour. Gradually stir in milk. Stir sour cream mixture into onion mixture. Cook and stir until thickened and bubbly. Stir in cooked noodles and bacon.

3. Transfer noodle mixture to an ungreased 3-quart rectangular baking dish. Arrange chicken on top of noodle mixture. Sprinkle chicken lightly with additional paprika, salt, and pepper. Bake, uncovered, for 35 to 40 minutes or until chicken is no longer pink (170°F).

Per Serving: 493 cal., 19 g total fat (9 g sat. fat), 141 mg chol., 389 mg sodium, 33 g carbo., 2 g fiber, 45 g pro.

Chicken Supreme Casserole

Remember this chicken dish when you have all ages and all kinds of tastes to please.

Prep: 25 minutes *Bake:* 30 minutes *Stand:* 10 minutes
Makes 6 to 8 servings

8	ounces dried rotini pasta
1	16-ounce package frozen broccoli stir-fry vegetables
2	10.75-ounce cans condensed cream of chicken soup
2	cups milk
¼	cup mayonnaise or salad dressing
¼	teaspoon ground black pepper
2	cups chopped cooked chicken
2	cups cubed French bread
2	tablespoons butter or margarine, melted
¼	teaspoon garlic powder
1	tablespoon snipped fresh parsley

1. Preheat oven to 350°F. Cook pasta according to package directions, adding frozen vegetables during the last 5 minutes of cooking; drain.

2. Meanwhile, in a large bowl, combine soup, milk, mayonnaise, and pepper. Stir in pasta mixture and chicken.

3. Transfer chicken mixture to an ungreased 3-quart rectangular baking dish. In a medium bowl, combine bread cubes, melted butter, and garlic powder; toss gently to coat. Sprinkle over chicken mixture.

4. Bake, uncovered, for 30 to 35 minutes or until heated through and bread cubes are golden brown. Let stand for 10 minutes before serving. Sprinkle with parsley.

Per Serving: 584 cal., 25 g total fat (8 g sat. fat), 71 mg chol., 1123 mg sodium, 60 g carbo., 4 g fiber, 28 g pro.

MAKE IT A MENU
Chicken Paprikash, Romaine with Creamy Garlic Dressing (170), lemon sorbet

Chicken and Bow Ties

Start to Finish: 30 minutes
Makes 4 servings

- 8 ounces dried bow tie pasta
- 1 teaspoon bottled minced garlic (2 cloves)
- 2 tablespoons olive oil
- 1 pound skinless, boneless chicken breasts, cut into thin bite-size strips
- 1 teaspoon dried basil, crushed
- ⅛ teaspoon crushed red pepper
- ¾ cup chicken broth
- ½ cup oil-packed dried tomatoes, drained and cut into thin strips
- ¼ cup dry white wine or chicken broth
- ½ cup whipping cream
- ¼ cup grated Parmesan cheese
  Grated Parmesan cheese (optional)

1. Cook pasta according to package directions; drain.

2. Meanwhile, in a large skillet, cook garlic in hot oil over medium-high heat for 30 seconds. Add chicken, basil, and crushed red pepper. Cook or 3 minutes or until chicken is no longer pink. Stir in broth, dried tomatoes, and wine. Bring to boiling; reduce heat. Simmer, uncovered, for 10 minutes. Stir in cream and the ¼ cup cheese. Simmer, uncovered, for 2 minutes more. Stir in pasta. If desired, serve with cheese.
Per Serving: 574 cal., 24 g total fat (10 g sat. fat), 112 mg chol., 414 mg sodium, 48 g carbo., 2 g fiber, 38 g pro.

Chicken and Pasta Salad

Prep: 30 minutes *Chill:* 4 to 24 hours
Makes 6 servings

- 1½ cups dried radiatore, mostaccioli, and/or medium shell pasta
- 3 cups chopped cooked chicken
- 3 cups seedless grapes, halved
- 1½ cups halved small strawberries
- 1 8-ounce can sliced water chestnuts, drained
- ⅔ cup bottled cucumber ranch salad dressing
- ⅛ teaspoon cayenne pepper
- 1 to 2 tablespoons milk (optional)
  Leaf lettuce
  Sliced almonds, toasted (optional)

1. Cook pasta according to package directions; drain. Rinse with cold water; drain again. In a large bowl, combine cooked pasta, chicken, grapes, strawberries, and drained water chestnuts.

2. For dressing, in a small bowl, stir together bottled dressing and cayenne pepper. Pour over pasta mixture; toss. Cover and chill 4 to 24 hours.

3. If necessary, stir enough of the milk into the pasta mixture to moisten. Line six large salad plates with lettuce. Mound pasta mixture on top of lettuce. If desired, sprinkle with almonds.
Per Serving: 447 cal., 19 g total fat (3 g sat. fat), 62 mg chol., 265 mg sodium, 44 g carbo., 3 g fiber, 25 g pro.

Pulled Chicken Sandwiches

This sandwich is great any time, but for the best flavor, make the filling a day ahead, chill, and reheat.
Start to Finish: 30 minutes
Makes 6 sandwiches

- 1 2- to 2¼-pound purchased roasted chicken
- 1 medium onion, cut into ¼-inch slices
- 1 tablespoon olive oil
- ⅓ cup cider vinegar or white wine vinegar
- ½ cup tomato sauce
- 3 to 4 tablespoons seeded and finely chopped fresh red and/or green chile pepper
- 2 tablespoons snipped fresh thyme
- 2 tablespoons molasses
- 2 tablespoons water
- ½ teaspoon salt
- 4 ciabatta buns or kaiser rolls, split
  Bread-and-butter pickle slices

1. Remove meat from chicken, discarding skin and bones. Shred chicken by pulling two forks through it in opposite directions; set aside.

2. In a large skillet, cook onion in hot oil over medium heat about 5 minutes or until tender, stirring occasionally to separate into rings. Add vinegar; cook and stir for 1 minute more.

3. Stir in tomato sauce, chile pepper, thyme, molasses, the water, and salt. Bring to boiling. Stir in shredded chicken; heat through. Serve chicken mixture on buns with pickle slices.
Per Sandwich: 44   total fat (3 g sat. fat), 84 mg chol., 990 mg sodium, 51 .   g fiber, 33 g pro.

Pulled Chicken
Sandwiches

Tarragon Chicken Linguine

Tarragon Chicken Linguine

Cooking broccoli with the linguine keeps everything in one pan, which cuts down on cleanup.

Start to Finish: 25 minutes
Makes 4 (1-½ cup) servings

6	ounces dried linguine or fettuccine
2	cups broccoli florets
½	cup reduced-sodium chicken broth
2	teaspoons cornstarch
¼	teaspoon lemon-pepper seasoning or ground black pepper
3	skinless, boneless chicken breast halves (12 ounces total), cut into bite-size strips
2	teaspoons olive oil or cooking oil
1	tablespoon snipped fresh tarragon or dill or ½ teaspoon dried tarragon or dill, crushed

1. Cook pasta according to directions, adding broccoli the last 4 minutes. Drain; keep warm. Combine broth, cornstarch, and seasoning; set aside.

2. In a large nonstick skillet, cook chicken in hot oil 4 minutes or until no longer pink, stirring often. Stir cornstarch mixture; add to skillet. Cook and stir until thickened. Stir in tarragon; cook for 2 minutes. Serve over pasta.

Per Serving: 293 cal., 4 g total fat (1 g sat. fat), 49 mg chol., 153 mg sodium, 36 g carbo., 2 g fiber, 27 g pro.

MAKE IT A MENU
Tarragon Chicken Linguine, crusty bread and butter, Berries and Brownies (180)

Chicken Taco Pasta

Substitute a Mexican cheese blend for the cheddar cheese, if you like.

Prep: 25 minutes *Bake:* 45 minutes
Makes 12 servings

8	ounces dried penne pasta
2	pounds uncooked ground chicken
1	cup chopped onion (1 large)
1½	cups water
1	1.25-ounce envelope taco seasoning mix
2	11-ounce cans whole kernel corn with sweet peppers, drained
2	cups shredded cheddar cheese (8 ounces)
1½	cups sliced, pitted ripe olives
1	cup bottled salsa
2	4-ounce cans diced green chile peppers, drained
8	cups shredded lettuce
2	medium tomatoes, cut into thin wedges
	Dairy sour cream (optional)
	Tortilla chips (optional)

1. Preheat oven to 350°F. Lightly grease a 3-quart rectangular baking dish; set aside. Cook pasta according to package directions; drain.

2. Meanwhile, in a 12-inch skillet, cook ground chicken and onion, half at a time, over medium heat until chicken is brown. Drain fat. Return all of the chicken mixture to skillet. Stir in the water and taco seasoning mix. Bring to boiling; reduce heat. Simmer, uncovered, for 2 minutes, stirring occasionally. Stir in cooked pasta, drained corn, half of the cheese, the olives, salsa, and drained chile peppers. Transfer chicken mixture to prepared baking dish.

3. Bake, covered, about 45 minutes or until heated through. Sprinkle with the remaining cheese. Serve with lettuce, tomato, and, if desired, sour cream and tortilla chips.

Per Serving: 365 cal., 20 g total fat (4 g sat. fat), 77 mg chol., 926 mg sodium, 27 g carbo., 4 g fiber, 23 g pro.

Chicken Tetrazzini

A clever way to use leftover cooked chicken that is so loved that no one thinks of it is a leftover.

Prep: 30 minutes *Bake:* 15 minutes
Makes 6 servings

8	ounces dried spaghetti or linguine
2	cups sliced fresh mushrooms
½	cup sliced green onion (4)
2	tablespoons butter or margarine
¼	cup all-purpose flour
⅛	teaspoon ground nutmeg
⅛	teaspoon ground black pepper
1¼	cups chicken broth
1¼	cups half-and-half, light cream, or milk
2	cups chopped cooked chicken
¼	cup grated Parmesan cheese
2	tablespoons dry sherry (optional)
¼	cup sliced almonds, toasted
2	tablespoons snipped fresh parsley

1. Preheat oven to 350°F. Cook pasta according to package directions; drain.

2. Meanwhile, in a large saucepan, cook mushrooms and green onion in hot butter over medium heat until tender. Stir in flour, nutmeg, and pepper. Gradually stir in broth and half-and-half. Cook and stir until thickened and bubbly. Stir in chicken, half of the cheese, and, if desired, sherry. Add cooked pasta; stir gently to coat.

3. Transfer pasta mixture to an ungreased 2-quart rectangular baking dish. Sprinkle with the remaining cheese and the almonds.

4. Bake, uncovered, about 15 minutes or until heated through. Before serving, sprinkle with parsley.

Per Serving: 404 cal., 18 g total fat (8 g sat. fat), 74 mg chol., 342 mg sodium, 37 g carbo., 2 g fiber, 24 g pro.

Jerk-Spiced Shrimp with Spinach

seafood favorites

Seafood is a natural choice for a fast, easy meal. Luckily, fish doesn't have to be pricey: Watch out for deals at your local supermarket and price club, and stock up on frozen seafood when you can!

Jerk-Spiced Shrimp with Spinach

To avoid overfilling the skillet, add the spinach half at a time. Once the first portion has wilted and you've removed it, you can cook the remaining spinach.

Start to Finish: 25 minutes
Makes 4 servings

12	ounces fresh or frozen peeled, deveined medium and/or large shrimp
1½	teaspoons Jamaican jerk seasoning
2	tablespoons olive oil
3	cloves garlic, minced, or 1½ teaspoons bottled minced garlic
8	cups torn fresh spinach

1. Thaw shrimp, if frozen. Rinse shrimp; pat dry with paper towels. Place shrimp in a small bowl. Sprinkle shrimp with jerk seasoning; toss to coat. Set shrimp aside.

2. In a large skillet, heat 1 tablespoon of the oil over medium-high heat. Add garlic and cook in the hot oil for 15 to 30 seconds. Add half of the spinach. Cook and stir about 1 minute or until spinach is just wilted. Transfer to a serving platter. Repeat with remaining spinach. Cover; keep warm.

3. Carefully add remaining oil to skillet. Add shrimp. Cook and stir for 2 to 3 minutes or until shrimp are opaque. Serve shrimp over wilted spinach.

Per Serving: 159 cal., 8 g fat (1 g sat. fat), 129 mg chol., 315 mg sodium, 2 g carbo., 6 g fiber, 19 g pro.

Sea Bass with Lemon-Caper Butter

If it's more convenient, make the lemon-caper butter in advance and store in the fridge. This recipe will work with any white, firm-fleshed fish, like cod.

Start to Finish: 20 minutes
Makes 4 servings

4	6-ounce fresh or frozen sea bass steaks, 1 inch thick
	Salt and ground black pepper
1	medium lemon
¼	cup butter, softened
1	tablespoon capers, drained
1	clove garlic, minced, or ½ teaspoon bottled minced garlic

1. Thaw fish, if frozen. Rinse fish; pat dry with paper towels. Preheat broiler. Sprinkle fish with salt and pepper. Place fish on the greased unheated rack of a broiler pan. Broil 4 inches from heat for 8 to 12 minutes or until fish flakes easily when tested with a fork, turning once halfway through broiling.

2. Meanwhile, finely shred 1 teaspoon peel from lemon. Cut lemon in half; squeeze one half to get 2 teaspoons juice. Cut remaining lemon half into wedges; set wedges aside.

3. For lemon-caper butter, in a small bowl, stir together lemon peel, lemon juice, butter, capers, and garlic. Top fish with lemon-caper butter. Serve with lemon wedges.

Per Serving: 277 cal., 16 g fat (8 g sat. fat), 102 mg chol., 449 mg sodium, 2 g carbo., 1 g fiber, 32 g pro.

Lime-Steamed Salmon

Use a rice steamer if you have one. If not, follow the directions for steaming using a skillet and a steamer basket.

Start to Finish: 30 minutes
Makes 3 servings

1	pound fresh or frozen salmon fillet, skinned
2	limes
2	tablespoons toasted sesame oil
1	tablespoon grated fresh ginger
⅛	teaspoon salt
⅛	teaspoon ground black pepper
2	cups trimmed small green beans (about 8 ounces) or one 9-ounce package frozen French-cut green beans
	Lime wedges (optional)

1. Thaw fish, if frozen. Rinse fish; pat dry with paper towels. Cut fish into three pieces; set aside.

2. Finely shred 2 teaspoons of peel from the limes; set limes aside. In a small bowl, stir together lime peel, sesame oil, ginger, salt, and pepper. Set mixture aside.

3. In a small covered saucepan, cook green beans in a small amount of boiling salted water about 15 minutes (5 to 6 minutes for frozen beans) or until crisp-tender.

4. Meanwhile, place 4 cups water in a very large skillet. Bring to boiling; reduce heat. Thinly slice limes. Place lime slices and fish in a steamer basket. Generously brush fish with oil mixture. Carefully place steamer basket in the skillet. Cover and steam over gently boiling water about 10 minutes or until fish flakes easily when tested with a fork.

5. To serve, arrange green beans in a serving dish; remove fish from lime slices and arrange fish on top of beans. If desired, serve with lime wedges.

Per Serving: 293 cal., 14 g fat (2 g sat. fat), 78 mg chol., 204 mg sodium, 11 g carbo., 4 g fiber, 32 g pro.

MAKE IT A MENU
Lime-Steamed Salmon with green beans, couscous, apple wedges, Boston Cream Pie (page 177)

Make it a point to *get acquainted with your fish mongers*. They can help you choose the best variety for your recipe and steer you to the *best seafood buys*.

Tossed Shrimp Salad

Start to Finish: 10 minutes

Makes 4 servings

- 2   8-ounce packages frozen peeled, cooked shrimp, thawed
- 1   10-ounce package torn mixed salad greens
- ¼   cup thinly sliced green onions (2)
- ⅓   cup bottled Italian salad dressing
     Salt (optional)
     Ground black pepper (optional)
- ¼   cup sliced toasted almonds

1. Drain shrimp; pat dry with paper towels.

2. In a large salad bowl, combine shrimp, salad greens, and green onions. Pour dressing over salad; toss to coat. If desired, season to taste with salt and pepper. Sprinkle with almonds.

Per Serving: 301 cal., 20 g fat (2 g sat. fat), 185 mg chol., 483 mg sodium, 6 g carbo., 2 g fiber, 26 g pro.

Cajun Catfish with Coleslaw

Salt-free Cajun seasoning has a zippier flavor and richer color than regular Cajun seasonings, most of which contain considerable salt. If you use regular Cajun seasoning, omit the salt.

Prep: 10 minutes   *Bake:* 15 minutes

Makes 4 servings

- 1   pound fresh or frozen skinless catfish fillets, ½ inch thick
- 2½ teaspoons salt-free Cajun seasoning
- ¼   teaspoon salt
- 2   cups shredded cabbage with carrot (coleslaw mix)
- 3   tablespoons mayonnaise or salad dressing
     Salt and ground black pepper (optional)
     Bottled hot pepper sauce (optional)

1. Thaw fish, if frozen. Preheat oven to 350°F. Rinse fish; pat dry with paper towels. If necessary, cut fish into four serving-size pieces.

2. Combine 2 teaspoons of the Cajun seasoning and the ¼ teaspoon salt; sprinkle both sides of fish with seasoning mixture. Arrange fish in a greased 3-quart rectangular baking dish. Tuck under any thin edges.

3. Bake for 15 to 20 minutes or until fish flakes easily when tested with a fork.

4. Meanwhile, in a medium bowl, stir together cabbage, mayonnaise, and the remaining ½ teaspoon Cajun seasoning. If desired, season to taste with salt and pepper. Cover and chill until serving time. Serve catfish with coleslaw and, if desired, hot pepper sauce.

Per Serving: 241 cal., 17 g fat (3 g sat. fat), 57 mg chol., 127 mg sodium, 3 g carbo., 1 g fiber, 18 g pro.

Buttery Sole with Almonds and Cilantro

Start to Finish: 15 minutes

Makes 4 to 6 servings

- 1½ pounds sole fillets
     Salt and freshly cracked black pepper
- 2   tablespoons butter, softened
- 2   tablespoons slivered almonds, toasted
- 2   teaspoons snipped fresh cilantro

1. Preheat the broiler. Season fish with salt and pepper. Rub 1 tablespoon of the butter on the inside of a 13×9×2-inch baking pan or a shallow broiler-proof baking dish.

2. Place the fillets in the pan in a single layer and spread with remaining butter. Broil about 4 inches from the heat for 4 to 6 minutes or until fish flakes easily when tested with a fork. Sprinkle with almonds and cilantro just before serving.

Per Serving: 228 cal., 9 g fat (4 g sat. fat), 97 mg chol., 325 mg sodium, 4 g carbo., 2 g fiber, 33 g pro.

Beer-Battered Cod

When you're buying frozen fish fillets, look for a package of individually wrapped fillets. You can remove just the number you need and save the rest for another meal.

Start to Finish: 35 minutes

Makes 4 servings

6	4- to 6-ounce fresh or frozen cod fillets
	Cooking oil for deep-fat frying
2	cups self-rising flour
½	teaspoon salt
½	teaspoon ground black pepper
1	12-ounce can beer

1. Thaw fish, if frozen. Rinse fish; pat dry with paper towels. In a heavy 3-quart saucepan or deep-fat fryer, heat 2 inches of oil to 365°F.

2. Meanwhile, in a large bowl stir together flour, salt, and pepper. Sprinkle both sides of fish with 2 tablespoons of the flour mixture. Add beer to remaining flour mixture and stir until combined. (Batter will be thick.) Dip fish pieces, one at a time, into the batter, coating well.

3. Fry fish, one or two pieces at a time, for 4 to 6 minutes or until golden and fish flakes easily when tested with a fork. Drain on paper towels; keep warm in a 300°F oven while frying remaining fish.

Per Serving: 635 cal., 29 g fat (4 g sat. fat), 72 mg chol., 1,181 mg sodium, 50 g carbo., 2 g fiber, 37 g pro.

Roasted Curried Shrimp

Thirty minutes is exactly the right time for marinating the shrimp. Less than that and they won't absorb enough flavor; more than that and they may toughen.

Prep: 10 minutes *Marinate:* 30 minutes

Bake: 8 minutes

Makes 4 to 6 servings

1½	pounds fresh or frozen medium shrimp, peeled and deveined
¼	cup reduced-sodium soy sauce
1	tablespoon lemon juice
2	teaspoons curry powder
2	cloves garlic, minced, or 1 teaspoon bottled minced garlic

1. Thaw shrimp, if frozen. Rinse shrimp; pat dry. In a shallow baking dish, whisk together soy sauce, lemon juice, curry powder, and garlic. Add shrimp and stir to coat. Cover and place in refrigerator for 30 minutes.

2. Preheat the oven to 350°F. Line a baking sheet with foil. Using a slotted spoon, remove shrimp from the marinade and spread in a single layer on the prepared baking sheet. Discard remaining marinade.

3. Bake for 8 to 9 minutes or until shrimp turn opaque.

Per Serving: 186 cal., 3 g fat (1 g sat. fat), 259 mg chol., 378 mg sodium, 2 g carbo., 0 g fiber, 35 g pro.

Halibut with Tomatoes and Olives

Fished from cold northern waters, halibut is white and firm with a mild flavor. It can be expensive, but watch out for specials at your supermarket.

Start to Finish: 20 minutes

Makes 4 servings

4	6-ounce fresh or frozen halibut steaks, 1 inch thick
2	tablespoons olive oil
	Salt and ground black pepper
⅓	cup coarsely chopped tomato
⅓	cup Greek black olives, pitted and coarsely chopped
2	tablespoons snipped fresh flat-leaf parsley or 1 tablespoon snipped fresh oregano or thyme
	Mixed salad greens (optional)

1. Thaw fish, if frozen. Rinse fish; pat dry with paper towels. Brush fish with 1 tablespoon of the oil; sprinkle with salt and pepper.

2. Preheat broiler. Place fish on the greased unheated rack of a broiler pan. Broil fish 4 inches from heat for 8 to 12 minutes or until fish flakes easily when tested with a fork, turning once halfway through broiling.

3. Meanwhile, stir together the remaining 1 tablespoon oil, tomato, olives, and parsley. Spoon tomato mixture over fish. If desired, serve with salad greens.

Per Serving: 262 cal., 12 g fat (2 g sat. fat), 54 mg chol., 264 mg sodium, 2 g carbo., 1 g fiber, 36 g pro.

Halibut
with Tomatoes
and Olives

Easy Baked Fish

Start to Finish: 30 minutes
Makes 4 servings

- ½ cup packaged herb-seasoned stuffing mix, finely crushed
- 2 tablespoons butter, melted
- 2 7.6-ounce packages frozen Caesar Parmesan or grill-flavored fish portions (4 portions)
- 2 teaspoons lemon juice

1. Preheat oven to 425°F. In a small bowl, combine dry stuffing mix and melted butter; toss until well mixed.

2. Place frozen fish portions in a greased 2-quart rectangular baking dish. Sprinkle with lemon juice. Sprinkle crumb mixture over fish.

3. Bake for 18 to 20 minutes or until fish flakes easily when tested with a fork.

Per Serving: 180 cal., 9 g fat (4 g sat. fat), 75 mg chol., 380 mg sodium, 6 g carbo., 1 g fiber, 18 g pro.

Salmon Caesar Salad

Smoked salmon is especially flavorful, but any form of salmon works well in this main-dish salad.

Start to Finish: 15 minutes
Makes 3 servings

- 1 10-ounce package Caesar salad (includes lettuce, dressing, croutons, and cheese)
- 1 small yellow, red, or green sweet pepper, cut into thin strips
- 1 small cucumber, quartered lengthwise and sliced
- 6 ounces smoked, poached, or canned salmon, skinned, boned, and broken into chunks (1 cup)
- ½ of a lemon, cut into 3 wedges

1. In a large bowl, combine the lettuce and dressing from the packaged salad, the sweet pepper strips, and cucumber; toss gently to coat.

2. Add salmon and the croutons and cheese from the packaged salad; toss gently to mix. Divide among three dinner plates. Before serving, squeeze juice from a lemon wedge over each salad.

Per Serving: 199 cal., 11 g fat (1 g sat. fat), 16 mg chol., 564 mg sodium, 10 g carbo., 2 g fiber, 14 g pro.

Spanish-Style Rice with Seafood

Prep: 15 minutes   *Stand:* 10 minutes
Makes 4 servings

- 1 5.6- to 6.2-ounce package Spanish-style rice mix
- 1¾ cups water
- 1 tablespoon butter or margarine
  Several dashes bottled hot pepper sauce
- 1 12-ounce package frozen peeled, deveined shrimp
- 1 cup frozen peas
- ½ cup chopped tomato (1 medium)

1. In a large skillet, stir together rice mix, water, butter, and hot pepper sauce. Bring to boiling; reduce heat. Cover and simmer for 5 minutes. Stir frozen shrimp into rice mixture. Return to boiling; reduce heat. Cover and simmer for 2 to 3 minutes more or until shrimp turn opaque. Remove from heat. Stir in peas. Cover and let stand for 10 minutes. Sprinkle with chopped tomato before serving.

Per Serving: 197 cal., 6 g fat (2 g sat. fat), 137 mg chol., 414 mg sodium, 15 g carbo., 2 g fiber, 21 g pro.

Fish Tacos

Start to Finish: 20 minutes
Makes 4 servings

- 1 11-ounce package frozen baked, breaded fish sticks (18)
- 1½ cups packaged shredded cabbage with carrot (coleslaw mix) or shredded cabbage
- 3 tablespoons low-fat mayonnaise or salad dressing
- 8 corn tortillas
  Purchased peach or other fruit salsa

1. Bake fish according to package directions. Cut each fish stick in half crosswise.

2. Meanwhile, in a medium bowl, combine coleslaw mix and mayonnaise; toss to coat. Divide cabbage mixture among tortillas. Add fish and top with peach salsa.

Per Serving: 334 cal., 12 g fat (2 g sat. fat), 22 mg chol., 655 mg sodium, 47 g carbo., 4 g fiber, 10 g pro.

Fish Tacos

Fish sticks are usually made from *cod, pollock,*
or other white fish. Typically, the fish fillet is frozen,
sliced into sticks, and breaded.

Snapper Veracruz

Prep: 15 minutes   *Bake:* 30 minutes
Makes 4 servings

- 1¼ to 1½ pounds fresh or frozen red snapper fillets or firm-textured whitefish fillets such as catfish, ½ to ¾ inch thick, skinned
- 1 14.5-ounce can Mexican-style stewed tomatoes, undrained
- 1 cup pitted ripe olives
- 2 tablespoons olive oil
- 1 10-ounce package seasoned yellow rice

1. Thaw fish, if frozen. Rinse fish; pat dry with paper towels. Cut fish into four serving-size pieces. Preheat oven to 300°F.

2. In a large ovenproof skillet, combine undrained tomatoes and olives. Top with fish fillets; drizzle with olive oil. Bake, uncovered, for 15 minutes. Spoon some of the tomato mixture over the fish and bake about 15 minutes more or until fish flakes easily when tested with a fork.

3. Meanwhile, prepare rice according to package directions. Serve fish and sauce with rice.
Per Serving: 566 cal., 19 g fat (3 g sat. fat), 52 mg chol., 1,466 mg sodium, 63 g carbo., 3 g fiber, 36 g pro.

Pesto Pasta with Shrimp

Mixing inexpensive pasta with pricier shrimp is a great way to enjoy these tasty crustaceans without breaking the budget.
Start to Finish: 20 minutes
Makes 4 servings

- 12 ounces fresh or frozen, peeled and deveined medium shrimp (leave tails intact, if desired)
- 1 9-ounce package refrigerated linguine
- 1 7-ounce container refrigerated basil pesto
- 2 teaspoons finely shredded lemon peel
- 2 tablespoons snipped fresh chives
- 1 teaspoon finely shredded lemon peel (optional)

1. Thaw shrimp, if frozen. Rinse shrimp; pat dry with paper towels. In a large saucepan, cook linguine in a large amount of boiling water for 1 minute. Add shrimp; cook about 2 minutes more or until shrimp turn opaque. Drain well.

2. Meanwhile, in a small bowl, stir together pesto and the 2 teaspoons lemon peel.

3. To serve, divide pasta mixture among four shallow bowls or dinner plates. Spoon pesto mixture over pasta mixture. Sprinkle with chives and, if desired, the 1 teaspoon lemon peel.
Per Serving: 497 cal., 23 g fat (6 g sat. fat), 186 mg chol., 562 mg sodium, 42 g carbo., 3 g fiber, 30 g pro.

No-Bake Tuna-Noodle Casserole

Cavatappi is a short spiral tube pasta with ridges, which are good for capturing the velvety sauce.
Start to Finish: 20 minutes
Makes 4 servings

- 8 ounces dried cavatappi, wagon wheel macaroni, or medium shell macaroni
- 1½ cups desired frozen vegetables (optional)
- ¼ to ½ cup milk
- 1 6.5-ounce container or two 4-ounce containers light semisoft cheese with garlic and herb or cucumber and dill
- 1 12.25-ounce can solid white tuna (water pack), drained and broken into chunks
  Salt and ground black pepper

1. Cook pasta in lightly salted water according to package directions. If desired, add frozen vegetables during the last 4 minutes of cooking. Drain and return to pan. Add ¼ cup milk and the cheese to pasta in pan. Cook and stir over medium heat until cheese melts and pasta is coated, adding additional milk as necessary for desired consistency. Gently fold in tuna; heat through. Season to taste with salt and pepper.
Per Serving: 417 cal., 10 g fat (7 g sat. fat), 66 mg chol., 552 mg sodium, 45 g carbo., 2 g fiber, 33 g pro.

No-Bake
Tuna-Noodle
Casserole

Citrus Scallops

Start to Finish: 15 minutes

Makes 4 servings

- 1 pound fresh or frozen sea scallops
- 1 medium orange
- 1 tablespoon olive oil
- 2 cloves garlic, minced, or 1 teaspoon bottled minced garlic
- ½ teaspoon snipped fresh thyme
   Salt and ground black pepper

1. Thaw scallops, if frozen. Rinse scallops; pat dry with paper towels. Set scallops aside. Finely shred 1 teaspoon peel from the orange. Cut orange in half; squeeze to get ⅓ cup juice.

2. In a large skillet, heat oil over medium-high heat. Add scallops. Cook, stirring frequently, for 2 to 3 minutes or until scallops turn opaque. Transfer scallops to a serving platter; keep warm.

3. For sauce, add garlic to skillet; cook and stir for 30 seconds (add more oil to skillet if necessary). Add orange peel, orange juice, and thyme to skillet. Bring to boiling; reduce heat. Simmer, uncovered, for 1 to 2 minutes or until desired consistency. Season to taste with salt and pepper. Pour over scallops.

Per Serving: 142 cal., 4 g fat (1 g sat. fat), 37 mg chol.,
218 mg sodium, 5 g carbo., 0 g fiber, 19 g pro.

Broiled Snapper with Fennel

Fennel has a mild, sweet flavor that may remind you of licorice. Save some of the delicate, fernlike tops to use as a garnish.

Prep: 15 minutes   *Broil:* 4 to 6 minutes per ½-inch thickness

Makes 4 servings

- 4 6- to 8-ounce fresh or frozen red snapper fillets
   Salt and ground black pepper
- 1 medium lemon
- 1 tablespoon butter
- 1 fennel bulb, trimmed and cut crosswise into thin slices (about 1¼ cups)
- 1 teaspoon snipped fresh dill or thyme

1. Thaw fish, if frozen. Rinse fish; pat dry with paper towels. Preheat broiler. Measure thickness of fish. Place fish on the greased unheated rack of a broiler pan. Sprinkle fish with salt and pepper. Broil 4 inches from heat until fish flakes easily when tested with a fork (allow 4 to 6 minutes per ½-inch thickness of fish).

2. Meanwhile, finely shred 1 teaspoon peel from lemon. Cut lemon in half; squeeze one half to get 4 teaspoons juice. Cut remaining half into wedges; set wedges aside.

3. In a small saucepan, melt butter over medium-high heat. Add fennel and cook in hot butter for 5 to 8 minutes or just until tender. Stir in lemon peel, lemon juice, and dill. Season to taste with salt and pepper. Spoon fennel over fish. Serve with lemon wedges.

Per Serving: 237 cal., 6 g fat (2 g sat. fat), 81 mg chol.,
318 mg sodium, 4 g carbo., 2 g fiber, 41 g pro.

Buttery Garlic Shrimp with Red Pepper

For extra color and flavor, add broccoli florets to the boiling pasta for the last 4 minutes of cooking time or sauté with the shrimp.

Start to Finish: 10 minutes

Makes 4 servings

- 1½ pounds fresh or frozen medium shrimp, peeled and deveined
- 8 ounces dried angel hair pasta
- 2 tablespoons butter
- 2 cloves garlic, minced, or 1 teaspoon bottled minced garlic
   Salt
- ¼ teaspoon crushed red pepper

1. Thaw shrimp, if frozen. Rinse shrimp; pat dry with paper towels. Cook pasta according to package directions. Drain pasta; keep warm.

2. Meanwhile, in a large skillet, melt butter over medium heat. Add garlic; cook for 30 seconds. Add the shrimp; sprinkle with salt. Cook and stir for 2 to 4 minutes or until shrimp turn opaque. Sprinkle with crushed red pepper. Serve over hot cooked pasta.

Per Serving: 444 cal., 10 g fat (4 g sat. fat), 274 mg chol.,
438 mg sodium, 44 g carbo., 1 g fiber, 42 g pro

Buttery Garlic Shrimp
with Red Pepper

Oven-Fried Fish

Fish fillets coated with a Parmesan crumb coating bake to golden goodness in as little as 4 minutes.

Prep: 15 minutes Bake: 4 to 6 minutes per ½-inch thickness
Makes 4 servings

- 1 pound fresh or frozen skinless cod, orange roughy, or catfish fillets
- ¼ cup milk
- ⅓ cup all-purpose flour
- ½ cup fine dry bread crumbs
- 2 tablespoons grated Parmesan cheese
- ¼ teaspoon lemon-pepper seasoning
- 2 tablespoons butter or margarine, melted
  Lemon wedges (optional)

1. Preheat oven to 450°F. Thaw fish, if frozen. Rinse fish; pat dry with paper towels. If necessary, cut into four serving-size pieces. Measure the thickness of each piece. Place milk in a shallow dish. Place flour in another shallow dish. In a third shallow dish, combine bread crumbs, Parmesan cheese, and lemon-pepper seasoning. Add melted butter to bread crumb mixture; stir until well mixed.

2. Grease a shallow baking pan; set aside. Dip fish in the milk; coat with flour. Dip again in the milk; dip in the crumb mixture, turning to coat all sides. Place fish in a single layer in prepared baking pan. Bake, uncovered, for 4 to 6 minutes per ½-inch thickness or until fish flakes easily when tested with a fork. If desired, serve with lemon wedges.

Per Serving: 254 cal., 9 g total fat (5 g sat. fat), 75 mg chol., 565 mg sodium, 15 g carbo., 1 g fiber, 26 g pro.

Spinach and Pasta Salad with Shrimp

Fresh dill is widely available in the produce section of most supermarkets. You can substitute with 1 teaspoon dried dill and 2 tablespoons snipped fresh parsley.

Start to Finish: 25 minutes
Makes 6 servings

- 1 cup dried medium shell pasta or elbow macaroni
- 1 10- to 12-ounce package frozen peeled, cooked shrimp, thawed
- 1 cup chopped red sweet pepper
- ⅓ cup bottled creamy onion or Caesar salad dressing
- 2 tablespoons snipped fresh dill (optional)
  Salt and ground black pepper
- 1 6-ounce package fresh baby spinach
- 4 ounces goat cheese (chévre), sliced, or feta cheese, crumbled

1. Cook pasta according to package directions; drain. Rinse with cold water; drain again.

2. In a very large bowl, combine cooked pasta, shrimp, and sweet pepper. Drizzle with salad dressing and, if desired, sprinkle with dill; toss gently to coat. Season to taste with salt and black pepper.

3. Divide spinach among six salad plates or bowls. Top with shrimp mixture and cheese.

Per Serving: 247 cal., 10 g total fat (4 g sat. fat), 156 mg chol., 435 mg sodium, 17 g carbo., 2 g fiber, 23 g pro.

Garlic-Broiled Shrimp and Tomatoes

Prep: 10 minutes Marinate: 2 to 4 hours Broil: 5 minutes
Makes 4 servings

- 1 pound fresh or frozen extra-large shrimp, peeled and deveined (about 20)
- 2 tablespoons olive oil
- 2 tablespoons dry vermouth or white wine
- 2 cloves garlic, minced
  Dash salt
  Dash pepper
- 2 medium tomatoes, halved crosswise

1. Place shrimp in a resealable plastic bag set in a deep bowl.

2. For marinade, in a small bowl combine oil, vermouth or white wine, garlic, salt, and pepper. Pour over shrimp in bag. Close bag and marinate in the refrigerator for 2 to 4 hours. Drain shrimp, reserving marinade.

3. Arrange shrimp on the unheated rack of a broiler pan. Place tomatoes, cut side up, next to shrimp. Brush shrimp and tomatoes with marinade. Discard remaining marinade. Broil 4 to 6 inches from the heat about 5 minutes or until shrimp turn opaque, turning shrimp over once.

Per Serving: 170 cal., 8 g total fat, 129 mg chol., 164 mg sodium, 4 g carb., 18 g protein.

Pan-Seared Tilapia
with Almond Browned Butter

Pan-Seared Tilapia with Almond Browned Butter

Pan-searing gives the fish a golden crust and locks in flavor and natural juices.

Start to Finish: 25 minutes
Makes 4 servings

4   4- to 5-ounce skinless fresh or frozen tilapia fillets or other white fish
3   cups fresh pea pods, trimmed
     Salt
     Freshly ground black pepper
1   teaspoon all-purpose flour
1   tablespoon olive oil
2   tablespoons butter
¼   cup coarsely chopped almonds
1   tablespoon snipped fresh parsley

1. Thaw fish, if frozen. Rinse fish; pat dry with paper towels. Set aside. In a large saucepan, bring a large amount of lightly salted water to boiling. Add pea pods; cook for 2 minutes. Drain and set aside.

2. Meanwhile, sprinkle one side of each fish fillet with salt and pepper; sprinkle with the flour. Preheat a large skillet over medium-high heat. When skillet is hot (a drop of water should sizzle or roll), remove from the heat; immediately add olive oil, tilting skillet to coat with oil. Return skillet to heat; add fish, floured side up (if necessary, cook fish half at a time). Cook fish for 4 to 5 minutes or until it is easy to remove with spatula. Gently turn fish and cook for 2 to 3 minutes more or until fish flakes easily when tested with a fork. Arrange pea pods on a serving platter; arrange fish on top of pea pods.

3. Reduce heat to medium. Add butter to the skillet. When butter begins to melt, stir in almonds. Cook for 30 to 60 seconds or until butter melts and nuts toast lightly (do not let butter burn). Spoon the butter mixture over fish fillets. Sprinkle with parsley.

Per Serving: 266 cal., 15 g total fat (5 g sat. fat), 71 mg chol., 210 mg sodium, 7 g carbo., 3 g fiber, 24 g pro.

Shrimp Alfredo

Start to Finish: 25 minutes

Makes 4 servings

3	cups water
1	cup milk
¼	cup butter or margarine
2	4.4-ounce packages noodles with Alfredo-style sauce
3	cups thinly sliced zucchini (3 small)
1	10- to 12-ounce package frozen peeled, cooked shrimp, thawed, or 12 ounces chunk-style imitation crabmeat

1. In a large saucepan, combine water, milk, and butter. Bring to boiling. Stir in noodle mixes. Return to boiling; reduce heat. Simmer, uncovered, for 5 minutes.

2. Stir in zucchini. Return to a gentle boil. Cook, uncovered, about 3 minutes or until noodles are tender. Gently stir in shrimp; heat through. Remove from heat. Let stand, covered, for 3 to 5 minutes or until slightly thickened.

Per Serving: 486 cal., 21 g total fat (12 g sat. fat), 264 mg chol., 1279 mg sodium, 44 g carbo., 2 g fiber, 30 g pro.

Basil-Buttered Salmon

Use the leftover basil-and-butter mixture to season your favorite cooked vegetables.

Start to Finish: 25 minutes

Makes 4 servings

4	5-ounce fresh or frozen skinless salmon, halibut, or sea bass fillets, about 1 inch thick
½	teaspoon salt-free lemon-pepper seasoning
1	tablespoon butter or margarine, softened
1	teaspoon snipped fresh basil or dill or ¼ teaspoon dried basil, crushed, or dried dill
1	teaspoon snipped fresh parsley or cilantro
¼	teaspoon finely shredded lemon peel or lime peel

1. Thaw fish, if frozen. Preheat broiler. Rinse fish; pat dry with paper towels. Sprinkle with lemon-pepper seasoning.

2. Place fish on the greased unheated rack of a broiler pan, tucking under any thin edges to make fish of uniform thickness. Broil about 4 inches from the heat for 8 to 12 minutes or until fish flakes easily when tested with a fork, carefully turning once halfway through broiling.

3. Meanwhile, in a small bowl, combine butter, basil, parsley, and lemon peel. To serve, spoon butter mixture on top of fish.

Per Serving: 284 cal., 18 g total fat (5 g sat. fat), 91 mg chol., 104 mg sodium, 0 g carbo., 0 g fiber, 28 g pro.

Watch for specials on frozen shrimp and stock up. It's a great thing to have in the freezer on reserve for special treat nights.

Black Bean and Corn Quesadillas

meatless dishes

Whether you eat meatless all the time or prepare an occasional meat-free dinner for variety, you have plenty of savory main dishes to choose from. Our recipes are based upon beans, cheese, grains, pasta, and vegetables—naturally delicious, naturally inexpensive.

Black Bean and Corn Quesadillas

Flour tortillas come in an array of flavors, sizes, and colors. Store opened bags of tortillas in the refrigerator and watch their expiration date or freeze sealed bags for up to 3 months.
Start to Finish: 20 minutes
Makes 4 servings

- 1 8-ounce package shredded 4-cheese Mexican blend cheese (2 cups)
- 8 8-inch whole wheat or flour tortillas
- 1½ cups bottled black bean and corn salsa
- 1 medium avocado, seeded, peeled, and chopped
  Dairy sour cream

1. Preheat oven to 300°F. Sprinkle cheese evenly over half of each tortilla. Top each tortilla with 1 tablespoon of the salsa. Divide avocado among tortillas. Fold tortillas in half, pressing gently.

2. Heat a large skillet over medium-high heat for 2 minutes; reduce heat to medium. Cook two of the quesadillas for 2 to 3 minutes or until lightly browned and cheese is melted, turning once. Transfer quesadillas to a baking sheet. Keep warm in the oven. Repeat with the remaining quesadillas, cooking two at a time.

3. Cut quesadillas into wedges. Serve with sour cream and the remaining salsa.
Per Serving: 647 cal., 35 g fat (16 g sat. fat), 61 mg chol., 1,405 mg sodium, 48 g carbo., 23 g fiber, 31 g pro.

Chili Corn Pie

Prep: 20 minutes   *Bake:* 20 minutes   *Stand:* 5 minutes
Makes 4 servings

- 2 11-ounce packages frozen chunky beef and bean chili
- 1 11.5-ounce package refrigerated corn bread twists
- ⅓ cup shredded cheddar cheese
- 1 tablespoon snipped fresh cilantro
- ¼ cup dairy sour cream

1. Preheat oven to 375°F. Heat the frozen chili according to microwave package directions.

2. Meanwhile, on a lightly floured surface, unroll sheet of corn bread twist dough (do not separate into strips). Press at perforations to seal. Roll into an 11×7-inch rectangle.

3. Spoon hot chili into a 2-quart rectangular baking dish. Immediately place corn bread dough on top of chili. Using a sharp knife, cut slits in corn bread dough to allow steam to escape.

4. Bake about 20 minutes or until corn bread is lightly browned. Sprinkle with cheese and cilantro. Let stand for 5 minutes before serving. Top individual servings with sour cream.
Per Serving: 512 cal., 24 g fat (9 g sat. fat), 44 mg chol., 1,429 mg sodium, 50 g carbo., 3 g fiber, 22 g pro.

Gardener's Pie

Prep: 15 minutes   *Bake:* 45 minutes
Makes 4 servings

- 1 16-ounce package frozen mixed vegetables (any combination), thawed
- 1 11-ounce can condensed cheddar cheese soup
- ½ teaspoon dried thyme, crushed
- 1 20-ounce package refrigerated mashed potatoes
- 1 cup shredded smoked cheddar cheese (4 ounces)

1. Preheat oven to 350°F. In a 1½-quart casserole, combine thawed vegetables, soup, and thyme. Stir mashed potatoes to soften. Spread mashed potatoes carefully over vegetable mixture to cover surface.

2. Bake, covered, for 30 minutes. Uncover and bake about 15 minutes more or until heated through, topping with cheese for the last 5 minutes of baking. Serve in shallow bowls.

Per Serving: 349 cal., 17 g fat (8 g sat. fat), 39 mg chol., 1,031 mg sodium, 40 g carbo., 4 g fiber, 15 g pro.

Sweet Beans and Pasta

Kids and adults alike have fallen for the nutty flavor of shelled edamame (sweet soybeans). Toss them with rosemary, carrot, linguine, and Alfredo sauce for a fresh twist on a pasta favorite.

Start to Finish: 30 minutes
Makes 4 servings

- 8 ounces dried linguine
- 1½ cups frozen sweet soybeans (shelled edamame)
- 2 medium carrots, shredded, or 1 cup purchased shredded carrot
- 1 10-ounce container refrigerated Alfredo pasta sauce
- 2 teaspoons snipped fresh rosemary

1. Cook the linguine according to package directions, adding the soybeans and carrot the last 10 minutes of cooking. Drain and return to pan.

2. Add Alfredo sauce and rosemary to linguine mixture in pan; toss to combine. Heat through.

Per Serving: 544 cal., 27 g fat (1 g sat. fat), 35 mg chol., 280 mg sodium, 57 g carbo., 5 g fiber, 20 g pro.

Couscous-Stuffed Peppers

Vary this vegetable-and-rice main dish according to your family's preferences. Use any color sweet pepper, any variety of pasta sauce, or another Italian-style cheese.

Prep: 15 minutes   *Bake:* 25 minutes
Makes 4 servings

- 1 6-ounce package toasted pine nut couscous mix
- 1 medium carrot, shredded, or ½ cup purchased shredded carrot
- 2 large or 4 small red, yellow, green, or orange sweet peppers
- ½ cup shredded Italian cheese blend (2 ounces)
- 1½ cups mushroom and olive or tomato basil pasta sauce

1. Preheat oven to 350°F. Prepare couscous mix according to package directions, omitting oil and adding the shredded carrot with the couscous.

2. Meanwhile, cut large peppers in half lengthwise (for small peppers, cut off tops and reserve). Remove seeds and membranes from peppers. Cook peppers (and tops, if using) in boiling water for 5 minutes. Drain on paper towels. Place peppers, cut sides up, in a 2-quart rectangular baking dish. Spoon cooked couscous mixture into peppers.

3. Bake, covered, for 20 to 25 minutes or until filling is heated through and peppers are tender. Sprinkle cheese over peppers. Bake, uncovered, about 5 minutes more or until cheese is melted.

4. Meanwhile, in a small saucepan, heat the pasta sauce. Serve peppers with sauce. (For small peppers, place pepper tops on top of couscous filling.)

Per Serving: 259 cal., 6 g fat (3 g sat. fat), 10 mg chol., 801 mg sodium, 42 g carbo., 7 g fiber, 11 g pro.

MAKE IT A MENU
Couscous-Stuffed Peppers, cornmeal rolls, apple wedges, Rocky Road Parfaits (page 184)

Couscous-
Stuffed Peppers

Chipotle Bean Enchiladas

Prep: 25 minutes   *Bake:* 30 minutes
Makes 5 servings

- 10 6-inch corn tortillas
- 1   15-ounce can pinto beans or black beans, rinsed and drained
- 1   tablespoon chopped chipotle pepper in adobo sauce
- 1   8-ounce package shredded Mexican cheese blend (2 cups)
- 2   10-ounce cans enchilada sauce

1. Preheat oven to 350°F. Grease a 2-quart rectangular baking dish; set aside. Stack the tortillas and wrap tightly in foil. Warm tortillas in the oven for 10 minutes.

2. Meanwhile, for filling, in a medium bowl, combine beans, chipotle pepper, 1 cup of the cheese, and ½ cup of the enchilada sauce. Spoon about ¼ cup of the filling onto one edge of each tortilla. Starting at the edge with the filling, roll up each tortilla.

3. Arrange tortillas, seam sides down, in the prepared baking dish. Top with remaining enchilada sauce. Cover with foil.

4. Bake about 25 minutes or until heated through. Remove foil. Sprinkle with remaining 1 cup cheese. Bake, uncovered, about 5 minutes more or until cheese melts.
Per Serving: 487 cal., 19 g fat (8 g sat. fat), 40 mg chol., 1,091 mg sodium, 63 g carbo., 14 g fiber, 23 g pro.

Cashew Vegetable Stir-Fry

Start to Finish: 10 minutes
Makes 4 servings

- 1   tablespoon cooking oil
- 1   16-ounce package frozen stir-fry vegetables
- ⅓   cup bottled stir-fry sauce
- 3   cups hot cooked rice
- ¾   cup dry roasted cashews

1. In a large skillet, heat oil over medium-high heat. Add vegetables; cook and stir about 3 minutes or until crisp-tender. Add the sauce; stir-fry for 1 to 2 minutes more or until heated through. Serve vegetable mixture over rice. Sprinkle with cashews.
Per Serving: 393 cal., 16 g fat (3 g sat. fat), 0 mg chol., 720 mg sodium, 54 g carbo., 4 g fiber, 9 g pro.

Pasta with Pepper-Cheese Sauce

Start to Finish: 25 minutes
Makes 4 to 6 servings

- 8   ounces dried medium shell pasta
- 1   0.9- to 1.25-ounce envelope hollandaise sauce mix
- 1   7-ounce jar roasted red sweet peppers, drained and chopped
- ½   cup shredded Monterey Jack cheese with jalapeño peppers (2 ounces)

1. Cook pasta according to package directions. Drain well and return pasta to pan. Meanwhile, for sauce, prepare hollandaise sauce according to package directions, except use only 2 tablespoons butter. Stir in roasted red peppers. Remove pan from heat. Add cheese to sauce, stirring until melted. Add sauce to pasta in pan; toss to coat.
Per Serving: 384 cal., 13 g fat (8 g sat. fat), 36 mg chol., 407 mg sodium, 53 g carbo., 2 g fiber, 13 g pro.

Tortellini Stir-Fry

Start to Finish: 20 minutes
Makes 4 servings

- 1   9-ounce package refrigerated cheese-filled tortellini
- 1   tablespoon cooking oil
- 1   16-ounce package fresh cut or frozen stir-fry vegetables (such as broccoli, pea pods, carrots, and celery)
- ¾   cup peanut stir-fry sauce
- ¼   cup chopped dry-roasted cashews

1. Cook tortellini according to package directions. Drain and set aside.

2. In a wok or large skillet, heat oil over medium-high heat. Add fresh-cut vegetables; cook and stir for 3 to 5 minutes (7 to 8 minutes for frozen vegetables) or until crisp-tender. Add tortellini and stir-fry sauce; toss gently to coat. Heat through. Sprinkle with cashews.
Per Serving: 400 cal., 16 g fat (3 g sat. fat), 30 mg chol., 1,256 mg sodium, 48 g carbo., 4 g fiber, 18 g pro.

Tortellini
Stir-Fry

Measure once for lots of flavor in bottled stir-fry sauce.
It provides a *dozen Asian seasoning ingredients*
in a single step. Keep convenient *peanut stir-fry sauce* and
one or two other varieties on hand.

Ramen Noodles With Vegetables

Saucy Pizza Skillet Dinner

Start to Finish: 30 minutes
Makes 4 servings

1   **6.4-ounce package lasagna dinner mix**
1   **4-ounce can (drained weight) mushroom stems and pieces, undrained**
½   **cup chopped green sweet pepper**
½   **cup sliced pitted ripe olives**
½   **cup shredded mozzarella cheese (2 ounces)**

1. If the noodles in the dinner mix are large, break them into bite-size pieces. In a large skillet, combine noodles and seasoning from dinner mix, 3 cups *water*, undrained mushrooms, and sweet pepper.

2. Bring to boiling, stirring occasionally; reduce heat. Cover and simmer about 13 minutes or until pasta is tender. Uncover and cook for 2 to 3 minutes more or until sauce is desired consistency. Sprinkle with olives and top with cheese. Remove from heat; let stand for 1 to 2 minutes or until cheese melts.
Per Serving: 198 cal., 3 g fat (1 g sat. fat), 9 mg chol., 1,285 mg sodium, 35 g carbo., 2 g fiber, 9 g pro.

Ramen Noodles with Vegetables

Start to Finish: 15 minutes
Makes 2 to 3 servings

1   **3-ounce package ramen noodles (any flavor)**
1   **tablespoon cooking oil**
6   **ounces fresh asparagus, trimmed and cut into 1-inch pieces (1 cup)**
1   **medium carrot, shredded, or ½ cup purchased shredded carrot**
¼   **cup light teriyaki sauce**

1. Cook noodles according to package directions (discard seasoning packet). Drain and keep warm.

2. Meanwhile, in a large skillet, heat oil over medium-high heat. Add asparagus and carrot. Cook and stir for 3 to 5 minutes or until asparagus is crisp-tender. Stir in teriyaki sauce and noodles; toss to coat.
Per Serving: 291 cal., 14 g fat (4 g sat. fat), 0 mg chol., 1,396 mg sodium, 36 g carbo., 3 g fiber, 7 g pro.

PASTA PRESTO
Ramen noodles are just one of the quick-cooking pastas you'll want to keep on hand. Remember: The skinnier the dried pasta, the faster it cooks. Skinny options include angel hair (capellini), vermicelli, and fine egg noodles. Refrigerated pasta cooks in about half the time as the same shape of dried pasta.

Oven Omelets with Artichokes and Spinach

Forget making individual omelets. This recipe bakes enough for six servings all at once.

Start to Finish: 25 minutes

Makes 6 servings

	Nonstick cooking spray
10	eggs
¼	cup water
½	teaspoon salt
¼	teaspoon ground black pepper
2	6-ounce jars marinated artichoke hearts, drained and chopped
4	cups chopped fresh spinach
¾	cup shredded Swiss or provolone cheese (3 ounces)

1. Preheat oven to 400°F. Coat a 15×10×1-inch baking pan with cooking spray; set pan aside.

2. In a medium bowl, combine eggs, water, salt, and pepper; beat lightly with a fork or rotary beater until combined but not frothy. Place the prepared pan on an oven rack. Carefully pour the egg mixture into the pan. Bake about 7 minutes or until egg mixture is set but still has a glossy surface.

3. Meanwhile, for filling, in a large skillet, cook artichoke hearts over medium heat until heated through, stirring occasionally. Add spinach; cook and stir until spinach is wilted.

4. Cut the baked egg mixture into six 5-inch-square omelets. Using a large spatula, remove omelet squares from pan. Invert omelet squares onto warm serving plates.

5. Spoon filling onto half of each omelet square. Sprinkle with cheese. Fold the other omelet half over the filled half, forming a triangle or rectangle.

Per Serving: 225 cal., 16 g fat (5 g sat. fat), 367 mg chol., 342 mg sodium, 7 g carbo., 2 g fiber, 16 g pro.

Tortilla Lasagna

Prep: 10 minutes   *Bake:* 35 minutes   *Stand:* 10 minutes

Makes 8 servings

1	7-ounce package Spanish rice mix
1	11-ounce can whole kernel corn with sweet peppers, undrained
2	15-ounce cans black beans, undrained
10	6-inch corn tortillas
2	cups shredded Monterey Jack cheese with jalapeño peppers (8 ounces)

1. Preheat oven to 400°F. Prepare the rice according to package directions, except substitute undrained corn for ½ cup of the liquid. Place undrained beans in a medium bowl; mash slightly.

2. Place five tortillas in the bottom of a greased 3-quart rectangular baking dish, overlapping and placing slightly up the sides of the dish (cut tortillas as necessary to fit). Spoon beans evenly over tortillas. Sprinkle with 1 cup of the cheese. Top with the remaining tortillas. Spoon cooked rice over tortillas.

3. Bake, covered, for 30 minutes. Uncover and sprinkle with remaining 1 cup cheese. Bake 5 minutes more or until cheese melts. Let stand 10 minutes before serving.

Per Serving: 406 cal., 12 g fat (7 g sat. fat), 34 mg chol., 1,101 mg sodium, 60 g carbo., 11 g fiber, 20 g pro.

Pasta with Broccoli and Asiago

Start to Finish: 25 minutes

Makes 2 servings

4	ounces dried spaghetti, linguine, fettuccine, or angel hair pasta
1	cup chopped broccoli
½	of a 5.2-ounce container semisoft cheese with garlic and herbs
¼	cup milk
	Finely shredded Asiago or Parmesan cheese

1. Cook pasta according to package directions, adding the broccoli the last 4 minutes of cooking. Drain and return pasta mixture to pan. In a small saucepan, combine semisoft cheese and milk. Cook and stir until smooth. Pour over pasta; toss to coat. Sprinkle individual servings with Asiago cheese.

Per Serving: 411 cal., 20 g fat (13 g sat. fat), 11 mg chol., 316 mg sodium, 47 g carbo., 3 g fiber, 14 g pro.

Linguine with Gorgonzola Sauce

Start to Finish: 20 minutes
Makes 4 servings

- 1   9-ounce package refrigerated linguine
- 1   pound fresh asparagus, trimmed and cut into 1-inch pieces, or one 10-ounce package frozen cut asparagus
- 1   cup half-and-half or light cream
- 1   cup crumbled Gorgonzola or other blue cheese (4 ounces)
- 2   tablespoons chopped walnuts, toasted

1. Cook linguine and asparagus according to package directions for the linguine; drain. Return pasta mixture to pan.

2. Meanwhile, in a medium saucepan, combine half-and-half, ¾ cup of the Gorgonzola cheese, and ¼ teaspoon *salt*. Bring to boiling over medium heat; reduce heat. Simmer, uncovered, for 3 minutes, stirring frequently.

3. Pour sauce over linguine mixture; toss gently to coat. Transfer to a warm serving dish. Sprinkle with the remaining ¼ cup Gorgonzola cheese and the walnuts.
Per Serving: 399 cal., 20 g fat (11 g sat. fat), 111 mg chol., 590 mg sodium, 39 g carbo., 3 g fiber, 18 g pro.

Asian Noodle Bowl

Start to Finish: 25 minutes
Makes 4 servings

- 8   ounces dried buckwheat soba noodles, udon noodles, or vermicelli noodles
- 2   cups vegetable broth
- ½   cup bottled peanut sauce
- 2   cups frozen Chinese-style stir-fry vegetables with seasonings
- ½   cup dry roasted peanuts, chopped

1. Cook noodles according to package directions. Drain noodles but do not rinse; set aside. In the same saucepan, combine vegetable broth and peanut sauce. Bring to boiling. Stir in frozen vegetables and cooked noodles. Return to boiling; reduce heat. Simmer for 2 to 3 minutes or until vegetables are heated through. Divide noodles and broth among four bowls. Sprinkle with peanuts.
Per Serving: 408 cal., 12 g fat (2 g sat. fat), 0 mg chol., 1,438 mg sodium, 62 g carbo., 7 g fiber, 19 g pro.

Two-Cheese Macaroni Bake

Prep: 20 minutes   *Bake:* 45 minutes   *Stand:* 10 minutes
Makes 8 servings

- 2   cups dried elbow macaroni (8 ounces)
- 4   eggs
- 2½ cups milk
- 8   ounces feta cheese, crumbled
- ¾   cup cream-style cottage cheese
- ½   teaspoon salt

1. Preheat oven to 375°F. Cook macaroni according to package directions; drain well. Place macaroni in a greased 2-quart square baking dish. In a medium bowl, lightly beat eggs with a fork; stir in milk, feta cheese, cottage cheese, and salt. Pour over macaroni. Bake for 45 minutes. Let stand for 10 minutes.
Per Serving: 267 cal., 11 g fat (6 g sat. fat), 136 mg chol., 609 mg sodium, 26 g carbo., 1 g fiber, 17 g pro.

Vegetable Curry

Start to Finish: 20 minutes
Makes 4 servings

- 1   16-ounce package frozen baby lima beans
- ½   cup water
- 1   15-ounce can tomato sauce with garlic and onion
- 1½   teaspoons curry powder
- 2   8.8-ounce pouches cooked Spanish-style rice
- ¼   cup sliced green onions or snipped fresh cilantro
      Olive oil (optional)

1. In a medium saucepan, combine lima beans and water. Bring to boiling; reduce heat. Cover and simmer for 5 minutes. Stir in tomato sauce and curry powder; return to boiling. Reduce heat. Simmer, covered, for 3 minutes.

2. Meanwhile, heat rice according to package directions. Spoon rice on one side of four dinner plates; spoon bean mixture alongside rice. Sprinkle with green onions. If desired, drizzle with olive oil.
Per Serving: 385 cal., 3 g fat (0 g sat. fat), 0 mg chol., 939 mg sodium, 72 g carbo., 9 g fiber, 14 g pro.

Vegetable
curry

Vegetarian Gumbo

Vegetarian Gumbo

Okra makes this stew taste special and also helps to thicken it.

Prep: 10 minutes Cook: 6 hours (low) or 3 hours (high)
Makes 6 servings

- 2 15-ounce cans black beans, rinsed and drained
- 1 28-ounce can diced tomatoes, undrained
- 1 16-ounce package frozen sweet pepper stir-fry vegetables
- 2 cups frozen cut okra
- 2 to 3 teaspoons Cajun seasoning
- 3 cups hot cooked white or brown rice (optional)
   Chopped green onion (optional)

1. In a 3½- to 4½-quart slow cooker, combine drained beans, undrained tomatoes, frozen stir-fry vegetables, frozen okra, and Cajun seasoning.

2. Cover and cook on low-heat setting for 6 to 8 hours or on high-heat setting for 3 to 4 hours. If desired, serve over hot cooked rice and sprinkle with green onion.

Per Serving: 153 cal., 0 g total fat (0 g sat. fat), 0 mg chol., 639 mg sodium, 31 g carbo., 10 g fiber, 12 g pro.

Brown Rice Primavera

Colorful zucchini, sweet peppers, and tomatoes dress up this cheesy one-dish meal.

Prep: 25 minutes Cook: 2 to 2½ hours (high)
Makes 6 servings

- 1 medium eggplant (1 pound), peeled (if desired) and cubed
- 2 medium zucchini, halved lengthwise and cut into ½-inch pieces
- 1 medium onion, cut into thin wedges
- 1 14-ounce can vegetable broth
- 2 cups thin bite-size strips red and/or yellow sweet pepper (2 medium)
- 1 14.5-ounce can diced tomatoes with basil, garlic, and oregano, drained
- 1 cup uncooked instant brown rice
- 2 cups crumbled feta cheese (8 ounces)

1. In a 5- to 6-quart slow cooker, combine eggplant, zucchini, and onion. Pour broth over mixture in cooker. Cover and cook on high-heat setting for 2 to 2½ hours.

2. Stir in sweet pepper, drained tomatoes, and rice. Cover and cook for 30 minutes more. Sprinkle each serving with cheese.

Per Serving: 212 cal., 9 g total fat (6 g sat. fat), 34 mg chol., 1045 mg sodium, 26 g carbo., 5 g fiber, 9 g pro.

Greek Pasta Casserole

Beans are a wonderful alternative for stretching the food dollar. They're high in fiber, low in fat, and also a great source of protein.

Prep: 25 minutes Bake: 20 minutes Stand: 10 minutes
Makes 6 servings

- 12 ounces dried rotini pasta
- 1 15-ounce can tomato sauce
- 1 10.75-ounce can condensed tomato soup
- 2 cups crumbled feta cheese (8 ounces)
- 1 15-ounce can cannellini beans (white kidney beans), rinsed and drained
- 1 cup coarsely chopped, pitted Greek black olives
- ½ cup seasoned fine dry bread crumbs
- 2 tablespoons butter or margarine, melted
- 2 tablespoons grated Parmesan cheese

1. Preheat oven to 375°F. Lightly grease a 3-quart rectangular baking dish; set aside. Cook pasta according to package directions; drain. In a very large bowl, combine cooked pasta, tomato sauce, and soup. Stir in feta cheese, drained beans, and olives. Transfer pasta mixture to the prepared baking dish.

2. In a small bowl, combine bread crumbs, melted butter, and Parmesan cheese; sprinkle over pasta mixture.

3. Bake, uncovered, for 20 to 25 minutes or until heated through and top is light brown. Let stand for 10 minutes before serving.

Per Serving: 553 cal., 19 g total fat (10 g sat. fat), 52 mg chol., 1890 mg sodium, 74 g carbo., 7 g fiber, 24 g pro.

Mediterranean Frittata

Mediterranean Frittata

Place the croutons in a resealable plastic bag and pound with a rolling pin to coarsely crush.

Start to Finish: 30 minutes

Makes 6 servings

- 3 tablespoons olive oil
- 1 cup chopped onion
- 1 teaspoon bottled minced garlic
- 8 eggs
- ¼ cup half-and-half, light cream, or milk
- ½ cup crumbled feta cheese (2 ounces)
- ½ of a 7-ounce jar (½ cup) roasted red sweet peppers, drained and chopped
- ½ cup sliced Kalamata or pitted ripe olives
- ¼ cup slivered fresh basil
- ⅛ teaspoon pepper
- ½ cup onion-and-garlic croutons, coarsely crushed
- 2 tablespoons finely shredded Parmesan cheese

1. Preheat broiler. In a 10-inch broilerproof skillet, heat 2 tablespoons of the oil over medium heat. Add onion and garlic; cook until onion is just tender.

2. Meanwhile, in a large mixing bowl, beat together eggs and half-and-half. Stir in feta cheese, sweet peppers, olives, basil, and ground pepper. Pour over onion mixture in skillet. Cook over medium heat. As mixture sets, run a spatula around the edge of the skillet, lifting egg mixture to allow the uncooked portion to flow underneath. Continue cooking and lifting edges till egg mixture is almost set (surface will be moist). Reduce heat as necessary to prevent overcooking.

3. Combine crushed croutons, Parmesan cheese, and the remaining tablespoon of oil; sprinkle mixture over frittata. Broil 4 to 5 inches from heat for 1 to 2 minutes or until top is set. Cut frittata in wedges to serve.

Per Serving: 242 cal., 19 g total fat (6 g sat. fat), 297 mg chol., 339 mg sodium, 7 g carbo., 1 g fiber, 12 g pro.

EGGS FOR DINNER

At a price of $2 to $3 a dozen in most grocery stores, eggs are an excellent source of protein at a bargain. They're also one of the most versatile sources of protein, taking well to all kinds of cooking methods and seasonings.

Roasted Vegetable Lasagna

Oven roasting the vegetables adds earthy flavors to each luscious layer.

Prep: 30 minutes Bake: 50 minutes
Broil: 12 minutes Stand: 10 minutes
Makes 9 servings

12	dried lasagna noodles
4	cups bite-size pieces zucchini
2½	cups thinly sliced carrot (5 medium)
2	cups fresh mushrooms, halved
1½	cups coarsely chopped red or green sweet pepper (2 medium)
¼	cup olive oil
1	tablespoon dried Italian seasoning, crushed
½	teaspoon salt
½	teaspoon ground black pepper
1	egg, lightly beaten
1	12-ounce carton cream-style cottage cheese, undrained
½	cup grated Parmesan cheese
1	26-ounce jar marinara sauce
3	cups shredded mozzarella cheese (12 ounces)

1. Cook lasagna noodles according to package directions; drain. Rinse with cold water; drain again. Place noodles in a single layer on a piece of foil; set aside.

2. Meanwhile, preheat broiler. In a very large bowl, combine zucchini, carrot, mushrooms, and sweet pepper. Drizzle vegetables with oil. Sprinkle with Italian seasoning, salt, and black pepper; toss gently to combine.

3. Transfer vegetables to a shallow roasting pan. Broil 5 to 6 inches from the heat for 12 to 14 minutes or until vegetables are tender and light brown, stirring once halfway through broiling. Set vegetables aside.

4. Reduce oven temperature to 375°F. Grease a 3-quart rectangular baking dish; set aside. In a medium bowl, combine egg, undrained cottage cheese, and ¼ cup of the Parmesan cheese.

5. To assemble, spread one-third of the marinara sauce in the bottom of the prepared baking dish. Layer 4 of the cooked noodles in the dish. Top with half of the roasted vegetables, one-third of the marinara sauce, and one-third of the mozzarella cheese. Add 4 more noodles, all of the cottage cheese mixture, and one-third of the mozzarella cheese. Add the remaining 4 noodles, the remaining vegetables, the remaining marinara sauce, and the remaining mozzarella cheese. Sprinkle with the remaining ¼ cup Parmesan cheese.

6. Bake, covered, for 30 minutes. Bake, uncovered, about 20 minutes more or until heated through. Let stand for 10 minutes before serving.

Per Serving: 420 cal., 21 g total fat (8 g sat. fat), 3 mg chol., 1,020 mg sodium, 37 g carbo., 3 g fiber, 22 g pro.

Fettuccine and Vegetables Alfredo

Keep all the ingredients for this satisfying dish on hand in the pantry for a fix-it-fast weeknight meal.

Start to Finish: 20 minutes
Makes 4 servings

1	16-ounce package frozen sugar snap pea stir-fry vegetables
1	cup frozen shelled sweet soybeans (edamame)
1	9-ounce package refrigerated fettuccine
1	16-ounce jar Alfredo pasta sauce
½	cup finely shredded Parmesan cheese (2 ounces)
¼	cup milk
2	tablespoons refrigerated basil pesto

1. In a 4-quart Dutch oven, bring a large amount of water to boiling. Add stir-fry vegetables and soybeans; cook for 3 minutes. Add fettuccine. Cook about 3 minutes more or until fettuccine is tender but still firm; drain. Return fettuccine mixture to Dutch oven.

2. Meanwhile, in a medium saucepan, combine pasta sauce, ¼ cup of the cheese, the milk, and pesto. Cook and stir until heated through. Add cheese mixture to fettuccine mixture; toss gently to coat.

3. Divide fettuccine mixture among four dinner plates. Sprinkle with the remaining ¼ cup cheese.

Per Serving: 691 cal., 37 g total fat (16 g sat. fat), 117 mg chol., 1,107 mg sodium, 61 g carbo., 7 g fiber, 28 g pro.

Vegetable-Beef Soup

soups & stews

Maybe it can't always cure what ails you, but a bowl of homemade soup is certainly cheering and comforting. It's a no-brainer for feeding a family inexpensively, and with these five-ingredient recipes you can enjoy homemade soup more often and with less effort.

Vegetable-Beef Soup

Although this soup simmers long and slow to blend flavors, using a blend of frozen vegetables eliminates time-consuming peeling and chopping.

Prep: 5 minutes *Cook:* 1 hour and 35 minutes
Makes 6 servings

- 1 tablespoon cooking oil
- 1 pound beef stew meat or boneless beef chuck roast, cut into ¾-inch cubes
- 3 14-ounce cans beef broth
- 1 14.5-ounce can diced tomatoes with basil, oregano, and garlic, undrained
- 1 16-ounce package frozen broccoli, green beans, pearl onions, and red sweet pepper

1. In a Dutch oven, heat oil over medium-high heat. Add half of the meat; cook until brown. Remove meat from Dutch oven. Add remaining meat to Dutch oven; cook until brown (add additional oil if necessary).

2. Return all meat to Dutch oven. Stir in beef broth and undrained tomatoes. Bring to boiling; reduce heat. Cover and simmer for 1½ to 1¾ hours or until meat is tender.

3. Stir in vegetables. Return to boiling; reduce heat. Cover and simmer about 5 minutes more or just until vegetables are tender.
Per Serving: 179 cal., 6 g fat (2 g sat. fat), 45 mg chol., 1,095 mg sodium, 11 g carbo., 2 g fiber, 20 g pro.

Double Chicken Tortellini Soup

If you don't have leftover roasted or grilled chicken on hand for this hearty soup, buy a deli-roasted chicken.

Start to Finish: 25 minutes
Makes 8 servings

- 5 14-ounce cans chicken broth
- 1 14.5-ounce can Italian-style diced tomatoes, undrained
- 1½ cups frozen whole kernel corn
- 1 9-ounce package refrigerated herb chicken tortellini
- 2½ cups cooked shredded chicken (about 12 ounces)
  Salt and ground black pepper
  Freshly shredded Parmesan cheese (optional)
  Sliced green onions (optional)

1. In a large saucepan, combine chicken broth, undrained tomatoes, and corn. Bring to boiling over medium-high heat.

2. Add tortellini and chicken to broth mixture; reduce heat to medium. Cook, uncovered, about 10 minutes or until pasta is tender, stirring occasionally. Season with salt and pepper. If desired, serve with Parmesan cheese and green onions.
Per Serving: 270 cal., 7 g fat (2 g sat. fat), 57 mg chol., 1,393 mg sodium, 30 g carbo., 2 g fiber, 20 g pro.

Manhattan-Style Clam Chowder

This hearty chowder contains tomatoes, unlike New England–style chowder, which is cream-based.

Start to Finish: 25 minutes
Makes 4 servings

- 2   6.5-ounce cans minced clams
- 2   slices bacon, coarsely chopped
- 1   cup chopped celery (2 stalks)
- 1   cup chopped onion (1 large)
- 1   14.5-ounce can diced tomatoes with basil, oregano, and garlic, undrained
- ¼   teaspoon salt
- ⅛   teaspoon ground black pepper

1. Drain canned clams, reserving juice. If necessary, add enough water to reserved clam juice to equal 2 cups. Set clams and juice aside.

2. In a large saucepan, cook bacon until crisp. Remove bacon from pan, reserving drippings in pan. Drain bacon on paper towels.

3. Cook celery and onion in reserved drippings until tender. Stir in the reserved clam juice and undrained tomatoes. Bring to boiling; reduce heat. Simmer, uncovered, for 5 minutes. Stir in clams, bacon, salt, and pepper; heat through.

Per Serving: 133 cal., 5 g fat (3 g sat. fat), 10 mg chol., 1,026 mg sodium, 14 g carbo., 2 g fiber, 4 g pro.

Quick Chili

Start to Finish: 15 minutes
Makes 4 servings

- 1   pound lean ground beef
- 2   15-ounce cans chili beans with chili gravy
- 1½ cups tomato juice
- 4   teaspoons chili powder
      Dairy sour cream

1. In a medium saucepan, cook ground beef until brown. Drain off fat. Stir chili beans, tomato juice, and chili powder into beef in pan. Bring to boiling; reduce heat. Simmer, uncovered, for 5 minutes. Top individual servings with sour cream.

Per Serving: 525 cal., 22 g fat (9 g sat. fat), 89 mg chol., 1,450 mg sodium, 36 g carbo., 8 g fiber, 38 g pro.

Easy Beef and Noodle Soup

Start to Finish: 25 minutes
Makes 4 servings

- 1   pound lean ground beef
- 2½ cups water
- 1   10.75-ounce can condensed cream of onion soup
- 1   10.5-ounce can condensed beef broth
- 1½ cups dried medium noodles
- 2   tablespoons dried parsley flakes
      Finely shredded Parmesan cheese (optional)

1. In a large saucepan or skillet, cook meat over medium-high heat until brown. Drain off fat. Stir in the water, onion soup, beef broth, uncooked noodles, and parsley flakes.

2. Bring to boiling; reduce heat. Cover and simmer about 5 minutes or until noodles are tender, stirring occasionally. If desired, sprinkle individual servings with Parmesan cheese.

Per Serving: 357 cal., 19 g fat (7 g sat. fat), 98 mg chol., 1,218 mg sodium, 19 g carbo., 1 g fiber, 27 g pro.

Pineapple Pork Chili

Start to Finish: 20 minutes
Makes 4 servings

- 1   pound ground pork or beef
- 1   16-ounce jar pineapple salsa*
- 1   15-ounce can red kidney beans, rinsed and drained
- 1   8-ounce can tomato sauce
- 1   tablespoon chili powder
      Pineapple slices (optional)

1. In a 3-quart saucepan, cook meat until brown. Drain off fat. Stir in salsa, beans, tomato sauce, and chili powder. Bring to boiling; reduce heat. Simmer, uncovered, for 10 minutes. If desired, garnish with pineapple slices.

*Note: If you can't find pineapple salsa, use regular salsa and add ⅓ to ½ cup crushed pineapple.

Per Serving: 329 cal., 9 g fat (4 g sat. fat), 53 mg chol., 852 mg sodium, 44 g carbo., 11 g fiber, 22 g pro.

Pineapple Pork Chili

Pineapple salsa is just one of the fruit salsas
you'll find alongside the more familiar tomato variety
in your supermarket. Fruit salsas are especially good
in *pork and chicken* dishes.

Sausage-Corn Chowder

Start to Finish: 20 minutes
Makes 4 servings

- 12 ounces cooked link smoked turkey sausage or frankfurters
- 1 10.75-ounce can condensed cream of potato soup
- 1⅓ cups milk
- 1 8.75-ounce can cream-style corn
- 2 or 3 slices American cheese, torn into pieces (2 or 3 ounces)

1. Cut sausage links in half lengthwise; cut into ½-inch-thick slices. Set aside. In a 2-quart saucepan, combine soup, milk, and corn. Stir in sausage and cheese. Cook and stir over medium heat until heated through.

Per Serving: 312 cal., 15 g fat (6 g sat. fat), 80 mg chol., 1,774 mg sodium, 24 g carbo., 1 g fiber, 21 g pro.

Oriental Chicken Soup

Chicken thighs are often overlooked in favor of breast halves, but they are just as convenient and even more flavorful.

Start to Finish: 20 minutes
Makes 3 servings

- 1 tablespoon cooking oil
- 8 ounces skinless, boneless chicken thighs or breasts, cut into thin bite-size strips
- 3 cups water
- 2 cups frozen broccoli, carrots, and water chestnuts (½ of a 16-ounce package)
- 1 3-ounce package chicken-flavor ramen noodles
- 2 tablespoons reduced-sodium soy sauce

1. In a large saucepan, heat oil over medium-high heat. Add chicken; cook and stir for 2 to 3 minutes or until no longer pink. Remove from heat. Drain off fat.

2. Add water, vegetables, and seasoning packet from ramen noodles to chicken in saucepan. Bring to boiling. Break up ramen noodles and add to soup. Reduce heat. Cover and simmer for 3 minutes. Stir in soy sauce.

Per Serving: 254 cal., 8 g fat (1 g sat. fat), 63 mg chol., 829 mg sodium, 22 g carbo., 5 g fiber, 22 g pro.

MAKE IT A MENU
Chicken Tortilla Soup, Pepper and Four-Bean Salad (page 172), Cereal-Coated Ice Cream Sundaes (page 178)

Turkey Chili with Hominy

Start to Finish: 20 minutes
Makes 4 to 5 servings

- 12 ounces bulk Italian turkey sausage or uncooked ground turkey
- 2 15-ounce cans chili beans with chili gravy
- 1 cup bottled salsa with lime
- 1 15.5-ounce can golden hominy, drained
- ⅔ cup water
- ⅓ cup sliced green onions

1. In a large saucepan, cook turkey sausage over medium heat until brown. Stir in undrained chili beans, salsa, hominy, and water. Heat through. Sprinkle individual servings with green onions.

Per Serving: 470 cal., 11 g fat (3 g sat. fat), 45 mg chol., 1,897 mg sodium, 64 g carbo., 16 g fiber, 28 g pro.

Chicken Tortilla Soup

Start to Finish: 25 minutes
Makes 4 servings

- 2 14-ounce cans chicken broth with roasted garlic
- 1 14.5-ounce can Mexican-style stewed tomatoes, undrained
- 2 cups chopped cooked chicken
- 2 cups frozen sweet pepper and onion stir-fry vegetables
  Tortilla chips
  Sliced fresh jalapeño chile peppers (optional)
  Lime wedges (optional)

1. In a large saucepan, combine chicken broth, undrained tomatoes, chicken, and frozen vegetables. Bring to boiling; reduce heat. Cover and simmer for 5 minutes.

2. To serve, ladle soup into warm soup bowls. Serve with tortilla chips. If desired, top with sliced jalapeño chile peppers and serve with lime wedges.

Per Serving: 266 cal., 9 g fat (2 g sat. fat), 65 mg chol., 1,260 mg sodium, 22 g carbo., 1 g fiber, 24 g pro.

Chicken
Tortilla Soup

Vegetable Cheese Chowder

Start to Finish: 20 minutes
Makes 4 servings

1	16-ounce package frozen broccoli, cauliflower, and carrots
½	cup water
2	cups milk
⅓	cup all-purpose flour
1	14-ounce can chicken broth
1	cup shredded smoked or regular Gouda cheese (4 ounces)

1. In a large saucepan, combine the frozen vegetables and water. Bring to boiling; reduce heat. Cover and simmer about 4 minutes or until vegetables are just tender. Do not drain.

2. Meanwhile, in a screw-top jar, combine ⅔ cup of the milk and the flour; cover and shake well. Add to vegetable mixture; add remaining 1⅓ cups milk and the broth. Cook and stir over medium heat until thickened and bubbly. Cook and stir for 1 minute more. Add the cheese; cook and stir over low heat until cheese nearly melts.

Per Serving: 370 cal., 20 g fat (13 g sat. fat), 81 mg chol., 942 mg sodium, 22 g carbo., 3 g fiber, 25 g pro.

Corn Chowder

Corn Chowder

Start to Finish: 20 minutes
Makes 4 servings

1	8-ounce tub cream cheese spread with chive and onion
2	cups milk
1	14.75-ounce can cream-style corn
1½	cups chopped smoked turkey breast (about 8 ounces)
1	cup frozen peas
	Ground black pepper

1. In a medium saucepan, heat cream cheese over medium heat to soften; add milk and corn, stirring until combined. Stir in turkey and peas; heat through. Season to taste with pepper.

Per Serving: 397 cal., 23 g fat (15 g sat. fat), 88 mg chol., 1,159 mg sodium, 27 g carbo., 3 g fiber, 19 g pro.

Curried Shrimp Soup

Who would believe a soup this tasty could be ready in 15 minutes? The sweetness of the apple contrasts with the spicy curry, and both complement the shrimp.

Start to Finish: 15 minutes

Makes 4 servings

- 12 ounces medium fresh or frozen shrimp, peeled and deveined
- 4 cups water
- 1 3-ounce package chicken-flavor ramen noodles
- 1 tablespoon curry powder
- 2 medium stalks bok choy, cut into ¼-inch slices
- 1 small apple, cored and chopped

1. Thaw shrimp, if frozen. Rinse shrimp; pat dry with paper towels.

2. In a medium saucepan, combine water, seasoning packet from ramen noodles, and curry powder. Bring to boiling.

3. Break up ramen noodles. Add noodles, shrimp, and bok choy to mixture in saucepan. Return to boiling. Reduce heat. Simmer, uncovered, about 3 minutes or until shrimp turn opaque. Stir in apple; heat through.

Per Serving: 237 cal., 3 g fat (0 g sat. fat), 129 mg chol., 861 mg sodium, 29 g carbo., 5 g fiber, 26 g pro.

Mashed Potato Soup

This soup is a great use for a relatively new food—refrigerated mashed potatoes.

Start to Finish: 15 minutes

Makes 3 servings

- 1 20-ounce package refrigerated mashed potatoes
- 1 14-ounce can chicken broth
- ¼ cup sliced green onions (2)
- ½ cup shredded Swiss, cheddar, or smoked Gouda cheese (2 ounces)
  Dairy sour cream (optional)

1. In a medium saucepan, combine mashed potatoes, chicken broth, and green onions. Cook over medium-high heat just until mixture reaches boiling, whisking to make nearly smooth. Add cheese; whisk until cheese is melted. If desired, serve with sour cream.

Per Serving: 239 cal., 9 g fat (4 g sat. fat), 17 mg chol., 917 mg sodium, 27 g carbo., 2 g fiber, 11 g pro.

Easy Sausage Soup

Start to Finish: 25 minutes

Makes 8 servings

- 1 pound bulk pork sausage
- 2 14.5-ounce cans onion-flavor beef broth
- 1 16-ounce package frozen mixed vegetables
- 1 14.5-ounce can diced tomatoes with basil, oregano, and garlic, undrained
- 1 cup water
- 2 tablespoons tomato paste
- ¼ teaspoon ground black pepper

1. In a 5- to 6-quart Dutch oven, cook sausage over medium heat until brown; drain off fat. Stir in beef broth, vegetables, undrained tomatoes, water, tomato paste, and pepper. Bring mixture to boiling; reduce heat. Cover and simmer about 15 minutes or until vegetables are tender, stirring occasionally.

Per Serving: 232 cal., 13 g fat (5 g sat. fat), 38 mg chol., 1,004 mg sodium, 14 g carbo., 3 g fiber, 12 g pro.

Speedy Southwestern-Style Tomato Soup

Southwestern-style seasonings give canned soup character and punch. If you wish, sprinkle additional snipped cilantro on top.

Start to Finish: 10 minutes

Makes 5 or 6 servings

- 1 32-ounce jar ready-to-serve tomato soup
- 1 14.5-ounce can Mexican-style chopped tomatoes, undrained
- ⅛ teaspoon ground cumin
  Dash cayenne pepper
- 2 tablespoons snipped fresh cilantro
- ¼ cup dairy sour cream (optional)

1. In a large saucepan, combine tomato soup, undrained tomatoes, cumin, and cayenne pepper. Cook, covered, over medium heat until heated through, stirring occasionally. Stir in cilantro. If desired, top individual servings with sour cream.

Per Serving: 125 cal., 2 g fat (1 g sat. fat), 7 mg chol., 787 mg sodium, 23 g carbo., 2 g fiber, 3 g pro.

MAKE IT A MENU
Corn Chowder (opposite), Pesto Biscuits (page 168), Baked Fruit Ambrosia (page 180)

Tomato and Turkey Soup

Fajita seasoning gives a south-of-the-border slant to smoked turkey soup. If you have leftover turkey, you can substitute it for the smoked variety.

Start to Finish: 20 minutes

Makes 4 servings

- 3 14-ounce cans reduced-sodium chicken broth
- 1 14-ounce can diced tomatoes with onion and garlic or one 10-ounce can chopped tomatoes and green chile peppers, undrained
- 2 teaspoons fajita seasoning
- ¼ teaspoon ground black pepper
- 2 cups chopped smoked turkey breast or chopped cooked chicken or turkey (about 10 ounces)
- 1 tablespoon snipped fresh cilantro

1. In a large saucepan, combine chicken broth, undrained tomatoes, fajita seasoning, and pepper. Bring to boiling; reduce heat. Cover and simmer for 10 minutes. Stir in turkey; heat through. Just before serving, stir in cilantro.

Per Serving: 125 cal., 1 g fat (0 g sat. fat), 30 mg chol., 2,062 mg sodium, 9 g carbo., 0 g fiber, 20 g pro.

Cream of Broccoli Soup

Start to Finish: 20 minutes

Makes 6 to 8 servings

- 2 cups chopped broccoli
- 2 cups boiling water
- 3 tablespoons butter
- ¼ cup all-purpose flour
- 2 teaspoons instant chicken bouillon granules
- 2 cups half-and-half, light cream, or milk
  Ground black pepper

1. In a large saucepan, cook the broccoli in the 2 cups boiling water for 8 to 10 minutes or until very tender. Drain broccoli, reserving cooking liquid. (Add additional water, if necessary, to make 1½ cups liquid.) In a blender, combine broccoli and the reserved cooking liquid. Cover and blend at low speed until smooth. Set aside.

2. In the same saucepan, melt the butter. Stir in the flour and bouillon granules. Add half-and-half all at once. Cook and stir over medium heat until thickened and bubbly. Cook and stir for 1 minute more. Stir in broccoli mixture; heat through. Season to taste with pepper.

Per Serving: 186 cal., 15 g fat (10 g sat. fat), 46 mg chol., 393 mg sodium, 9 g carbo., 1 g fiber, 4 g pro.

Speedy Beef Stew

Start to Finish: 25 minutes

Makes 4 servings

- 1 17-ounce package refrigerated cooked beef roast au jus
- 2 10.75-ounce cans condensed beefy mushroom soup
- 1 16-ounce package frozen stew vegetables
- 1½ cups milk
- 4 teaspoons snipped fresh basil or 1½ teaspoons dried basil, crushed

1. Cut beef into bite-size pieces if necessary. In a 4-quart Dutch oven, combine beef and au jus, soup, frozen vegetables, and dried basil, if using. Bring to boiling; reduce heat. Cover and simmer for 10 minutes. Stir in milk and fresh basil, if using. Heat through.

Per Serving: 386 cal., 15 g fat (7 g sat. fat), 80 mg chol., 1,688 mg sodium, 33 g carbo., 5 g fiber, 33 g pro.

Cajun Fish Soup

Start to Finish: 20 minutes

Makes 4 servings

- 12 ounces fresh or frozen sea bass, cod, or orange roughy fillets
- 4 cups assorted stir-fry vegetables from a salad bar or produce department or one 16-ounce package frozen stir-fry vegetables
- 4 cups reduced-sodium chicken broth
- 2 teaspoons Cajun seasoning
- 1 14.5-ounce can diced tomatoes, undrained

1. Thaw fish, if frozen. Rinse fish; cut into 1-inch pieces. Set fish aside.

2. In a large saucepan, combine vegetables, chicken broth, and Cajun seasoning. Bring to boiling; reduce heat. Cover and simmer for 3 to 5 minutes or until vegetables are crisp-tender. Stir in fish and undrained tomatoes. Return to boiling; reduce heat. Simmer, covered, for 2 to 3 minutes or until fish flakes easily when tested with a fork.

Per Serving: 157 cal., 2 g fat (0 g sat. fat), 35 mg chol., 968 mg sodium, 12 g carbo., 3 g fiber, 21 g pro.

Cajun Fish Soup

Tomato-Tortellini Soup

Start to Finish: 15 minutes
Makes 4 servings

2   14-ounce cans reduced-sodium chicken broth or vegetable broth
1   9-ounce package refrigerated tortellini
½   of an 8-ounce tub cream cheese spread with chive and onion
1   10.75-can condensed tomato soup or one 11-ounce can tomato bisque
    Snipped fresh chives (optional)

1. In a medium saucepan, bring broth to boiling. Add tortellini; reduce heat. Simmer, uncovered, for 5 minutes.

2. In a small bowl, whisk ⅓ cup of the hot broth into the cream cheese spread until smooth. Return all to saucepan. Stir in tomato soup; heat through. If desired, sprinkle individual servings with chives.
Per Serving: 363 cal., 14 g fat (8 g sat. fat), 57 mg chol., 1,264 mg sodium, 44 g carbo., 1 g fiber, 14 g pro.

Chicken-Vegetable Soup

Keep several cans of seasoned tomatoes on hand. The spices and herbs they contain lend bonus flavor to whatever you're making.
Start to Finish: 25 minutes
Makes 4 servings

1   16-ounce package frozen Italian vegetables (zucchini, carrots, cauliflower, lima beans, and Italian beans)
1   14.5-ounce can Italian-style stewed tomatoes, undrained
1   12-ounce can vegetable juice
1   cup chicken broth
1½   cups chopped cooked chicken or turkey (about 8 ounces)

1. In a large saucepan, combine frozen vegetables, undrained tomatoes, vegetable juice, and chicken broth.

2. Bring to boiling; reduce heat. Cover and simmer about 10 minutes or until vegetables are tender. Stir in chicken. Heat through.
Per Serving: 186 cal., 4 g fat (1 g sat. fat), 47 mg chol., 888 mg sodium, 17 g carbo., 5 g fiber, 18 g pro.

Stuffed Green Pepper Soup

Love stuffed peppers? Try this soup that combines the same ingredients in a brand-new way.
Start to Finish: 30 minutes
Makes 6 servings

8   ounces lean ground beef
2   14.5-ounce cans diced tomatoes with green peppers and onions, undrained
3   cups water
1   14-ounce can beef broth
1   5.7-ounce package tomato basil risotto mix
¾   cup chopped green sweet pepper (1 medium)

1. In a large saucepan, cook beef until meat is brown. Drain off fat. Stir undrained tomatoes, water, beef broth, risotto mix and seasoning packet, and sweet pepper into meat in saucepan. Bring to boiling; reduce heat. Cover and simmer about 20 minutes or until rice is tender.
Per Serving: 245 cal., 6 g fat (2 g sat. fat), 23 mg chol., 990 mg sodium, 33 g carbo., 2 g fiber, 11 g pro.

Pumpkin and Bean Soup

The five ingredients in this soup might seem mismatched, but the combination works like a charm, producing complex, subtle flavor that pleases with every spoonful.
Start to Finish: 15 minutes
Makes 4 servings

1   15-ounce can pumpkin
1   15-ounce can cannellini (white kidney) beans, rinsed and drained
1   14-ounce can unsweetened coconut milk
1   14-ounce can vegetable broth
1   teaspoon dried sage, crushed
    Salt and ground black pepper
    Cracked black peppercorns (optional)
    Fresh lime slices (optional)

1. In a medium saucepan, combine pumpkin, beans, unsweetened coconut milk, vegetable broth, and sage. Heat through. Season to taste with salt and pepper. If desired, sprinkle individual servings with black peppercorns and serve with lime slices.
Per Serving: 285 cal., 19 g fat (17 g sat. fat), 0 mg chol., 729 mg sodium, 28 g carbo., 8 g fiber, 9 g pro.

Pumpkin and Bean Soup

Salmon Confetti Chowder

Asian-Style Beef Soup

Fresh ginger adds the right amount of spice when using leftover roast beef or beef from the deli.

Start to Finish: 15 minutes

Makes 4 servings

- 3 14-ounce cans beef broth
- 1 16-ounce package frozen broccoli stir-fry vegetables
- 3 tablespoons teriyaki sauce
- 2 teaspoons grated fresh ginger or ½ teaspoon ground ginger
- 1 9-ounce package frozen cooked seasoned beef strips, thawed and cut up, or 2 cups chopped cooked beef

1. In a large saucepan, bring broth to boiling. Stir in frozen vegetables, teriyaki sauce, and ginger. Return to boiling; reduce heat. Simmer, covered, for 3 to 5 minutes or until vegetables are tender. Stir in cooked beef; heat through.

Per Serving: 177 cal., 6 g total fat (2 g sat. fat), 41 mg chol., 1,885 mg sodium, 10 g carbo., 2 g fiber, 21 g pro.

Salmon Confetti Chowder

Canned salmon is a true economic value—low in cost, nutritious, and delicious.

Start to Finish: 25 minutes

Makes 4 servings

- 2 cups frozen sweet pepper stir-fry vegetables
- 2 tablespoons seeded and finely chopped fresh jalapeño chile pepper
- 1 tablespoon butter or margarine
- 2 tablespoons all-purpose flour
- 2 cups milk
- 1 cup half-and-half
- 2 cups refrigerated diced potatoes with onions
- 1 15-ounce can salmon, drained, flaked, and skin and bones removed
- ¼ cup snipped watercress
- 2 tablespoons lemon juice
- ½ teaspoon salt
- ½ teaspoon ground black pepper

1. In a large saucepan, cook frozen vegetables and jalapeo pepper in hot butter over medium heat for 3 to 5 minutes or until tender, stirring occasionally. Stir in flour. Gradually stir in milk and half-and-half. Cook and stir until slightly thickened. Cook and stir for 2 minutes more.

2. Stir in potatoes, salmon, watercress, lemon juice, salt, and black pepper; heat through.

Per Serving: 349 cal., 10 g total fat (3 g sat. fat), 68 mg chol., 1,174 mg sodium, 33 g carbo., 3 g fiber, 29 g pro.

Goulash Soup

This Hungarian paprika tomato-and-beef soup is a hearty and satisfying meal in a bowl.

Prep: 25 minutes *Cook:* 75 minutes

Makes 6 to 8 servings

- 1 pound beef top round, cut into ½-inch cubes
- 1 medium onion, chopped
- 2 tablespoons cooking oil
- 2 tablespoons all-purpose flour
- 1 tablespoon Hungarian paprika
- 2 cloves garlic, minced
- 3 14-ounce cans chicken broth
- 1 14½-ounce can diced tomatoes, undrained
- 3 medium carrots, sliced
- 2 tablespoons tomato paste
- 1 bay leaf
- ½ teaspoon dried marjoram, crushed
- ½ teaspoon caraway seeds, crushed
- ½ teaspoon freshly ground black pepper
- 2 medium potatoes, peeled and cubed
   Dairy sour cream (optional)

1. In a 4- to 5-quart Dutch oven, cook and stir beef and onion in hot oil over medium-high heat about 5 minutes or until beef is brown and onion is tender.

2. Add flour, paprika, and garlic; cook, stirring constantly, for 3 minutes. Carefully stir in chicken broth, undrained tomatoes, carrots, tomato paste, bay leaf, marjoram, caraway seeds, and pepper. Bring to boiling; reduce heat. Cover and simmer for 50 minutes, stirring occasionally. Stir in potatoes. Cover and simmer for 25 to 30 minutes more or until potatoes and beef are tender. Discard bay leaf. If desired, top individual servings with sour cream.

Per Serving: 244 cal., 9 g total fat (2 g sat. fat), 42 mg chol., 996 mg sodium, 19 g carbo., 3 g fiber, 21 g pro.

Chunky Chipotle
Pork Chili

Chunky Chipotle Pork Chili

Chipotle peppers, cumin, and picante sauce spice up the flavor in short order.

Start to Finish: 30 minutes
Makes 4 servings

12	ounces pork tenderloin
2	teaspoons chili powder
2	teaspoons ground cumin
⅓	cup chopped onion (1 small)
4	cloves garlic, minced
1	tablespoon cooking oil
1	cup beer or beef broth
¾	cup bite-size pieces yellow or red sweet pepper (1 medium)
½	cup picante sauce or bottled salsa
1	to 2 tablespoons finely chopped canned chipotle chile pepper in adobo sauce
1	15-ounce can small red beans or pinto beans, rinsed and drained
½	cup dairy sour cream
	Fresh cilantro sprigs or Italian (flat-leaf) parsley sprigs (optional)

1. Trim fat from meat. Cut meat into ¾-inch pieces. In a medium bowl combine meat, chili powder, and cumin; toss gently to coat. Set aside.

2. In a large saucepan, cook onion and garlic in hot oil over medium-high heat about 3 minutes or until tender. Add meat; cook and stir until meat is brown. Stir in beer, sweet pepper, picante sauce, and chipotle pepper.

3. Bring to boiling; reduce heat. Simmer, covered, about 5 minutes or until meat is tender. Stir in drained beans; heat through.

4. Top each serving with sour cream and, if desired, garnish with cilantro sprigs.

Per Serving: 328 cal., 11 g total fat (4 g sat. fat), 65 mg chol., 625 mg sodium, 29 g carbo., 7 g fiber, 26 g pro.

CHILI POWDER POINTER
Substitute a few dashes of bottled hot pepper sauce along with some dried oregano and cumin powder. Start with small amounts, then taste.

Smoked pork hocks are more *readily available,* but a meaty ham bone is the traditional—*and most economical*—way to flavor thick and hearty Split Pea Soup.

Split Pea Soup

Prep: 20 minutes *Cook:* 1¼ hours
Makes 4 servings

2¾ **cups water**
1½ **cups dry split peas, rinsed and drained**
 1 **14-ounce can reduced-sodium chicken broth**
 1 **to 1½ pounds meaty smoked pork hocks or**
    one 1- to 1½-pound meaty ham bone
 ¼ **teaspoon dried marjoram, crushed**
    Dash black pepper
 1 **bay leaf**
 ½ **cup chopped carrot (1 medium)**
 ½ **cup chopped celery (1 stalk)**
 ½ **cup chopped onion (1 medium)**

1. In a large saucepan, combine water, split peas, chicken broth, pork hocks, marjoram, pepper, and bay leaf. Bring to boiling; reduce heat. Simmer, covered, for 1 hour, stirring occasionally. Remove pork hocks.

2. When cool enough to handle, cut meat off bones; coarsely chop meat. Discard bones. Return meat to saucepan. Stir in carrot, celery, and onion. Return to boiling; reduce heat. Simmer, covered, for 20 to 30 minutes more or until vegetables are tender. Discard bay leaf.

Per 1½ cups: 320 cal., 4 g total fat (1 g sat. fat), 19 mg chol., 713 mg sodium, 49 g carbo., 20 g fiber, 25 g pro.

Quick Hamburger Soup

Using extra-lean ground beef and ground turkey makes this heart healthy.

Start to Finish: 30 minutes
Makes 12 servings

 8 **ounces extra-lean ground beef**
 8 **ounces uncooked ground turkey breast**
 2 **medium onions, finely chopped**
 2 **carrots, coarsely shredded**
 2 **stalks celery, sliced**
 2 **cloves garlic, minced**
 6 **cups reduced-sodium beef broth**
 2 **14.5-ounce cans diced tomatoes, undrained**
 1 **tablespoon snipped fresh sage or 1 teaspoon**
    dried sage, crushed
 2 **teaspoons snipped fresh thyme or 1 teaspoon**
    dried thyme, crushed
 1 **teaspoon snipped fresh rosemary or**
    ½ teaspoon dried rosemary, crushed
 ¼ **teaspoon salt**
 ¼ **teaspoon ground black pepper**
 2 **medium potatoes, chopped (2 cups)**

1. In a Dutch oven, combine beef, turkey, onion, carrot, celery, and garlic; cook until meat is brown and onion is tender. Drain off fat. Stir beef broth, undrained tomatoes, 1 tablespoon sage, thyme, rosemary, salt, and pepper into beef mixture in Dutch oven. Bring to boiling; stir in potatoes. Reduce heat. Simmer, covered, for 10 to 15 minutes or until vegetables are tender.

Per Serving: 103 cal., 2 g total fat (1 g sat. fat), 19 mg chol., 418 mg sodium, 10 g carbo., 1 g fiber, 10 g pro.

Top Loins with Gorgonzola Butter

from the grill

Grilling is America's favorite way to cook and entertain—
and no wonder. Hot coals bring out so much succulent flavor
in food that few extra ingredients are needed.
Look here for an innovative recipe to wow your cookout guests.

Top Loins with Gorgonzola Butter

Prep: 15 minutes *Grill:* 10 minutes
Makes 4 servings

- 2 tablespoons crumbled Gorgonzola or blue cheese
- 2 tablespoons tub-style cream cheese spread with chive and onion
- 1 to 2 tablespoons butter, softened
- 1 tablespoon chopped pine nuts or walnuts, toasted
- 4 boneless beef top loin steaks, cut 1 inch thick
    Salt

1. For Gorgonzola butter, in a small bowl, combine Gorgonzola cheese, cream cheese spread, butter, and pine nuts. Shape cheese mixture into a 1-inch-diameter log. Wrap in plastic wrap. Refrigerate until firm.

2. Trim fat from steaks. For a charcoal grill, grill steaks on the rack of an uncovered grill directly over medium coals until steaks reach desired doneness, turning once halfway through grilling. Allow 10 to 12 minutes for medium rare (145°F) or 12 to 15 minutes for medium (160°F). (For a gas grill, preheat grill. Reduce heat to medium. Place steaks on grill rack over heat. Cover and grill as above.)

3. To serve, halve each steak. Season with salt to taste. Cut Gorgonzola butter log into eight slices. Place one slice of butter on each steak piece.

Per Serving: 268 cal., 19 g fat (8 g sat. fat), 82 mg chol., 110 mg sodium, 0 g carbo., 0 g fiber, 23 g pro.

Texas Rib Sandwiches with Coleslaw

Coleslaw is an indispensable ingredient for this down-home classic. Pick up a creamy- or vinaigrette-base slaw from your supermarket deli.

Prep: 10 minutes *Grill:* 1½ hours
Makes 6 servings

- 2 pounds boneless pork country-style ribs
- ¾ cup bottled barbecue sauce
- 6 crusty dinner rolls or hamburger buns, split and toasted
    Bottled hot pepper sauce (optional)
- 1 cup purchased deli coleslaw

1. Trim fat from ribs. For a charcoal grill, arrange medium-hot coals around a drip pan. Test for medium heat above pan. Place ribs on grill rack over pan. (Or place ribs in a rib rack; place on grill rack.) Cover and grill for 1½ to 2 hours or until ribs are tender, brushing occasionally with barbecue sauce during the last 10 minutes of grilling. (For a gas grill, preheat grill. Reduce heat to medium. Adjust for indirect cooking. Grill as above.) Remove ribs from grill and brush with the remaining sauce.

2. Thinly slice ribs. To serve, top the roll bottoms with rib slices and, if desired, sprinkle with hot pepper sauce. Spoon coleslaw on top of sandwiches. Add roll tops.

Per Serving: 464 cal., 22 g fat (7 g sat. fat), 89 mg chol., 635 mg sodium, 37 g carbo., 1 g fiber, 28 g pro.

Caesar Beef-Vegetable Kabobs

Named for the Caesar salad dressing used here as a marinade, this meat and veggie combo is also tasty when marinated in Italian salad dressing.

Prep: 30 minutes *Marinate:* 2 hours *Grill:* 12 minutes
Makes 4 servings

1	pound boneless beef sirloin steak, cut 1 inch thick
8	cherry tomatoes
8	whole fresh button mushrooms
1	large yellow or green sweet pepper, cut into 1-inch pieces
½	cup bottled Caesar salad dressing
½	teaspoon ground black pepper

1. Cut steak into 1-inch cubes. Place steak cubes, tomatoes, mushrooms, and sweet pepper pieces in a resealable plastic bag set in a shallow dish. For marinade, combine salad dressing and pepper. Pour marinade over steak and vegetables. Seal bag; turn to coat steak and vegetables. Marinate in the refrigerator for 2 to 4 hours, turning bag occasionally.

2. Remove steak and vegetables from marinade; discard marinade. On eight 6- to 8-inch metal skewers, alternately thread steak, tomatoes, mushrooms, and sweet pepper pieces, leaving a ¼-inch space between pieces.

3. For a charcoal grill, grill kabobs on the rack of an uncovered grill directly over medium coals for 12 to 14 minutes for medium doneness, turning once. (For a gas grill, preheat grill. Reduce heat to medium. Place kabobs on grill rack over heat. Cover and grill as above.)
Per Serving: 338 cal., 23 g fat (4 g sat. fat), 69 mg chol., 385 mg sodium, 7 g carbo., 1 g fiber, 26 g pro.

MARINATING

When used properly, marinades impart wonderful flavor to grilled foods. Always marinate food in the refrigerator. If the marinade is to be used later for basting, reserve some before it comes into contact with any raw meat or poultry. If it is to be served as a sauce, boil it for several minutes to destroy any harmful bacteria.

Teriyaki Beef Spirals

Score the steak with a sharp knife and pound it with a meat mallet to make it more tender and easier to roll into a spiral.

Prep: 20 minutes *Grill:* 12 minutes
Makes 4 servings

1	cup loosely packed fresh spinach leaves
½	cup finely chopped water chestnuts
¼	cup chopped green onions (2)
¼	cup reduced-sodium teriyaki sauce
¾	to 1 pound beef flank steak
	Salt and ground black pepper
	Cooked rice noodles (optional)
	Sliced green onions (optional)

1. Remove stems from spinach leaves. Layer leaves on top of each other; slice crosswise into thin strips. In a medium bowl, combine spinach, water chestnuts, the ¼ cup green onions, and 2 tablespoons of the teriyaki sauce.

2. Trim fat from steak. Score steak on both sides by making shallow cuts at 1-inch intervals in a diamond pattern. Place meat between two pieces of plastic wrap. Using the flat side of a meat mallet, pound lightly into a 10×8-inch rectangle. Remove plastic wrap. Sprinkle steak with salt and pepper.

3. Spread spinach mixture over steak. Starting from a short side, roll steak up. Secure with wooden toothpicks at 1-inch intervals, starting ½ inch from one end. Slice between toothpicks into eight 1-inch-thick slices. Thread two slices onto each of four long wooden* or metal skewers. Brush slices with some of the remaining teriyaki sauce.

4. For a charcoal grill, grill slices on the rack of an uncovered grill directly over medium coals for 12 to 14 minutes for medium doneness, turning once and brushing with remaining teriyaki sauce halfway through grilling. (For a gas grill, preheat grill. Reduce heat to medium. Place slices on grill rack over heat. Cover and grill as above.) If desired, toss noodles with sliced green onions and serve with meat.
*Note: If using wooden skewers, soak in water for 30 minutes; drain.
Per Serving: 135 cal., 6 g fat (2 g sat. fat), 42 mg chol., 135 mg sodium, 2 g carbo., 1 g fiber, 18 g pro.

Teriyaki Beef
Spirals

Cheesy Tuscan Chicken Pockets

Prep: 15 minutes   *Grill:* 12 minutes

Makes 4 servings

- 4   skinless, boneless chicken breast halves
- ¼   cup semisoft cheese with garlic and herb
- 3   to 4 ounces thinly sliced prosciutto
- ⅓   cup bottled Parmesan Italian salad dressing with basil

1. Using a sharp knife, cut a pocket in the side of each chicken breast half. Spread 1 tablespoon of the cheese in each pocket; top with a folded slice of prosciutto. Secure pockets with wooden toothpicks. Brush chicken with some of the salad dressing.

2. For a charcoal grill, grill chicken on the rack of an uncovered grill directly over medium coals for 12 to 15 minutes or until chicken is no longer pink (170°F), turning once and brushing with remaining salad dressing halfway through grilling. (For a gas grill, preheat grill. Reduce heat to medium. Place chicken on grill rack over heat. Cover and grill as above.)

Per Serving: 312 cal., 15 g fat (5 g sat. fat), 113 mg chol., 888 mg sodium, 2 g carbo., 0 g fiber, 40 g pro.

Turkey with Onion-Cilantro Relish

Start to Finish: 20 minutes

Makes 4 servings

- ½   cup chopped onion (1 medium)
- ¼   cup cilantro sprigs
- 2   turkey breast tenderloins, halved horizontally (about 1 pound total)
- 3   tablespoons lime or lemon juice

1. In a blender or food processor, combine onion, cilantro, ⅛ teaspoon *salt*, and ⅛ teaspoon *ground black pepper*; cover and blend or process until mixture is very finely chopped. Dip tenderloins in lime juice.

2. For a charcoal grill, grill turkey on the rack of an uncovered grill directly over medium coals for 7 minutes. Turn and brush with lime juice; spread with onion mixture. Grill for 8 to 11 minutes more or until turkey is no longer pink (170°F). (For a gas grill, preheat grill. Reduce heat to medium. Place turkey on grill rack over heat. Cover and grill as above.)

Per Serving: 141 cal., 2 g fat (1 g sat. fat), 68 mg chol., 130 mg sodium, 3 g carbo., 1 g fiber, 27 g pro.

Bull's-Eye Onion Burgers

These scrumptious burgers not only are shaped with a bull's-eye on top, but they're also tastefully targeted to hit the spot.

Prep: 20 minutes   *Grill:* 10 minutes

Makes 4 servings

- 1   large sweet onion
- 1   pound lean ground beef
- 1½   teaspoons garlic powder
- ½   teaspoon salt
- ¼   teaspoon ground black pepper
- 4   slices Swiss cheese (4 ounces)
- 4   ¾-inch-thick slices hearty bread or Texas toast, toasted
       Lettuce (optional)
       Sliced tomatoes (optional)

1. Peel and cut onion into four ¼-inch slices; refrigerate remaining onion for another use. Shape meat loosely into four ½-inch-thick patties; sprinkle with garlic powder, salt, and pepper. Press one onion slice into the center of each patty and shape meat around onion until top of onion is flush with the surface of the meat patty.

2. For a charcoal grill, place patties, onion sides up, on the rack of an uncovered grill directly over medium coals. Grill for 10 to 13 minutes or until meat is done (160°F), turning once halfway through grilling. Top with cheese slices before the last minute of grilling. (For a gas grill, preheat grill. Reduce heat to medium. Place patties on grill rack over heat. Cover and grill as above.)

3. Serve burgers on toast and, if desired, with lettuce and tomato slices.

Per Serving: 475 cal., 24 g fat (10 g sat. fat), 147 mg chol., 648 mg sodium, 31 g carbo., 2 g fiber, 36 g pro.

MAKE IT A MENU
Bull's-Eye Onion Burgers, potato or corn chips, cucumber salad, Berries and Brownies (page 180)

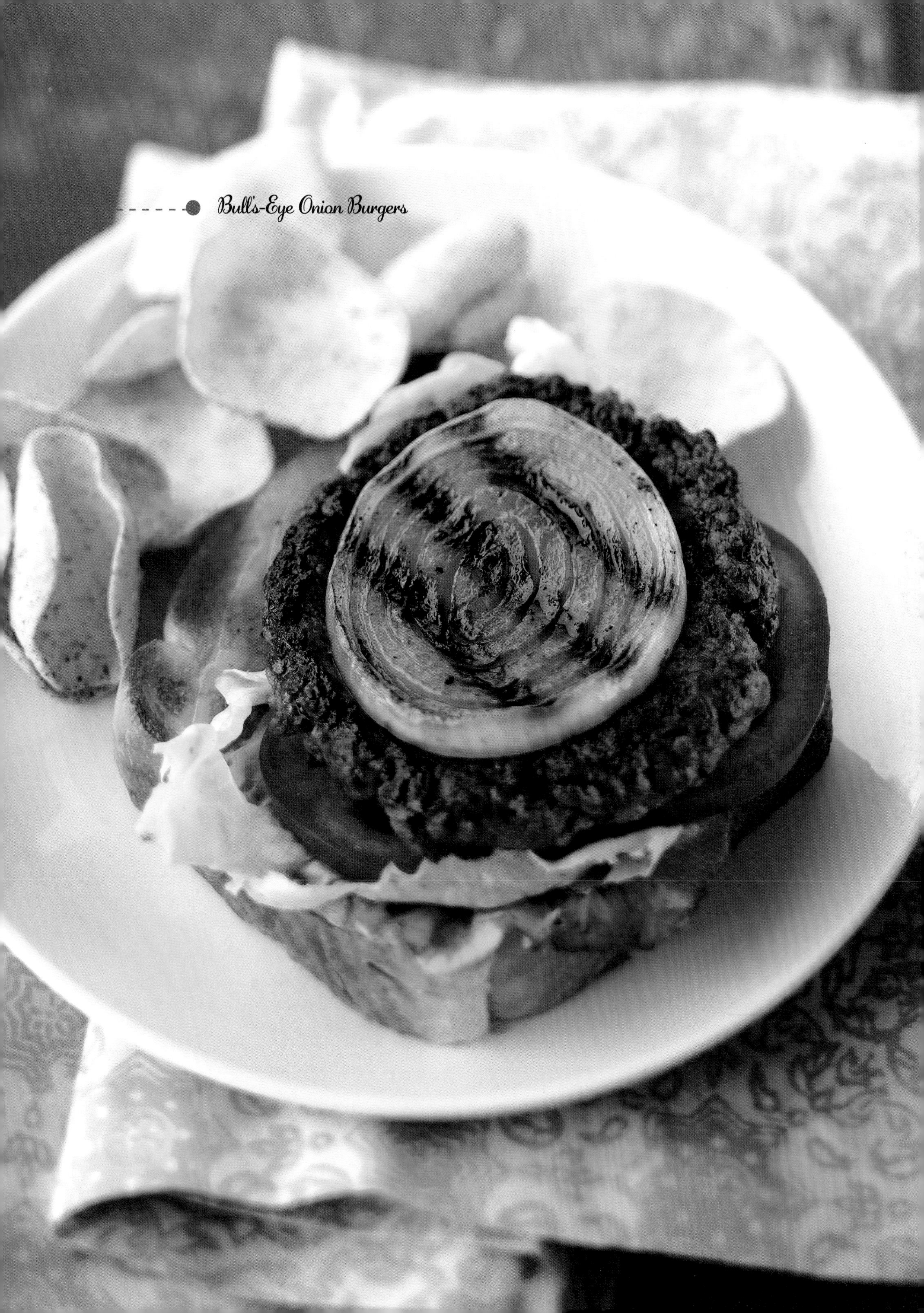

Bull's-Eye Onion Burgers

Balsamic-Glazed Lamb Chops

Balsamic-Glazed Lamb Chops

Check your supermarket for specials on lamb, and make mealtime special with this succulent recipe.

Prep: 15 minutes   *Marinate:* 4 hours
Cook: 15 minutes   *Grill:* 12 minutes
Makes 4 servings

8	lamb rib chops, cut 1 inch thick (1½ pounds total)
¼	teaspoon salt
¼	teaspoon ground black pepper
½	cup orange juice
¼	cup balsamic vinegar
1	tablespoon honey
1	tablespoon reduced-sodium soy sauce

1. Trim fat from chops. Season chops with salt and pepper. Place chops in a resealable plastic bag set in a shallow dish. For marinade, in a small bowl, stir together orange juice, balsamic vinegar, honey, and soy sauce. Pour marinade over chops. Seal bag; turn to coat chops. Marinate in the refrigerator for 4 to 24 hours, turning bag occasionally.

2. Drain lamb, reserving marinade. For glaze, pour marinade into a heavy small saucepan. Bring to boiling; reduce heat. Boil gently, uncovered, about 15 minutes or until reduced to about ⅓ cup; set aside.

3. For a charcoal grill, grill chops on the rack of an uncovered grill directly over medium coals until chops reach desired doneness, turning once and brushing with glaze halfway through grilling. Allow 12 to 14 minutes for medium rare (145°F) or 15 to 17 minutes for medium (160°F). (For a gas grill, preheat grill. Reduce heat to medium. Place chops on grill rack over heat. Cover and grill as above.) Discard any remaining glaze.

Per Serving: 161 cal., 6 g fat (2 g sat. fat), 48 mg chol., 334 mg sodium, 10 g carbo., 0 g fiber, 15 g pro.

MAKE IT A MENU
Balsamic-Glazed Lamb Chops, potato-onion packets, Romaine with Creamy Garlic Dressing (page 170), Praline Crunch Bars (page 182)

THE RIB STUFF

Pork spareribs come from the belly of the hog and are large and meaty; they contain more fat and flavor than pork loin back ribs. Most racks weigh 2 to 4 pounds. Pork loin back ribs come from the loin of the hog and are leaner than spareribs. The leanest, most tender—and highest priced—portion is called baby back ribs.

Stout-Glazed Ribs

Stout beer glazes the ribs with gorgeous, dark color and deep, rich flavor. The darker the beer the better.

Prep: 15 minutes   *Marinate:* 6 hours
Cook: 10 minutes   *Grill:* 1½ hours
Makes 4 servings

4	pounds pork loin back ribs or meaty pork spareribs
1	12-ounce bottle stout
½	cup chopped onion (1 medium)
¼	cup honey mustard
3	cloves garlic, minced, or 1½ teaspoons bottled minced garlic
1	teaspoon caraway seeds (optional)
	Salt and ground black pepper

1. Trim fat from ribs. Place ribs in a resealable plastic bag set in a shallow dish. For marinade, in a medium bowl, combine stout, onion, honey mustard, garlic, and, if desired, caraway seeds. Pour marinade over ribs. Seal bag; turn to coat ribs. Marinate in the refrigerator for 6 to 24 hours, turning bag occasionally.

2. Drain ribs, reserving marinade. Sprinkle ribs with salt and pepper. Pour marinade into a small saucepan. Bring to boiling; reduce heat. Simmer, uncovered, for 10 minutes.

3. For a charcoal grill, arrange medium-hot coals around a drip pan. Test for medium heat above pan. Place ribs, bone sides down, on grill rack over drip pan. (Or place ribs in a rib rack; place on grill rack.) Cover and grill for 1½ to 1¾ hours or until ribs are tender, brushing frequently with marinade during the last 10 minutes of grilling. Discard any remaining marinade. (For a gas grill, preheat grill. Adjust for indirect cooking. Grill as above.)

Per Serving: 482 cal., 20 g fat (7 g sat. fat), 135 mg chol., 296 mg sodium, 5 g carbo., 0 g fiber, 63 g pro.

Zesty Grilled Sirloin

Marinate beef sirloin steak in a paste of dried chile peppers and cumin overnight before grilling. The finished steak will be mouthwatering with just the right flavor.

Prep: 20 minutes   *Soak:* 30 minutes
Marinate: 24 hours   *Grill:* 24 minutes
Makes 12 servings

1½	ounces dried red chile peppers, such as guajillo, ancho, or pasilla (7 or 8 chiles)
1	tablespoon ground cumin
½	cup olive oil
1	2¾- to 3-pound beef sirloin steak, cut 2 inches thick

1. Wearing plastic or rubber gloves, use scissors or a sharp knife to remove the stalk ends from the peppers. Split peppers; remove and discard seeds. In a heavy skillet, toast peppers (without oil) over medium heat for 3 to 4 minutes or until they become fragrant, turning once or twice with tongs.

2. Transfer peppers to a small bowl. Cover with hot water and soak for 30 minutes. Drain, reserving 1 cup soaking water. Place peppers in a blender or food processor.

3. In the same skillet, toast cumin over medium heat for 1 to 2 minutes or until it becomes fragrant, stirring often. Add cumin and olive oil to peppers in blender or food processor. Blend or process until nearly smooth, adding enough of the soaking water to make a medium-thick paste; set aside.

4. Trim fat from steak. Place steak in a resealable plastic bag set in a shallow dish. Spread pepper paste on both sides of steak. Seal bag. Marinate in the refrigerator for 24 hours, turning bag occasionally.

5. Drain the steak, reserving marinade. For a charcoal grill, grill steak on the rack of an uncovered grill directly over medium coals for 22 to 26 minutes for medium rare (145°F) or 26 to 30 minutes for medium (160°F), turning once halfway through grilling and brushing occasionally with reserved marinade during the first half of grilling. (For a gas grill, preheat grill. Reduce heat to medium. Place steak on grill rack. Cover and grill as above.) Discard remaining marinade. To serve, thinly slice meat across the grain.

Per Serving: 233 cal., 14 g fat (3 g sat. fat), 63 mg chol., 56 mg sodium, 3 g carbo., 1 g fiber, 23 g pro.

Apple-Smoked
Pork Loin

Apple-Smoked Pork Loin

Flavored wood chips are sold in a variety of flavors, from hickory and mesquite to cherry and pecan. In this oregano-rubbed pork recipe, apple wood chips impart a subtle sweetness and full-bodied smoky flavor.

Prep: 10 minutes   *Soak:* 1 hour
Grill: 1 hour   *Stand:* 15 minutes
Makes 8 servings

3	cups apple wood or orange wood chips or 6 to 8 apple wood or orange wood chunks
1	2- to 2½-pound boneless pork top loin roast (single loin)
2	teaspoons dried oregano, crushed
4	cloves garlic, minced, or 2 teaspoons bottled minced garlic
½	teaspoon salt
½	teaspoon coarsely ground black pepper

1. At least 1 hour before cooking, soak wood chips or chunks in enough water to cover.

2. Meanwhile, trim fat from roast. Place roast in a shallow dish. In a small bowl, stir together oregano, garlic, salt, and pepper. Sprinkle evenly over all sides of roast; rub in with your fingers.

3. Drain wood chips. For a charcoal grill, arrange medium coals around a drip pan. Test for medium-low heat above drip pan. Sprinkle half of the drained wood chips over the coals. Place roast on grill rack directly over drip pan. Cover and grill for 1 to 1½ hours or until done (155°F). Add more coals and remaining wood chips as needed during grilling. (For a gas grill, preheat grill. Reduce heat to medium. Adjust for indirect cooking. Grill as above following manufacturer's directions for use of wood chips.)

4. Remove roast from grill. Cover with foil; let stand for 15 minutes before slicing. (The temperature of the roast will rise 5°F during standing.)

Per Serving: 190 cal., 9 g fat (3 g sat. fat), 74 mg chol., 214 mg sodium, 1 g carbo., 0 g fiber, 24 g pro.

MAKE IT A MENU
Apple-Smoked Pork Loin, Creamy Lemon-Pepper Coleslaw (page 166), Black Forest Trifle (page 184)

Weather conditions can affect *outdoor grilling times*, so keep an *instant-read thermometer* handy to double-check the doneness of meat and poultry.

Spiced Cider Salmon

This salty-sweet brine features allspice for exotic flavor and delectable moistness.

Prep: 10 minutes   *Chill:* 2 hours   *Grill:* 10 minutes
Makes 6 servings

- 1   1½-pound fresh or frozen skinless salmon fillet, ¾ inch thick
- 4   cups apple cider or apple juice
- 3   tablespoons coarse salt
- 2   tablespoons brown sugar
- 1   teaspoon ground allspice
      Nonstick cooking spray
- 2   tablespoons apple jelly (optional)

1. Thaw fish, if frozen. For brine, in a large bowl combine apple cider, salt, brown sugar, and allspice. Stir until salt and brown sugar dissolve. Add salmon. Cover and chill for 2 to 3 hours, turning salmon occasionally.

2. Drain salmon, discarding brine. Rinse salmon; pat dry with paper towels. Cut salmon into six serving-size pieces. Tear off a 28×12-inch piece of heavy foil; fold in half to make a 14×12-inch rectangle. Cut several slits in the foil rectangle. Lightly coat one side of the foil with cooking spray. Place salmon on the coated side of the foil.

3. For a charcoal grill, arrange medium-hot coals around a drip pan. Test for medium heat above pan. Place salmon on foil over drip pan. Cover and grill about 10 minutes or until salmon flakes easily when tested with a fork. (For a gas grill, preheat grill. Reduce heat to medium. Adjust for indirect cooking. Cover and grill as above.) If desired, spread apple jelly over salmon just before serving.

Per Serving: 223 cal., 12 g fat (2 g sat. fat), 66 mg chol., 550 mg sodium, 4 g carbo., 0 g fiber, 23 g pro.

Balsamic Chicken over Greens

Cut into strips and served over greens, these tangy chicken breasts make a refreshing dinner or lunch.

Prep: 15 minutes   *Marinate:* 1 hour   *Grill:* 12 minutes
Makes 4 servings

- 4   skinless, boneless chicken breast halves
- 1   cup bottled balsamic vinaigrette salad dressing
- 3   cloves garlic, minced, or 1½ teaspoons bottled minced garlic
- ¼   teaspoon crushed red pepper
- 8   cups torn mixed greens

1. Place the chicken breast halves in a resealable plastic bag set in a shallow dish. For marinade, stir together ½ cup of the vinaigrette, the garlic, and crushed red pepper. Pour marinade over the chicken. Seal bag; turn to coat chicken. Marinate in the refrigerator for 1 to 4 hours, turning bag occasionally.

2. Drain chicken, reserving marinade. For a charcoal grill, grill chicken on the rack of an uncovered grill directly over medium coals for 12 to 15 minutes or until chicken is no longer pink (170°F), turning once and brushing with marinade halfway through grilling. (For a gas grill, preheat grill. Reduce heat to medium. Place chicken on grill rack over heat. Cover and grill as above.)

3. Divide greens among four dinner plates. Cut chicken into strips. Place chicken on top of greens. Serve with remaining ½ cup vinaigrette.

Broiling Directions: Prepare and marinate chicken as directed. Drain chicken, reserving marinade. Place chicken breasts on the unheated rack of a broiler pan. Broil 4 to 5 inches from heat for 12 to 15 minutes or until chicken is no longer pink (170°F), turning once and brushing once with marinade halfway through broiling. Discard any remaining marinade.

Per Serving: 284 cal., 13 g fat (2 g sat. fat), 82 mg chol., 525 mg sodium, 7 g carbo., 1 g fiber, 34 g pro.

Grilled Tomato and Chicken Kabobs

Grill the tomatoes separately to keep them from overcooking and possibly dropping off the skewer into the coals.

Prep: 20 minutes *Marinate:* 4 hours *Grill:* 10 minutes
Makes 6 servings

1	pound skinless, boneless chicken breast halves, cut into 1-inch pieces
12	fresh small white mushrooms or button mushrooms, stems removed
¼	cup reduced-sodium soy sauce
1	tablespoon sesame oil
12	cherry tomatoes
1	tablespoon sesame seeds, toasted (optional)

1. Place chicken pieces and mushrooms in a resealable plastic bag set in a shallow dish. For marinade, in a small bowl, combine soy sauce and sesame oil. Pour over chicken and mushrooms. Seal bag; turn bag to coat chicken and mushrooms. Marinate in the refrigerator for 4 to 6 hours, turning bag occasionally.

2. Drain chicken and mushrooms, reserving marinade. On five 10-inch metal skewers, alternately thread chicken and mushrooms, leaving ¼-inch space between pieces. Thread tomatoes on another 10-inch metal skewer.

3. For a charcoal grill, grill chicken and mushroom kabobs on the rack of an uncovered grill directly over medium coals for 10 to 12 minutes or until chicken is no longer pink, turning once and brushing occasionally with reserved marinade the last 5 minutes of grilling. Add tomato kabob to the grill during the last 3 to 4 minutes, grilling until softened and heated through. (For a gas grill, preheat grill. Reduce heat to medium. Place kabobs on grill rack over heat. Cover and grill kabobs as above.) Discard any remaining marinade. If desired, sprinkle kabobs with sesame seeds.

Per Serving: 124 cal., 3 g fat (1 g sat. fat), 44 mg chol., 436 mg sodium, 3 g carbo., 1 g fiber, 20 g pro.

PERFECT POULTRY

When you're grilling skinless chicken or turkey pieces, take care to not overcook them. Turn with tongs, not a fork. A marinade or basting sauce will help keep the poultry moist. Grill chicken or turkey breasts to 170°F or until no longer pink. Cook whole birds, thighs, legs, and drumsticks to an internal temperature of 180°F.

Grilled Lemon Chicken

Instead of using oil to keep the chicken moist while cooking, spritz it occasionally with broth.

Prep: 20 minutes *Marinate:* 1 hour *Grill:* 12 minutes
Makes 4 servings

3	lemons
4	skinless, boneless chicken breast halves
½	cup reduced-sodium chicken broth
1	tablespoon snipped fresh lemon thyme or thyme
¼	teaspoon ground black pepper
	Fresh lemon thyme or thyme sprigs (optional)

1. Finely shred enough lemon peel from one lemon to make 1 tablespoon peel. Cut the lemon in half and squeeze both halves to make ¼ cup juice. Set lemon peel and juice aside.

2. Place the chicken in a resealable plastic bag in a shallow bowl. For marinade, in a small bowl, stir together chicken broth, the lemon peel, the lemon juice, the 1 tablespoon snipped thyme, and pepper. Pour over chicken. Seal bag; turn to coat chicken. Marinate in the refrigerator for 1 to 2 hours, turning bag occasionally.

3. Drain chicken, reserving marinade. Cut remaining 2 lemons in half. For a charcoal grill, grill chicken on the rack of an uncovered grill directly over medium coals for 12 to 15 minutes or until no longer pink (170°F), turning once and brushing with marinade halfway through grilling. Add lemon halves to grill for the last 3 minutes of grilling. (For a gas grill, preheat grill. Reduce heat to medium. Place chicken on grill rack over heat. Cover and grill chicken and lemon halves as above.) Discard any remaining marinade.

4. Serve chicken with grilled lemons and, if desired, garnish with additional fresh thyme.

Per Serving: 161 cal., 2 g fat (0 g sat. fat), 82 mg chol., 140 mg sodium, 1 g carbo., 0 g fiber, 33 g pro.

Grilled Lemon
Chicken

Spice-Rubbed Ribeyes

Start to Finish: 20 minutes

Makes 4 servings

4 teaspoons chili powder
1 teaspoon ground coriander
1 teaspoon cumin seeds
½ teaspoon ground black pepper
4 6-ounce boneless beef ribeye steaks, cut 1 inch thick

1. For spice rub, in a small nonstick skillet, cook and stir chili powder, coriander, cumin seeds, and pepper over medium heat for 1 minute; cool. Rub spice mixture onto both sides of steaks.

2. For a charcoal grill, grill steaks on the rack of an uncovered grill directly over medium coals until desired doneness, turning once halfway through grilling. Allow 11 to 15 minutes for medium rare (145°F) and 14 to 18 minutes for medium (160°F). (For a gas grill, preheat grill. Reduce heat to medium. Place steaks on grill rack over heat. Cover and grill as above.)

Per Serving: 267 cal., 11 g fat (4 g sat. fat), 81 mg chol., 115 mg sodium, 2 g carbo., 1 g fiber, 38 g pro.

Spicy Orange-Glazed Pork Chops

Start to Finish: 25 minutes

Makes 4 servings

¼ cup orange marmalade
2 teaspoons Dijon-style mustard
1 teaspoon lemon juice
⅛ to ¼ teaspoon cayenne pepper
4 boneless pork loin chops, cut ¾ inch thick

1. For glaze, stir together orange marmalade, mustard, lemon juice, and cayenne pepper. Set glaze aside.

2. Trim fat from chops. Sprinkle chops with *salt* and *ground black pepper*. For a charcoal grill, grill chops on the greased rack of an uncovered grill directly over medium coals for 12 to 15 minutes or until done (160°F), turning once and brushing frequently with glaze during the last few minutes of grilling. (For a gas grill, preheat grill. Reduce heat to medium. Place chops on greased grill rack over heat. Cover and grill as above.)

Per Serving: 263 cal., 10 g fat (3 g sat. fat), 92 mg chol., 126 mg sodium, 5 g carbo., 0 g fiber, 37 g pro.

Herb-and-Lemon-Crusted Game Hens

Game hens look fancy, but they're actually almost the same price as chicken.

Prep: 30 minutes   *Chill:* 12 hours
Grill: 50 minutes   *Stand:* 10 minutes
Makes 4 servings

4 1¼- to 1½-pound Cornish game hens
2 lemons
1½ cups snipped fresh herbs (such as oregano and basil)
2 teaspoons coarse salt or 1½ teaspoons salt
½ teaspoon ground black pepper

1. Remove giblets from game hens, if present. If desired, remove skin from hens. Rinse hens and pat dry with paper towels. Place hens on a plate or in a baking dish.

2. Finely shred enough lemon peel from one lemon to make 2 teaspoons peel. In a small bowl, combine the lemon peel, herbs, salt, and pepper; set aside. Cut 1½ of the lemons into slices; cut remaining lemon half into four wedges. Place one lemon wedge into each hen cavity.

3. For each hen, tie drumsticks to tail with 100-percent-cotton kitchen string. Twist wing tips under back. Generously rub outside of game hens with herb mixture. Place lemon slices on top of hens. Cover tightly with plastic wrap and chill in the refrigerator for 12 to 24 hours.

4. For a charcoal grill, arrange medium-hot coals around a drip pan. Test for medium heat above pan. Unwrap game hens. Place game hens, breast sides up, on grill rack over drip pan. Cover and grill for 50 to 60 minutes or until hens are no longer pink (180°F in thigh muscle). (For a gas grill, preheat grill. Reduce heat to medium. Adjust for indirect cooking. Place game hens on grill rack; grill as above.)

5. Remove game hens from grill. Cover tightly with foil and let stand 10 minutes before carving.

Per Serving: 676 cal., 45 g fat (12 g sat. fat), 346 mg chol., 1,134 mg sodium, 3 g carbo., 0 g fiber, 60 g pro.

Herb-and-Lemon-
Crusted Game Hens

Cilantro-Lime
Orange Roughy

Cilantro-Lime Orange Roughy

The distinctive flavor of fresh cilantro goes beautifully with fish.

Start to Finish: 30 minutes
Makes 4 servings

1¼ pounds fresh or frozen orange roughy,
      ocean perch, cod, or haddock fillets,
      ¾ to 1 inch thick
      Salt and ground black pepper
¼   cup snipped fresh cilantro
1   tablespoon butter, melted
1   teaspoon finely shredded lime peel
1   tablespoon lime juice
      Lime and/or radish wedges (optional)

1. Thaw fish, if frozen. Rinse fish; pat dry with paper towels. Cut fish into four serving-size pieces, if necessary. Sprinkle fish with salt and pepper.

2. Place fish in a well-greased grill basket, tucking under any thin edges. For a charcoal grill, grill fish on the rack of an uncovered grill directly over medium coals for 4 to 6 minutes per ½-inch thickness of fish or until fish flakes easily when tested with a fork, turning basket once halfway through grilling. (For a gas grill, preheat grill. Reduce heat to medium. Place fish on grill rack over heat. Cover and grill as above.)

3. Meanwhile, in a small bowl stir together cilantro, melted butter, lime peel, and lime juice. Spoon cilantro mixture over fish. If desired, serve with lime wedges.

Per Serving: 127 cal., 4 g fat (2 g sat. fat), 36 mg chol., 259 mg sodium, 1 g carbo., 0 g fiber, 21 g pro.

IS IT DONE YET?
When checking fish doneness, check the flesh at the thickest part of a fillet, steak, or whole fish. When cooked, the flesh will be opaque and moist and will begin to pull away from the bones. A fork can pull cooked fish apart into large flakes. To test thick fish steaks, insert an instant-read thermometer horizontally; it should read 140°F.

Beer-Glazed Pork Chops

Prep: 15 minutes *Marinate:* 6 hours *Cook:* 15 minutes
Grill: 30 minutes
Makes 4 servings

- 4 boneless pork top loin chops, cut 1¼ inches thick (about 1¾ pounds total)
- 1 12-ounce bottle stout
- ¼ cup honey mustard
- 3 cloves garlic, minced, or 1½ teaspoons bottled minced garlic
- 1 teaspoon caraway seeds

1. Trim fat from chops. Place chops in a resealable plastic bag set in a shallow dish. For the marinade, stir together stout, mustard, garlic, and caraway seeds. Pour marinade over chops. Seal bag; turn to coat chops. Marinate in the refrigerator for 6 to 24 hours, turning the bag occasionally.

2. Drain chops, reserving marinade. Pour marinade into a small saucepan Bring to boiling; reduce heat. Simmer, uncovered, about 15 minutes or until marinade is reduced by about half; set aside.

3. For a charcoal grill, arrange medium-hot coals around a drip pan. Test for medium heat above pan. Place chops on grill rack over pan. Cover and grill for 30 to 35 minutes or until done (160°F), brushing chops frequently with marinade during last 10 minutes of grilling. (For a gas grill, preheat grill. Reduce heat to medium. Adjust for indirect cooking. Place chops on grill rack. Grill as above.) Discard remaining marinade.
Per Serving: 327 cal., 11 g fat (4 g sat. fat), 108 mg chol., 90 mg sodium, 5 g carbo., 0 g fiber, 44 g pro.

Gorgonzola-and-Herb-Stuffed Burgers

Gorgonzola is pricey but packed with flavor, so you only need a little bit to make these irresistible burgers.
Prep: 20 minutes *Grill:* 14 minutes
Makes 4 servings

- ½ cup crumbled Gorgonzola cheese or other blue cheese
- ¼ cup snipped fresh basil
- 1 teaspoon clove garlic, minced
- 1¼ pounds lean ground beef
  Salt and ground black pepper
- 4 kaiser rolls, split and toasted

- 1½ cups arugula or fresh spinach leaves (optional)
- 1 large tomato, sliced (optional)

1. In a small bowl, combine Gorgonzola cheese, basil, and garlic; shape into four slightly flattened mounds. Shape ground beef into eight ¼-inch-thick patties. Place a cheese mound in the center of four of the patties. Top with remaining patties; press gently to seal edges. Season with salt and pepper.

2. For a charcoal grill, grill burgers on the rack of an uncovered grill directly over medium coals for 14 to 18 minutes or until meat is done (160°F), turning once halfway through grilling. (For a gas grill, preheat grill. Reduce heat to medium. Place burgers on grill rack over heat. Cover and grill as above.)

3. Serve burgers on kaiser rolls with, if desired, arugula and tomato.
Per Serving: 448 cal., 20 g fat (8 g sat. fat), 100 mg chol., 704 mg sodium, 31 g carbo., 1 g fiber, 34 g pro.

Indian-Style Chicken

Prep: 5 minutes *Grill:* 35 minutes
Makes 6 servings

- ½ cup bottled barbecue sauce
- ¼ cup peanut butter
- ½ teaspoon finely shredded orange peel
- 1 to 2 tablespoons orange juice
- 1½ pounds chicken drumsticks and/or thighs

1. For sauce, in a small bowl, stir together barbecue sauce, peanut butter, orange peel, and enough orange juice to make desired consistency. Set sauce aside.

2. For a charcoal grill, grill chicken on the rack of an uncovered grill directly over medium coals for 35 to 45 minutes or until chicken is no longer pink (180°F), turning once and brushing with sauce during the last 5 minutes of grilling. (For a gas grill, preheat grill. Reduce heat to medium. Place chicken on grill rack over heat. Cover and grill as above.)

3. If desired, place any remaining sauce in a 1-cup glass measure. Microwave on 100% power (high) for 30 to 60 seconds or until boiling. Serve with chicken.
Per Serving: 171 cal., 8 g fat (2 g sat. fat), 49 mg chol., 338 mg sodium, 10 g carbo., 1 g fiber, 16 g pro.

Hot Barbecued Chicken

Prep: 10 minutes *Marinate:* 2 hours *Grill:* 50 minutes
Makes 6 servings

2½ to 3 pounds meaty chicken pieces
   (breast halves, thighs, and drumsticks)
1 2-ounce bottle (¼ cup) hot pepper sauce
3 tablespoons ketchup
3 tablespoons Worcestershire sauce

1. Place chicken pieces in a resealable plastic bag set in a shallow bowl. For marinade, in a small bowl, combine hot pepper sauce, ketchup, and Worcestershire sauce. Pour marinade over chicken pieces in bag. Seal bag; turn to coat chicken. Marinate in the refrigerator for 2 to 3 hours.

2. Drain chicken, discarding marinade. For a charcoal grill, arrange medium-hot coals around a drip pan. Test for medium heat above the pan. Place chicken pieces, bone sides down, on a grill rack over drip pan. Cover and grill for 50 to 60 minutes or until chicken is no longer pink (170°F for breasts; 180°F for thighs and drumsticks). (For a gas grill, preheat grill. Reduce heat to medium. Adjust for indirect cooking. Grill as above.)
Per Serving: 285 cal., 17 g fat (5 g sat. fat), 110 mg chol., 201 mg sodium, 2 g carbo., 0 g fiber, 29 g pro.

Mustard-Glazed Halibut Steaks

Start to Finish: 20 minutes
Makes 4 servings

4 6-ounce fresh or frozen halibut steaks, 1 inch thick
2 tablespoons butter or margarine
2 tablespoons lemon juice
1 tablespoon Dijon-style mustard
2 teaspoons snipped fresh basil

1. Thaw fish, if frozen. Rinse fish and pat dry. Heat butter, lemon juice, mustard, and basil over low heat until butter melts; brush mixture on both sides of fish.

2. For a charcoal grill, grill fish on greased rack of an uncovered grill directly over medium coals for 8 to 12 minutes or until fish flakes easily, turning once halfway through grilling and brushing occasionally with mustard mixture. (For a gas grill, preheat grill. Reduce heat to medium. Place fish on greased rack over heat. Cover and grill as above.)
Per Serving: 243 cal., 10 g fat (4 g sat. fat), 70 mg chol., 254 mg sodium, 1 g carbo., 0 g fiber, 36 g pro.

Spicy Grilled Shrimp

Prep: 15 minutes *Marinate:* 1 hour *Grill:* 7 minutes
Makes 4 servings

1½ pounds fresh or frozen peeled and deveined
    extra-large shrimp
¼ cup orange marmalade
¼ cup honey
2 to 3 teaspoons Cajun seasoning
1 tablespoon olive oil
2 cups hot cooked rice (optional)

1. Thaw shrimp, if frozen. (If using wooden skewers, soak in water for 1 hour.) Rinse shrimp; pat dry with paper towels. For sauce, in a small saucepan, stir together marmalade, honey, and ½ teaspoon of the Cajun seasoning; set aside.

2. Place shrimp in a resealable plastic bag set in a shallow bowl. For marinade, in a small bowl, combine oil and remaining Cajun seasoning. Pour marinade over shrimp; seal bag. Marinate in refrigerator for 1 hour, turning bag occasionally.

3. Drain shrimp, discarding marinade. Thread shrimp onto skewers, leaving ¼-inch space between shrimp. For a charcoal grill, grill skewers on the greased rack of an uncovered grill directly over medium coals for 7 to 9 minutes or until shrimp turn opaque, turning once halfway through grilling. (For a gas grill, preheat grill. Reduce heat to medium. Place skewers on greased grill rack over heat. Cover and grill as above.)

4. Stir marmalade sauce over low heat for 2 to 3 minutes or until melted. Place skewers on plates. Drizzle sauce over shrimp on skewers. If desired, serve with hot cooked rice.
Per Serving: 327 cal., 6 g fat (1 g sat. fat), 259 mg chol., 353 mg sodium, 33 g carbo., 0 g fiber, 35 g pro.

MAKE IT A MENU
Spicy Grilled Shrimp, rice, Grilled Asparagus with Lemon (page 168), Tropical Angel Cake (page 190)

Spicy Grilled Shrimp

Thai-Spiced Chicken Kabobs

Double the action of the bold-flavored sauce by brushing some on the chicken during grilling and reserving a separate portion to pass at the table.

Prep: 30 minutes Grill: 12 minutes
Makes 4 servings

- ⅔ cup sweet-and-sour sauce
- 2 tablespoons snipped fresh basil
- 1 teaspoon Thai seasoning or five-spice powder
- 1 clove garlic, minced
- 1 small fresh pineapple (3 to 3½ pounds)
  Nonstick cooking spray
- 1 pound skinless, boneless chicken breast halves, cut into 1-inch pieces
- 1 tablespoon butter, melted

1. For sauce, combine sweet-and-sour sauce, basil, Thai seasoning, and garlic. Reserve ¼ cup sauce to brush on kabobs. Set remaining sauce aside.

2. Cut off pineapple ends. Halve pineapple lengthwise; cut each half crosswise into 4 slices. Lightly coat pineapple slices with cooking spray; set aside.

3. Thread chicken pieces onto 4 long skewers, leaving a ¼-inch space between pieces. For a charcoal grill, grill skewers on the rack of an uncovered grill directly over medium heat for 7 minutes. Turn skewers; brush with reserved sauce. Discard any remaining brush-on sauce. Arrange pineapple slices on grill rack directly over medium heat. Grill chicken and pineapple for 6 to 8 minutes or until chicken is no longer pink (170°F) and pineapple is heated through, turning once.

4. In a small bowl, combine remaining sauce and melted butter; serve with chicken and pineapple. Makes 4 servings.

Per Serving: 285 cal., 4 g total fat (2 g sat. fat), 73 mg chol., 292 mg sodium, 35 g carbo., 3 g fiber, 27 g pro.

DOUBLE THE FLAVOR
The bold-flavored Asian-style sauce does double duty here—as a brush-on during grilling and as a sauce to pass at the table. Be sure to set the reserved sauce aside to avoid any contact with the raw chicken.

Chicken thighs are an *economical alternative* to chicken breasts. And when they're boneless and skinless, they're a *perfectly healthful* choice, too.

Barbecued Chicken Thighs

Serve this lip-smacking-good chicken with coleslaw and baked beans.

Prep: 10 minutes *Grill:* 12 minutes
Makes 4 servings

- ¼ cup packed brown sugar
- 2 tablespoons finely chopped onion
- 2 tablespoons vinegar
- 1 tablespoon yellow mustard
- ¼ teaspoon celery seeds
- ⅛ teaspoon garlic powder
- 1 teaspoon paprika
- ¼ teaspoon salt
- ¼ teaspoon ground black pepper
- 8 skinless, boneless chicken thighs

1. For the sauce, in a small saucepan, combine brown sugar, onion, vinegar, mustard, celery seeds, and garlic powder. Bring to boiling, stirring until sugar dissolves. Set aside.

2. In a small bowl, combine paprika, salt, and pepper. Sprinkle paprika mixture evenly over chicken thighs; rub in with your fingers.

3. For a charcoal grill, grill chicken on the rack of an uncovered grill over medium coals for 12 to 15 minutes or until no longer pink (180°F), turning once halfway through grilling and brushing with sauce during the last 5 minutes of grilling. (For a gas grill, preheat grill. Reduce heat to medium. Place chicken on rack over heat. Cover and grill as above.)

Per Serving: 305 cal., 8 g total fat (2 g sat. fat), 158 mg chol., 329 mg sodium, 16 g carbo., 0 g fiber, 40 g pro.

Grilled Chicken and Wild Rice Salad

Purchase an unseasoned rice mix to keep sodium at a reasonable level.

Prep: 30 minutes *Grill:* 12 minutes *Chill:* 2 hours
Makes 6 servings

- 1 6-ounce package long grain and wild rice mix
- ⅔ cup bottled fat-free Italian salad dressing
- 6 skinless, boneless chicken breast halves
- 1 cup loose-pack frozen French-cut green beans
- 1 14-ounce can artichoke hearts, drained and quartered
- 2½ cups packaged shredded cabbage with carrot (coleslaw mix)

1. Prepare rice mix according to package directions; transfer to a medium bowl. Cover and chill for 2 hours. Place 3 tablespoons of the salad dressing in a small bowl; set aside remaining dressing.

2. For a charcoal grill, grill chicken on the rack of an uncovered grill directly over medium coals for 12 to 15 minutes or until chicken is tender and no longer pink (170°F), turning once and brushing chicken with the 3 tablespoons dressing during the last 2 minutes of grilling. (For a gas grill, preheat grill. Reduce heat to medium. Place chicken on grill rack over heat. Cover and grill as above.)

3. Meanwhile, rinse beans with cool water for 30 seconds; drain. In a large bowl, toss together beans, chilled rice, artichoke hearts, and coleslaw mix. Add the reserved salad dressing; toss to gently coat.

4. Remove chicken from grill. Slice chicken and serve with salad.

Per Serving: 262 cal., 2 g total fat (0 g sat. fat), 66 mg chol., 982 mg sodium, 29 g carbo., 3 g fiber, 31 g pro.

Southwest Chicken Burgers

Southwest Chicken Burgers

Chili powder and pepper-flavored cheese make chicken burgers a tasty alternative to traditional beef burgers.

Prep: 20 minutes Grill: 15 minutes
Makes 4 servings

3	tablespoons finely chopped green sweet pepper
¾	teaspoon chili powder
¼	teaspoon salt
¼	teaspoon ground black pepper
1	pound uncooked ground chicken
1	cup shredded Monterey Jack cheese with jalapeño peppers (4 ounces)
4	kaiser rolls, split and toasted
1	medium avocado, seeded, peeled, and sliced (optional)
	Bottled salsa (optional)

1. In a large bowl, combine sweet pepper, chili powder, salt, and black pepper. Add ground chicken; mix well. Shape chicken mixture into four ¾-inch-thick patties.

2. For a charcoal grill, grill patties on the rack of an uncovered grill directly over medium coals for 14 to 18 minutes or until no longer pink (165°F), turning once halfway through grilling. Sprinkle with cheese. Grill for 1 to 2 minutes more or until cheese melts. (For a gas grill, preheat grill. Reduce heat to medium. Place patties on grill rack over heat. Cover and grill as above.)

3. Serve burgers on rolls. If desired, top with avocado and salsa.

Per Serving: 497 cal., 26 g total fat (6 g sat. fat), 25 mg chol., 683 mg sodium, 31 g carbo., 2 g fiber, 32 g pro.

HEALTHY SPLURGE
While ground chicken made solely from breast meat is more expensive, it may be worth the extra money if you're concerned about fat and calories. Regular ground chicken is made from a mix of white and dark meat, plus the skin.

Grilled Chicken with Cucumber Yogurt Sauce

Compliment grilled chicken with a tangy, refreshing sauce flavored with mint and cumin.

Prep: 20 minutes Grill: 12 minutes
Makes 4 servings

1	6-ounce carton plain low-fat yogurt
¼	cup thinly sliced green onions
2	teaspoons snipped fresh mint
½	teaspoon ground cumin
¼	teaspoon salt
⅛	teaspoon ground black pepper
1	cup chopped, seeded cucumber
4	skinless, boneless chicken breast halves
⅛	teaspoon ground black pepper

1. In a medium bowl, combine yogurt, green onions, mint, cumin, salt, and ⅛ teaspoon pepper. Reserve half of the yogurt mixture to use as a brush-on sauce. Stir cucumber into remaining yogurt mixture; set aside.

2. Sprinkle chicken breasts with ⅛ teaspoon pepper. For a charcoal grill, grill chicken on the rack of an uncovered grill directly over medium coals for 12 to 15 minutes or until chicken is no longer pink (170°F), turning once halfway through grilling and brushing with yogurt brush-on sauce during the last half of grilling. Discard any remaining yogurt mixture. (For a gas grill, preheat grill. Reduce heat to medium. Place chicken on grill rack over heat. Cover and grill as above.)

3. Serve chicken with the cucumber-yogurt sauce.

Per Serving: 159 cal., 2 g total fat (1 g sat. fat), 68 mg chol., 251 mg sodium, 5 g carbo., 0 g fiber, 29 g pro.

Grilled Chicken Sandwiches with Lime Dressing

Spice up the lime dressing by stirring in ¹/₈ teaspoon cayenne pepper before chilling.

Prep: 15 minutes Grill: 12 minutes
Makes 4 servings

¼	cup fat-free mayonnaise dressing or salad dressing
½	teaspoon finely shredded lime peel or lemon peel
1	medium zucchini, cut lengthwise into ¼-inch-thick slices
3	tablespoons Worcestershire sauce for chicken
4	skinless, boneless chicken breast halves
4	whole wheat hamburger buns, split and toasted

1. For lime dressing, combine mayonnaise dressing and lime peel; cover and chill until serving time. Brush zucchini slices with 1 tablespoon of the Worcestershire sauce; set aside. Brush chicken with remaining Worcestershire sauce.

2. For a charcoal grill, grill chicken on the rack of an uncovered grill directly over medium coals for 12 to 15 minutes or until no longer pink (170°F), turning once halfway through grilling. Add zucchini slices to grill for the last 6 minutes of grilling time for chicken, turning once and grilling until zucchini softens and lightly browns. (For a gas grill, preheat grill. Reduce heat to medium. Place chicken on grill rack over heat. Cover and grill as above.)

3. To serve, spread lime dressing onto cut sides of toasted buns. If desired, halve zucchini slices crosswise. Place chicken and zucchini slices on bun bottoms; add bun tops.

Per Serving: 259 cal., 2 g total fat (0 g sat. fat), 66 mg chol., 488 mg sodium, 27 g carbo., 3 g fiber, 31 g pro.

To get the best buy on boneless, skinless *chicken breasts,* buy them frozen in large 6-pound bags. Then thaw *just the number you need* in the refrigerator.

Peanut-Crusted Chops

Be sure to cover the grill after adding the peanut crust so it gets slightly crispy.

Prep: 15 minutes *Grill:* 11 minutes
Makes 4 servings

⅓	cup creamy peanut butter
⅓	cup pineapple juice
2	tablespoons finely chopped green onion
1	tablespoon soy sauce
1	tablespoon honey
1	teaspoon grated fresh ginger or ¼ teaspoon ground ginger
½	teaspoon dry mustard
	Several dashes bottled hot pepper sauce
⅓	cup finely chopped honey-roasted peanuts
2	tablespoons fine dry bread crumbs
1	tablespoon toasted sesame seeds
4	boneless pork sirloin chops, cut ¾ inch thick
4	ounces Chinese egg noodles or dried angel hair pasta

1. For peanut sauce, in a small saucepan, heat peanut butter until melted; gradually whisk in pineapple juice, green onion, soy sauce, honey, ginger, mustard, and hot pepper sauce. Set aside 2 tablespoons of the peanut sauce; keep remaining sauce warm. For crust, in a small bowl, combine peanuts, bread crumbs, and sesame seeds; set aside.

2. For a charcoal grill, grill chops on the rack of an uncovered grill directly over medium coals for 6 minutes. Turn chops and brush with the reserved 2 tablespoons peanut sauce. Sprinkle chops with crust mixture. With the back of a metal spatula, press crust onto chops. Cover and grill for 5 to 7 minutes more or until chops are slightly pink in center and juices run clear (160°F). (For a gas grill, preheat grill. Reduce heat to medium. Place chops on grill rack over heat. Cover and grill as above.)

3. Meanwhile, cook noodles according to package directions; drain. Toss noodles with the remaining peanut sauce. Serve with chops.

Per Serving: 510 cal., 23 g total fat (5 g sat. fat), 89 mg chol., 518 mg sodium, 39 g carbo., 6 g fiber, 42 g pro.

CUT YOUR OWN CHOPS

To save money, purchase whole pork loins on sale and cut into chops and/or cut the loin into thirds to cut your own roasts. Freeze what you don't use for use at a later date.

Curried Apricot Pork Pockets

Shape these pork-and-fruit patties into ovals so they tuck into the pita bread halves easily.

Prep: 30 minutes *Grill:* 14 minutes
Makes 4 servings

1	egg
¼	cup finely snipped dried apricots
¼	cup mango chutney (finely chop large pieces of fruit)
¼	cup finely crushed whole wheat crackers
1¼	teaspoons curry powder
¼	teaspoon salt
1	pound lean ground pork
2	tablespoons apricot preserves
1	teaspoon lemon juice
2	large pita bread rounds, halved crosswise
1	cup shredded spinach or romaine

1. In a large bowl, beat egg with a whisk; stir in apricots, chutney, wheat crackers, 1 teaspoon of the curry powder, and the salt. Add ground pork; mix well. Shape into four ¾-inch-thick oval patties. In a small bowl, combine apricot preserves, lemon juice, and remaining ¼ teaspoon curry powder; set aside.

2. For a charcoal grill, place patties on the rack of an uncovered grill directly over medium heat; grill for 14 to 18 minutes or until done (160°F), turning once halfway through grilling and brushing with the preserves mixture during the last 2 minutes of grilling. (For a gas grill, preheat grill. Reduce heat to medium. Place patties on grill rack over heat. Cover and grill as above.)

3. Serve patties in pita bread halves with shredded spinach.

Per Serving: 519 cal., 26 g total fat (10 g sat. fat), 134 mg chol., 584 mg sodium, 43 g carbo., 2 g fiber, 25 g pro.

SAVE ON SKEWERS
Although it's tempting to buy the already-cut pork loin for stir-fry or skewers to save a little time, you'll save money if you buy on-sale pork chops—especiallly the thinner ones—and cut them into bite-size slices or pieces.

Skewered Five-Spice Pork

Oyster sauce and five-spice powder boost flavors while the pork marinates.

Prep: 30 minutes *Grill:* 10 minutes *Marinate:* 4 to 24 hours
Makes 4 servings

1	pound boneless pork loin, cut into bite-size strips
¼	cup bottled salsa
2	tablespoons soy sauce
2	tablespoons bottled oyster sauce
1	tablespoon sugar
1	teaspoon five-spice powder
⅛	to ¼ teaspoon ground red pepper
1	medium red sweet pepper, cut into 1-inch pieces
4	green onions, cut diagonally into 1½-inch pieces
8	large fresh mushrooms
1	tablespoon cooking oil

1. Place pork in a plastic bag set in a medium bowl. In a small bowl, stir together the salsa, soy sauce, oyster sauce, sugar, five-spice powder, and ground red pepper. Pour over meat in bag; close bag. Turn to coat meat. Marinate in the refrigerator for 4 to 24 hours, turning bag occasionally. Drain meat, reserving marinade.

2. Brush vegetables lightly with cooking oil. Alternately thread pork, sweet pepper, green onions, and mushrooms onto four 12- to 14-inch metal skewers, leaving a ¼-inch space between pieces.

3. For charcoal grill, grill kabobs on the rack of an uncovered grill directly over medium coals for 10 to 12 minutes or until meat is done (160°F) and vegetables are tender, turning and brushing with marinade halfway through grilling. Discard any remaining marinade. (For gas grill, preheat grill. Reduce heat to medium. Place kabobs on grill rack over heat. Cover; grill as above.)

Per Serving: 318 cal., 19 g total fat (6 g sat. fat), 67 mg chol., 829 mg sodium, 11 g carbo., 2 g fiber, 26 g pro.

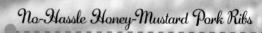
No-Hassle Honey-Mustard Pork Ribs

slow & simple

For busy families on a budget, this is the way to cook:
Put all the ingredients in a slow cooker, cover, and turn it on.
You can get a dozen things done while dinner cooks the no-tend way.

No-Hassle Honey-Mustard Pork Ribs

Boneless country-style ribs offer more meat with less mess than regular ribs.

Prep: 15 minutes
Cook: 8 to 10 hours (low) or 4 to 5 hours (high)
Makes 6 to 8 servings

- 3½ pounds boneless pork country-style ribs
- 1 cup bottled barbecue sauce
- 1 8-ounce jar honey mustard
- 2 teaspoons zesty herb grill seasoning blend

1. Place ribs in a 3½- or 4-quart slow cooker. In a small bowl, stir together barbecue sauce, honey mustard, and seasoning blend. Pour over ribs in cooker. Stir to coat.

2. Cover and cook on low-heat setting for 8 to 10 hours or on high-heat setting for 4 to 5 hours.

3. Transfer ribs to a serving platter. Strain sauce; skim fat from sauce. Drizzle some of the sauce over the ribs and pass remaining sauce.

Per Serving: 322 cal., 12 g fat (4 g sat. fat), 94 mg chol., 497 mg sodium, 18 g carbo., 1 g fiber, 29 g pro.

Minestrone Plus

Ordinary canned soup becomes extraordinary when cooked slowly with your choice of beef, pork, or sausage. Come the end of the day, all you have to do is add some cheese.

Prep: 20 minutes
Cook: 7 to 8 hours (low) or 3½ to 4 hours (high)
Makes 6 servings

- 1 pound lean ground beef, ground pork, or sweet Italian sausage
- ½ cup chopped onion (1 medium)
- 2 19-ounce cans chunky minestrone
- 1 15.5-ounce can navy beans, rinsed and drained
- 2 cups water
- ¼ cup finely shredded Parmesan cheese (1 ounce)

1. In a large skillet, cook ground meat and onion until meat is brown; drain off fat.

2. In a 3½- or 4-quart slow cooker, combine the cooked meat mixture, minestrone, navy beans, and the water.

3. Cover and cook on low-heat setting for 7 to 8 hours or on high-heat setting for 3½ to 4 hours. Ladle soup into bowls. Sprinkle individual servings with Parmesan cheese.

Per Serving: 424 cal., 18 g fat (9 g sat. fat), 67 mg chol., 1,408 mg sodium, 33 g carbo., 8 g fiber, 33 g pro.

Texas Two-Step Stew

Prep: 20 minutes
Cook: 5 to 7 hours (low) or 2¾ to 3¾ hours (high)
Makes 6 servings

8	ounces bulk chorizo sausage
½	cup chopped onion (1 medium)
1	15-ounce can Mexican-style or Tex-Mex–style chili beans
1	11-ounce can whole kernel corn with sweet peppers, drained
1	6-ounce package regular Spanish-style rice mix
6	cups water

1. In a medium skillet, cook sausage and onion over medium heat until sausage is brown. Drain off fat. Transfer sausage mixture to a 3½- or 4-quart slow cooker. Stir in undrained chili beans, drained corn, and the seasoning packet contents of the rice mix, if present (set aside remaining rice mix). Pour the water over all.

2. Cover and cook on low-heat setting for 4 to 6 hours or on high-heat setting for 2 to 3 hours.

3. Stir in remaining rice mix. Cover and cook on low-heat setting for 1 hour more or on high-heat setting for 45 minutes more.

Per Serving: 371 cal., 16 g fat (6 g sat. fat), 33 mg chol., 1,424 mg sodium, 43 g carbo., 5 g fiber, 16 g pro.

Easy Beef Stroganoff

Prep: 15 minutes *Cook:* 8 to 10 hours (low) or 4 to 5 hours (high)
Makes 6 servings

2	pounds boneless beef round, cut into 1-inch cubes
2	10.75-ounce cans condensed golden mushroom soup
1	medium onion, sliced
1	8-ounce container dairy sour cream chive dip
3	cups hot cooked noodles

1. In a 3½- or 4-quart slow cooker, stir together beef, soup, and onion.

2. Cover and cook on low-heat setting for 8 to 10 hours or on high-heat setting for 4 to 5 hours. Stir in dip. Serve over hot cooked noodles.

Per Serving: 450 cal., 16 g fat (7 g sat. fat), 131 mg chol., 1,155 mg sodium, 33 g carbo., 2 g fiber, 42 g pro.

Sweet Pork Sandwiches

Root beer concentrate adds rich flavor and pleasant sweetness. You'll find it in the spice section of your supermarket.

Prep: 15 minutes
Cook: 8 to 10 hours (low) or 4 to 5 hours (high)
Makes 8 to 10 servings

1	2½- to 3-pound boneless pork shoulder roast
½	teaspoon salt
½	teaspoon ground black pepper
2	medium onions, cut into thin wedges
3	12-ounce bottles or cans root beer*
1	cup bottled chili sauce
¼	teaspoon root beer concentrate (optional)
	Several dashes bottled hot pepper sauce (optional)
8	to 10 hamburger buns, split (toasted, if desired)
	Lettuce leaves (optional)
	Tomato slices (optional)

1. Trim fat from meat. If necessary, cut meat to fit into a 3½- to 5-quart slow cooker. Sprinkle meat with salt and pepper. Place meat in cooker. Add onions and one bottle root beer.

2. Cover and cook on low-heat setting for 8 to 10 hours or on high-heat setting for 4 to 5 hours.

3. Meanwhile, for sauce, in a medium saucepan, combine 2 bottles root beer and chili sauce. Bring to boiling; reduce heat. Boil gently, uncovered, for 30 to 35 minutes or until desired consistency, stirring occasionally. If desired, stir in root beer concentrate and hot pepper sauce.

4. Transfer meat to a bowl. Using a slotted spoon, remove onions from cooking liquid and place in bowl with meat. Discard cooking liquid. Using two forks, gently shred the meat.

5. If desired, line buns with lettuce leaves and tomato slices. Add shredded meat and onions; spoon on sauce.
*Note: Do not use diet root beer.

Per Serving: 399 cal., 10 g fat (3 g sat. fat), 92 mg chol., 884 mg sodium, 42 g carbo., 3 g fiber, 33 g pro.

Less tender cuts, such as *pork shoulder roast*, are perfect for slow cooking because they're *flavorful*, *economical*, and become extra tender during slow cooking.

Beef Fajitas

Shredded carrot and lettuce provide a fresh note to slow-simmered meat and vegetables.

Prep: 25 minutes
Cook: 7 to 8 hours (low) or 3 1/2 to 4 hours (high)
Makes 8 servings

- 1 large onion, cut into thin wedges
- 2 pounds boneless beef sirloin steak
- 1 teaspoon ground cumin
- 1 teaspoon ground coriander
- ½ teaspoon salt
- ½ teaspoon ground black pepper
- 2 medium red or green sweet peppers, cut into thin bite-size strips
- ¼ cup beef broth
- 8 7- to 8-inch whole wheat or plain flour tortillas
- 1 cup shredded carrot
- 1 cup shredded coarsely lettuce
  Salsa, guacamole, and sour cream

1. Place onion in a 3½- to 4-quart slow cooker. Trim fat from steak. Sprinkle one side of the steak with cumin, coriander, salt, and black pepper; rub in with your fingers. Cut steak across the grain into thin bite-size strips. Add beef strips to cooker. Top with sweet pepper. Pour broth over all.

2. Cover and cook on low-heat setting for 7 to 8 hours or on high-heat setting for 3½ to 4 hours.

3. To serve, use a slotted spoon to spoon beef-vegetable mixture onto tortillas. Top each serving with carrot and lettuce. Fold tortillas over. Serve with salsa, guacamole, and sour cream.

Per Serving: 327 cal., 10 g total fat (3 g sat. fat), 70 mg chol., 642 mg sodium, 22 g carb., 12 g fiber, 33 g protein.

MAKE IT A MENU
French Dips with Mushrooms, Southern Succotash (page 164), Angel Food Cake with Lemon Cream and Berries (page 190)

French Dips with Mushrooms

Meaty portobello mushrooms add a new dimension to classic French dip sandwiches. Serve the seasoned broth in bowls just large enough to dunk a corner of the sandwich.

Prep: 25 minutes
Cook: 8 to 9 hours (low) or 4 to 4½ hours (high)
Stand: 10 minutes
Makes 8 servings

- 1 3- to 3½-pound beef bottom round or rump roast
  Nonstick cooking spray
- 4 portobello mushrooms (3 to 4 inches in diameter)
- 1 14-ounce can onion-flavor beef broth
- 1 large red onion, cut into ½-inch slices (optional)
- 8 hoagie buns, split and toasted

1. Trim fat from roast. If necessary, cut roast to fit into a 3½- to 6-quart slow cooker. Lightly coat a large skillet with cooking spray; heat over medium heat. Brown roast on all sides in hot skillet. Place roast in the prepared cooker.

2. Clean mushrooms; remove and discard stems. Cut mushrooms into ¼-inch slices. Add to cooker. Pour broth over roast and mushrooms.

3. Cover and cook on low-heat setting for 8 to 9 hours or on high-heat setting for 4 to 4½ hours. Remove roast from cooker; cover and let stand for 10 minutes.

4. Meanwhile, using a slotted spoon, remove mushrooms and set aside. Thinly slice roast. Arrange meat, mushroom slices, and, if desired, onion slices on toasted buns. Pour cooking juices into a measuring cup; skim off fat. Drizzle a little of the juices onto each sandwich and pour the remaining juices into bowls to serve with sandwiches for dipping.

Per Serving: 646 cal., 17 g fat (4 g sat. fat), 98 mg chol., 970 mg sodium, 74 g carbo., 4 g fiber, 50 g pro.

Pork Chops and Corn Bread Stuffing

Try this when you get a craving for Thanksgiving-type fare. Browned chops slow-cook over vegetables, mushroom soup, and corn bread stuffing mix.

Prep: 20 minutes
Cook: 5 to 6 hours (low) or 2½ to 3 hours (high)
Makes 4 servings

	Nonstick cooking spray
4	pork rib chops, cut ¾ inch thick
1	10.75-ounce can condensed golden mushroom or cream of mushroom soup
¼	cup butter or margarine, melted
1	16-ounce package frozen broccoli, cauliflower, and carrots
½	of a 16-ounce package corn bread stuffing mix (about 3 cups)

1. Lightly coat a 5½- or 6-quart slow cooker with cooking spray; set aside. Lightly coat a 10-inch skillet with cooking spray; heat over medium heat. Brown the chops, half at a time, in the hot skillet. Remove chops from skillet; set aside.

2. In a very large bowl, stir together the soup and melted butter. Add frozen vegetables and stuffing mix; stir to combine. Transfer mixture to prepared cooker. Arrange chops on top of stuffing mixture.

3. Cover and cook on low-heat setting for 5 to 6 hours or on high-heat setting for 2½ to 3 hours.
Per Serving: 558 cal., 22 g fat (10 g sat. fat), 89 mg chol., 1,533 mg sodium, 56 g carbo., 7 g fiber, 30 g pro.

Cola Pot Roast

Different and delicious, this chuck pot roast with veggies and brown gravy gets its sweet kick from a can of cola. The meat is tender, and the gravy is thick.

Prep: 15 minutes
Cook: 7 to 8 hours (low) or 3½ to 4 hours (high)
Makes 6 servings

1	2½- to 3-pound boneless beef chuck pot roast
	Nonstick cooking spray
2	16-ounce packages frozen stew vegetables
1	12-ounce can cola
1	envelope (1 ounce) onion soup mix
2	tablespoons quick-cooking tapioca

1. Trim fat from roast. Coat a large skillet with cooking spray; heat over medium heat. Brown roast on all sides in hot skillet.

2. Place roast in a 4½ or 5-quart slow cooker. Top with frozen vegetables. In a small bowl, stir together cola, soup mix, and tapioca. Pour over roast and vegetables in cooker.

3. Cover and cook on low-heat setting for 7 to 8 hours or on high-heat setting for 3½ to 4 hours.
Per Serving: 278 cal., 5 g fat (2 g sat. fat), 75 mg chol., 582 mg sodium, 28 g carbo., 2 g fiber, 29 g pro.

MAKE IT A MENU
Taco Chili, toasted tortilla wedges, Creamy Lemon-Pepper Coleslaw (page 166), Granola-Topped Pudding (page 178)

Taco Chili

It looks like chili but tastes like a taco.

Prep: 20 minutes
Cook: 4 to 6 hours (low) or 2 to 3 hours (high)
Makes 4 to 6 servings

1	pound lean ground beef
2	15-ounce cans seasoned tomato sauce with diced tomatoes
1	15-ounce can chili beans with chili gravy
1	15-ounce can hominy or whole kernel corn, undrained
1	1.25-ounce package taco seasoning mix
	Dairy sour cream (optional)
	Shredded cheddar cheese (optional)

1. In a large skillet, cook ground beef over medium heat until brown; drain off fat.

2. In a 3½- or 4-quart slow cooker, combine the meat, tomato sauce, beans with chili gravy, undrained hominy, and taco seasoning mix.

3. Cover and cook on low-heat setting for 4 to 6 hours or on high-heat setting for 2 to 3 hours. If desired, top individual servings with sour cream and cheddar cheese.
Per Serving: 477 cal., 18 g fat (6 g sat. fat), 71 mg chol., 1,998 mg sodium, 49 g carbo., 12 g fiber, 35 g pro.

Taco Chili

Ginger Chicken

Sweet and Sour Beef Stew

Prep: 10 minutes   Cook: 10 to 11 hours (low) or 5 to 5½ hours (high)
Makes 6 to 8 servings

1½ pounds beef stew meat, cut into ¾- to 1-inch cubes
1 16-ounce package frozen stew vegetables (3 cups)
2 10.75-ounce cans condensed beefy mushroom soup
½ cup bottled sweet and sour sauce
½ cup water
⅛ to ¼ teaspoon cayenne pepper

1. In a 3½- or 4-quart slow cooker, place meat and frozen vegetables. Stir in soup, sweet and sour sauce, water, and cayenne pepper. Cover and cook on low-heat setting for 10 to 11 hours or on high-heat setting for 5 to 5½ hours.

Per Serving: 291 cal., 9 g fat (3 g sat. fat), 62 mg chol., 1,019 mg sodium, 19 g carbo., 2 g fiber, 30 g pro.

Ginger Chicken

Serve rice alongside to soak up every last drop.
Prep: 20 minutes
Cook: 5 to 6 hours (low) or 2½ to 3 hours (high)
Makes 6 servings

½ cup mango chutney or orange marmalade
¼ cup bottled chili sauce
2 tablespoons quick-cooking tapioca
1½ teaspoons grated fresh ginger or ½ teaspoon ground ginger
12 chicken thighs, skinned (about 4 pounds)
Hot cooked brown rice (optional)
Sliced green onions (optional)

1. Cut up any large pieces of fruit in the chutney. In a 4- to 5-quart slow cooker, combine chutney, chili sauce, tapioca, and ginger. Add chicken, turning pieces in mixture to coat.

2. Cover and cook on low-heat setting for 5 to 6 hours or on high-heat setting for 2½ to 3 hours. If desired, serve chicken over rice and sprinkle with green onions.

Per Serving: 264 cal., 7 g fat (2 g sat. fat), 143 mg chol., 494 mg sodium, 16 g carbo., 1 g fiber, 34 g pro.

VOLUME IS VITAL

A slow cooker works best when it's half to two-thirds full. Most of our recipes give a range of cooker sizes. Be sure to use a cooker that's within the range. If you decide to skip an ingredient (the potatoes in a stew, for example), increase another ingredient (such as the carrots) to keep the volume in the cooker at the optimal level.

Slow cooker recipes generally do not require stirring so **no peeking**. *Lifting the lid drops the temperature inside the cooker and* **extends the cooking time**.

Beer Brisket

Beer and chili sauce do great things to beef brisket and sliced onions. Fork slices of meat onto kaiser rolls for a hearty sandwich.

Prep: 15 minutes   *Cook:* 10 to 12 hours (low) or 5 to 6 hours (high)
Makes 9 to 12 servings

- 1   3- to 4-pound fresh beef brisket
- 2   large onions, sliced
- 1   12-ounce bottle or can beer
- ½   cup bottled chili sauce
- 2   teaspoons dried steak seasoning
- 9   to 12 kaiser rolls, split and toasted (optional)

1. Trim fat from meat. If necessary, cut brisket to fit into a 3½- or 4-quart slow cooker. Place onions in the cooker. Top with brisket. In a medium bowl, stir together beer, chili sauce, and steak seasoning. Pour over onions and meat in cooker.

2. Cover and cook on low-heat setting for 10 to 12 hours or on high-heat setting for 5 to 6 hours.

3. To serve, remove meat from cooking liquid. Thinly slice meat across the grain. Using a slotted spoon, remove the onions from the cooking liquid and place on top of the meat. Drizzle with some of the cooking liquid. If desired, serve sliced meat and onions on kaiser rolls.

Per Serving: 265 cal., 10 g fat (4 g sat. fat), 94 mg chol., 378 mg sodium, 8 g carbo., 2 g fiber, 31 g pro.

Ham and Potatoes au Gratin

Prep: 15 minutes   *Cook:* 7 to 8 hours (low) or 3½ to 4 hours (high)
Makes 6 servings

-      Nonstick cooking spray
- 2   5.5-ounce packages dry au gratin potato mix
- 2   cups diced cooked ham
- ¼   cup bottled roasted red sweet pepper, drained and chopped
- 3   cups water
- 1   10.75-ounce can condensed cheddar cheese soup

1. Lightly coat a 3½- or 4-quart slow cooker with cooking spray. Place au gratin potato mixes with contents of seasoning packets, the ham, and roasted red pepper in the prepared cooker. In a large bowl, stir together water and soup. Pour over potato mixture in cooker.

2. Cover and cook on low-heat setting for 7 to 8 hours or on high-heat setting for 3½ to 4 hours.

Per Serving: 255 cal., 7 g fat (3 g sat. fat), 29 mg chol., 2,087 mg sodium, 45 g carbo., 3 g fiber, 15 g pro.

Italian Sausage Stew

Prep: 15 minutes
Cook: 5½ to 6½ hours (low) or 2¾ to 3¼ hours (high)
Makes 6 servings

- 1   pound Italian sausage
- 2   14-ounce cans seasoned chicken broth with Italian herbs
- 1   15- to 19-ounce can white kidney (cannellini) beans, rinsed and drained
- 1   14.5-ounce can diced tomatoes with basil, oregano, and garlic, undrained
- 1   9-ounce package refrigerated cheese-filled tortellini
       Finely shredded Parmesan cheese (optional)

1. In a large skillet, cook sausage over medium heat until brown; drain off fat.

2. In a 3½- to 4½-quart slow cooker, combine cooked sausage, broth, beans, and undrained tomatoes.

3. Cover and cook on low-heat setting for 5 to 6 hours or on high-heat setting for 2½ to 3 hours. Stir in tortellini. Cover and cook on low-heat setting for 30 minutes more or on high-heat setting for 15 minutes more. Ladle soup into bowls. If desired, sprinkle individual servings with Parmesan cheese.

Per Serving: 441 cal., 20 g fat (8 g sat. fat), 72 mg chol., 1,597 mg sodium, 40 g carbo., 5 g fiber, 24 g pro.

Chicken and Bean Burritos

You'll get a different burrito each time you try a new blend of salsa—experiment!

Prep: 5 minutes   Cook: 5 to 6 hours (low) or 2½ to 3 hours (high)
Makes 8 servings

- 2 pounds skinless, boneless chicken breast halves
- 1 15-ounce can pinto beans in chili sauce
- 1 16-ounce bottle salsa with chipotle peppers (1⅔ cups)
- 8 10-inch flour tortillas, warmed*
- 1½ cups shredded Monterey Jack cheese (6 ounces)
  Shredded lettuce, chopped tomato, and/or dairy sour cream (optional)

1. In a 3½-quart slow cooker, place chicken and undrained beans. Pour salsa over chicken and beans.

2. Cover and cook on low-heat setting for 5 to 6 hours or on high-heat setting for 2½ to 3 hours.

3. Remove chicken breast halves from cooker. On a cutting board, use two forks to shred chicken into bite-size pieces. Using a potato masher, mash beans slightly in slow cooker. Return chicken to cooker, stirring to mix.

4. Divide chicken mixture evenly among the warmed tortillas. Top with shredded cheese. Fold bottom edge of each tortilla over filling. Fold in opposite sides just until they meet. Roll up from the bottom. If necessary, secure with wooden toothpicks. If desired, serve with lettuce, tomato, and/or sour cream.

*Note:** To warm tortillas, stack tortillas and wrap tightly in foil. Heat in a 350°F oven about 10 minutes or until heated through.

Per Serving: 400 cal., 12 g fat (5 g sat. fat), 84 mg chol., 662 mg sodium, 34 g carbo., 5 g fiber, 38 g pro.

Spicy Chicken with Peppers and Olives

Spicy red pepper sauce is the choice for this recipe. If you can't find it, use a favorite variety of pasta sauce.
Prep: 20 minutes
Cook: 6 to 7 hours (low) or 3 to 3½ hours (high)
Makes 6 servings

- 2½ to 3 pounds meaty chicken pieces (breasts, thighs, and drumsticks), skinned
  Salt and ground black pepper
- ½ cup coarsely chopped yellow sweet pepper (1 small)
- ½ cup sliced, pitted ripe olives and/or pimiento-stuffed green olives
- 1 26-ounce jar spicy red pepper pasta sauce
  Hot cooked pasta (optional)

1. Place the chicken pieces in a 3½- or 4-quart slow cooker. Sprinkle lightly with salt and black pepper. Add sweet pepper and olives to cooker. Pour pasta sauce over chicken mixture in cooker.

2. Cover and cook on low-heat setting for 6 to 7 hours or on high-heat setting for 3 to 3½ hours. If desired, serve chicken and sauce over hot cooked pasta.

Per Serving: 239 cal., 10 g fat (2 g sat. fat), 77 mg chol., 592 mg sodium, 10 g carbo., 3 g fiber, 27 g pro.

Pesto Meatball Stew

When you're ready for spring but winter temperatures linger, let this meatball stew warm you from the inside with its warmth and fresh-tasting basil pesto.
Prep: 10 minutes
Cook: 5 to 7 hours (low) or 2½ to 3½ hours (high)
Makes 6 servings

- 1 16-ounce package frozen cooked Italian-style meatballs (32), thawed
- 2 14.5-ounce cans Italian-style stewed tomatoes, undrained
- 1 15- to 19-ounce can white kidney (cannellini) beans, rinsed and drained
- ½ cup water
- ¼ cup purchased basil pesto
- ½ cup finely shredded Parmesan cheese (2 ounces)

1. In a 3½- or 4-quart slow cooker, combine the meatballs, undrained tomatoes, beans, water, and pesto.

2. Cover and cook on low-heat setting for 5 to 7 hours or on high-heat setting for 2½ to 3½ hours. Ladle soup into bowls. Sprinkle with Parmesan cheese.

Per Serving: 408 cal., 27 g fat (10 g sat. fat), 34 mg chol., 1,201 mg sodium, 24 g carbo., 6 g fiber, 17 g pro.

Pesto
Meatball
Stew

Smoky Turkey and Cheesy Potato Casserole

Prep: 20 minutes   *Cook:* 5 to 6 hours (low)
Makes 6 servings

	Nonstick cooking spray
1	10.75-ounce can condensed cream of chicken with herbs soup
1	8-ounce carton dairy sour cream
1½	cups shredded smoked cheddar cheese (6 ounces)
1	28-ounce package frozen loose-pack diced hash brown potatoes with onion and peppers, thawed
3	cups chopped smoked or roasted turkey or chicken
	Crushed croutons (optional)

1. Lightly coat the inside of a 3½- or 4-quart slow cooker with cooking spray. In the cooker, stir together soup, sour cream, cheese, potatoes, and turkey.

2. Cover and cook on low-heat setting for 5 to 6 hours. If desired, top each serving with crushed croutons.

Per Serving: 402 cal., 21 g fat (12 g sat. fat), 84 mg chol., 1,384 mg sodium, 29 g carbo., 3 g fiber, 26 g pro.

Cranberry Chicken

Rice and steamed Brussels sprouts make taste-tempting partners for this savory chicken.

Prep: 15 minutes
Cook: 5 to 6 hours (low) or 2½ to 3 hours (high)
Makes 6 servings

2½	to 3 pounds chicken thighs and/or drumsticks, skinned
1	16-ounce can whole cranberry sauce
2	tablespoons dry onion soup mix
2	tablespoons quick-cooking tapioca
3	cups hot cooked rice

1. Place chicken in 3½- or 4-quart slow cooker. In a small bowl, combine cranberry sauce, dry soup mix, and tapioca. Pour over chicken.

2. Cover and cook on low-heat setting for 5 to 6 hours or on high-heat setting for 2½ to 3 hours. Serve chicken and sauce over hot cooked rice.

Per Serving: 357 cal., 4 g fat (1 g sat. fat), 89 mg chol., 289 mg sodium, 55 g carbo., 1 g fiber, 23 g pro.

Orange-Sesame Ribs

Try ribs done the Asian-flavor way with an aromatic, sweet, dark sauce that glazes the meat.

Prep: 15 minutes
Cook: 8 to 10 hours (low) or 4 to 5 hours (high)
Makes 4 servings

2½	to 3 pounds boneless country-style pork ribs
	Nonstick cooking spray
1	10-ounce jar orange marmalade
1	7.25-ounce jar hoisin sauce
3	cloves garlic, minced, or 1½ teaspoons bottled minced garlic
1	teaspoon toasted sesame oil
	Hot cooked rice (optional)

1. Trim fat from ribs. Lightly coat a large skillet with cooking spray; heat over medium heat. Brown ribs on all sides in hot skillet; drain off fat. Place ribs in a 3½- or 4-quart slow cooker.

2. In a medium bowl, stir together marmalade, hoisin sauce, garlic, and sesame oil. Pour over ribs in cooker; stir to coat meat with sauce.

3. Cover and cook on low-heat setting for 8 to 10 hours or on high-heat setting for 4 to 5 hours. Transfer meat to a serving platter. Skim fat from sauce. Spoon some of the sauce over the meat. Pass remaining sauce. If desired, serve with hot cooked rice.

Per Serving: 532 cal., 16 g fat (5 g sat. fat), 101 mg chol., 696 mg sodium, 66 g carbo., 0 g fiber, 33 g pro.

PLAY IT SAFE

Thaw raw meat and poultry completely in the refrigerator before adding it to the cooker. If it thaws as it cooks, it will not reach a safe temperature quickly enough. Do not leave leftovers in the cooker to cool, but transfer quickly to storage containers, cover, and refrigerate or freeze. Never reheat leftovers in the slow cooker.

Cowboy Beef

Prep: 10 minutes

Cook: 10 to 12 hours (low) or 5 to 6 hours (high)

Makes 6 servings

- 1 2- to 2½-pound boneless beef chuck pot roast
- 1 15-ounce can chili beans with chili gravy
- 1 11-ounce can whole kernel corn with sweet peppers, drained
- 1 10-ounce can chopped tomatoes and green chile peppers, undrained
- 1 to 2 teaspoons chipotle peppers in adobo sauce, finely chopped

1. Trim fat from roast. If necessary, cut roast to fit into a 3½- or 4-quart slow cooker. Place roast in the cooker. In a medium bowl, combine undrained beans, drained corn, undrained tomatoes, and chipotle peppers. Pour bean mixture over roast in cooker.

2. Cover and cook on low-heat setting for 10 to 12 hours or on high-heat setting for 5 to 6 hours.

3. Remove roast from cooker and place on cutting board. Slice roast and arrange in a shallow serving bowl. Using a slotted spoon, spoon bean mixture over roast. Drizzle some of the cooking liquid over all.

Per Serving: 307 cal., 7 g fat (2 g sat. fat), 89 mg chol., 655 mg sodium, 23 g carbo., 5 g fiber, 37 g pro.

Mexican Meatball Stew

Eat this stew with warm corn bread.

Prep: 10 minutes

Cook: 6 to 7 hours (low) or 3 to 3½ hours (high)

Makes 8 to 10 servings

- 2 14.5-ounce cans Mexican-style stewed tomatoes
- 2 12-ounce packages frozen cooked turkey meatballs (24), thawed
- 1 15-ounce can black beans, rinsed and drained
- 1 14-ounce can chicken broth with roasted garlic
- 1 10-ounce package frozen corn, thawed

1. In a 4- to 5-quart slow cooker, combine tomatoes, meatballs, beans, broth, and corn.

2. Cover and cook on low-heat setting for 6 to 7 hours or on high-heat setting for 3 to 3½ hours.

Per Serving: 268 cal., 10 g fat (3 g sat. fat), 66 mg chol., 1,328 mg sodium, 30 g carbo., 8 g fiber, 20 g pro.

Bloody Mary Steak

Prep: 20 minutes

Cook: 8 to 9 hours (low) or 4 to 4½ hours (high)

Makes 6 servings

- 1 2-pound beef round steak, cut ¾ inch thick
   Nonstick cooking spray
- ¾ cup hot-style tomato juice
- 2 cloves garlic, minced
- ¼ cup water
- 4 teaspoons cornstarch
- 2 tablespoons water
- 2 teaspoons prepared horseradish
   Salt and ground black pepper

1. Trim fat from steak. Cut steak into six serving-size pieces. Lightly coat an unheated large skillet with cooking spray; heat skillet over medium-high heat. Add steak pieces; cook until brown, turning once. Place steak in a 2½- to 3½-quart slow cooker. Add tomato juice, garlic, and the ¼ cup water.

2. Cover and cook on low-heat setting for 8 to 9 hours or on high-heat setting for 4 to 4½ hours.

3. Transfer steak to a serving platter, reserving cooking juices. If desired, slice steak; cover and keep warm.

4. For gravy, pour cooking juices into a glass measuring cup; skim off fat. Measure juices; add water if necessary to reach 1½ cups liquid. In a small saucepan, combine cornstarch and 2 tablespoons cold water; stir in cooking juices. Cook and stir over medium heat until thickened and bubbly. Cook and stir for 2 minutes more. Stir in horseradish. Season to taste with salt and pepper. Serve steak with gravy.

Per Serving: 196 cal., 4 g fat (1 g sat. fat), 85 mg chol., 272 mg sodium, 3 g carbo., 0 g fiber, 35 g pro.

MAKE IT A MENU
Bloody Mary Steak, sautéed summer squash, mesclun salad, Simple Lemon-Sugar Snaps (page 182) with vanilla ice cream

Bloody Mary Steak

Saucy and lively—just like the *classic cocktail*—easy-fixing
Bloody Mary Steak is a sensational company dish. After the
meat is cooked, thicken the *savory liquid*.

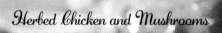
Herbed Chicken and Mushrooms

Ginger-Plum Chicken

This Asian-style chicken recipe gets its irresistible flavor from a lively mix of plum sauce, ground ginger, and dry mustard.

Prep: 20 minutes *Cook:* 5 to 6 hours (low) or 2½ to 3 hours (high)
Makes 6 servings

- 1½ cups thinly sliced carrot (3 medium) or packaged fresh julienned carrot
- 1⅓ cups thinly sliced leek (4 medium) or 1 cup chopped onion (1 large)
- 6 skinless, boneless chicken breast halves (about 2 pounds total)

- ¾ cup plum sauce
- 2 tablespoons quick-cooking tapioca, crushed
- ½ teaspoon ground ginger
- ½ teaspoon dry mustard
- 3 cups hot cooked white rice or wild rice (optional)
  Peanut Topper or sesame seeds, toasted

1. In a 3½- or 4-quart slow cooker, combine carrot and leek. Add chicken. In a small bowl, combine plum sauce, tapioca, ginger, and dry mustard. Pour over chicken.

2. Cover and cook on low-heat setting for 5 to 6 hours or on high-heat setting for 2½ to 3 hours. If desired, serve chicken mixture over hot cooked rice. Sprinkle with Peanut Topper.

Peanut Topper: In a small bowl combine ¼ cup chopped honey-roasted peanuts, ¼ cup thinly sliced green onions, and 2 tablespoons finely shredded fresh basil.

Per Serving: 301 cal., 5 g total fat (1 g sat. fat), 88 mg chol., 309 mg sodium, 26 g carbo., 2 g fiber, 38 g pro.

Herbed Chicken and Mushrooms

An herbed wine sauce makes this chicken-and-pasta dish a satisfying meal. Steamed green beans are the perfect accompaniment.

Prep: 30 minutes *Cook:* 7 to 8 hours (low) 3½ to 4 hours (high)
Makes 6 servings

- 5 cups sliced assorted fresh mushrooms (such as shiitake, button, crimini, and oyster)
- 1 medium onion, chopped (½ cup)
- 1 medium carrot, chopped (½ cup)
- ¼ cup dried tomato pieces (not oil-packed)
- ¾ cup chicken broth
- ¼ cup dry white wine or chicken broth
- 3 tablespoons quick-cooking tapioca, crushed
- 1 teaspoon dried thyme, crushed
- ½ teaspoon dried basil, crushed
- ½ teaspoon garlic salt
- ¼ to ½ teaspoon ground black pepper
- 3 pounds chicken thighs and/or drumsticks, skinned
- 4½ cups hot cooked plain and/or spinach linguine or fettuccine, or hot cooked rice

1. In a 4- to 5-quart slow cooker, combine mushrooms, onion, carrot, and dried tomato. Pour the ¾ cup chicken broth and the wine over mixture in cooker. Sprinkle with tapioca, thyme, basil, garlic salt, and pepper. Place chicken pieces on mixture in cooker.

2. Cover and cook on low-heat setting for 7 to 8 hours or on high-heat setting for 3½ to 4 hours. To serve, arrange chicken and vegetables over pasta; drizzle with cooking juices.

Per Serving: 360 cal., 7 g total fat (2 g sat. fat), 107 mg chol., 350 mg sodium, 39 g carbo., 3 g fiber, 34 g pro.

Chicken with Creamy Chive Sauce

Cooking the chicken in a wine-flavored soup sauce ensures that it will remain extra moist.

Prep: 15 minutes *Cook:* 4 to 5 hours (low)
Makes 6 servings

- 6 skinless, boneless chicken breast halves (about 2 pounds total)
- ¼ cup butter or margarine, melted
- 1 0.7-ounce envelope Italian dry salad dressing mix
- 1 10.75-ounce can condensed golden mushroom soup
- ½ cup dry white wine
- ½ of an 8-ounce tub cream cheese spread with chive and onion
- 3 cups hot cooked angel hair pasta
  Snipped fresh chives (optional)

1. Place chicken in a 3½- or 4-quart slow cooker. In a medium bowl, stir together melted butter and dry salad dressing mix. Stir in soup, wine, and cream cheese. Pour soup mixture over chicken.

2. Cover and cook on low-heat setting for 4 to 5 hours. Serve chicken mixture over hot cooked pasta. If desired, sprinkle with chives.

Per Serving: 448 cal., 18 g total fat (9 g sat. fat), 132 mg chol., 1064 mg sodium, 26 g carbo., 1 g fiber, 41 g pro.

Turkey with Creamy Alfredo Sauce

Turkey with Creamy Alfredo Sauce

The velvety sauce for this tender chicken is a tantalizing blend of golden mushroom soup, white wine, and cream cheese with chives and onion.

Prep: 20 minutes *Cook:* 5½ to 6½ hours (low)
Makes 6 to 8 servings

- 1 2½- to 3½-pound boneless turkey breast portion, rolled and tied
- 1 10¾-ounce can reduced-fat and reduced-sodium condensed cream of chicken soup
- 1 1.25-ounce envelope Alfredo sauce mix
- ½ of an 8-ounce tub cream cheese with chives and onion, softened
- 1 5-ounce can evaporated milk
- ½ cup water
- 4 cups hot cooked red pepper fettuccine, plain fettuccine, or angel hair pasta
   Shredded Parmesan cheese (optional)
   Steamed sugar snap peas (optional)

1. Place turkey in a 3½- or 4-quart slow cooker. In a medium bowl, stir together soup, sauce mix and cream cheese; whisk in milk and water. Pour over the chicken. Cover and cook on low-heat setting for 5½ to 6½ hours.

2. Remove turkey from slow cooker; remove string. Slice turkey. Whisk sauce in cooker until nearly smooth. Serve turkey and sauce over hot cooked pasta. If desired, sprinkle with Parmesan cheese and serve with sugar snap peas.

Per Serving: 489 cal., 13 g total fat (7 g sat. fat), 150 mg chol., 600 mg sodium, 34 g carbo., 2 g fiber, 55 g pro.

SAVINGS STRATEGY
Purchase turkeys and whole boneless turkey breasts during the holiday season and tuck them in the freezer. Both whole turkeys and breasts are more economically priced that time of year.

Once limited to Thanksgiving dinner, turkey in all its forms is now readily available every day of the year. Thankfully, turkey is always a good value.

Greek Chicken with Olives

Tapioca is used for thickening. To ensure a smooth-textured sauce, crush or finely grind the tapioca before adding it to the slow cooker.

Prep: 15 minutes Cook: 6 to 7 hours (low) or 3 to 3½ hours (high)

Makes 4 servings

- 3 large tomatoes, coarsely chopped
- 1 large onion, halved and thinly sliced
- ¼ cup Greek olives or ripe olives, pitted and sliced
- ¼ cup dry red wine or reduced-sodium chicken broth
- 1 tablespoon quick-cooking tapioca
- 1 tablespoon capers, drained
- 2 cloves garlic, minced
- ¼ teaspoon salt
- ⅛ teaspoon ground black pepper
- 4 skinless, boneless chicken breast halves (about 1¼ pounds total)
- ¼ cup snipped fresh basil
- 2 cups hot cooked couscous

1. In a 3½- or 4-quart slow cooker, combine tomato, onion, olives, wine, tapioca, capers, garlic, salt, and pepper. Add chicken, spooning some of the tomato mixture over chicken.

2. Cover and cook on low-heat setting for 6 to 7 hours or on high-heat setting for 3 to 3½ hours. Before serving, stir in basil. Serve chicken mixture over hot cooked couscous.

Per Serving: 326 cal., 4 g total fat (1 g sat. fat), 82 mg chol., 373 mg sodium, 32 g carbo., 4 g fiber, 38 g pro.

Fruited Couscous and Beans

Golden raisins and mixed dried fruit bits lend subtle sweetness to this pinto bean and couscous combo.

Prep: 20 minutes Cook: 6 hours (low) or 3 hours (high)

Stand: 5 minutes

Makes 6 servings

- 2 15-ounce cans Great Northern beans or pinto beans, rinsed and drained
- 1 cup finely chopped onion (1 large)
- 1 cup golden raisins
- 1 cup mixed dried fruit bits
- 2 teaspoons grated fresh ginger
- ¾ teaspoon salt
- ¼ teaspoon crushed red pepper
- 1 14-ounce can vegetable broth or chicken broth
- 1¾ cups unsweetened pineapple juice
- 1 10-ounce package couscous
- 1 tablespoon olive oil
- ½ cup sliced almonds, toasted
  Sliced green onion (optional)

1. In a 3½- or 4-quart slow cooker, combine drained beans, onion, raisins, fruit bits, ginger, salt, and crushed red pepper. Pour broth and pineapple juice over mixture in cooker.

2. Cover and cook on low-heat setting for 6 to 7 hours or on high-heat setting for 3 to 3½ hours.

3. Remove liner from cooker, if possible, or turn off cooker. Stir in couscous and oil. Let stand, covered, for 5 to 10 minutes or until couscous is tender. Fluff with a fork. Sprinkle each serving with almonds and, if desired, green onion.

Per Serving: 623 cal., 9 g total fat (1 g sat. fat), 0 mg chol., 596 mg sodium, 120 g carbo., 14 g fiber, 22 g pro.

Cranberry-Chipotle Beef

Canned cranberry sauce and canned chipotle chile pepper make up the fiery chipotle-seasoned sauce used to cook the chuck roast.

Prep: 10 minutes   *Cook:* 6 to 8 hours (low) or 3 to 4 hours (high)
Makes 4 servings

1½	pounds boneless beef chuck pot roast
1	medium onion, cut into thin wedges
2	cloves garlic, minced
¼	teaspoon salt
¼	teaspoon ground black pepper
1	16-ounce can whole cranberry sauce
1	to 2 teaspoons finely chopped canned chipotle chile pepper in adobo sauce
2	cups uncooked instant brown rice

1. Trim fat from meat. If necessary, cut meat to fit into a 4-quart slow cooker. Place onion in cooker; add meat. Sprinkle with garlic, salt, and black pepper. In a small bowl, combine cranberry sauce and chipotle pepper; pour over mixture in cooker.

2. Cover and cook on low-heat setting for 6 to 8 hours or on high-heat setting for 3 to 4 hours. To serve, cook rice according to package directions, except omit butter and salt. Serve meat mixture with rice.

Per Serving: 506 cal., 7 g total fat (2 g sat. fat), 101 mg chol., 296 mg sodium, 71 g carbo., 4 g fiber, 40 g pro.

Greek Beef and Orzo

Cinnamon, orzo, and artichoke hearts give this hearty stew its Greek flair.

Prep: 15 minutes   *Cook:* 8 to 9 hours (low) or 4 to 4½ hours (high) plus 30 minutes (high)
Makes 4 servings

	Nonstick cooking spray
2	large onions, cut into thin wedges (1 cup)
1	pound beef stew meat cut into 1-inch pieces
¼	teaspoon salt
¼	teaspoon ground black pepper
1	14-ounce can beef broth
½	of a 6-ounce can tomato paste (⅓ cup)
¼	teaspoon ground cinnamon
¾	cup dried orzo
1	9-ounce package frozen artichoke hearts, thawed

1. Lightly coat a 3½- to 4-quart slow cooker with cooking spray. Place onions in cooker; top with beef. Sprinkle with salt and pepper. In a medium bowl, whisk together beef broth, tomato paste and cinnamon; pour over beef.

2. Cover and cook on low-heat setting for 8 to 9 hours or on high-heat setting for 4 to 4½ hours. If using low-heat setting, turn to high. Stir in orzo and artichoke hearts. Cover and cook 30 minutes more.

Per Serving: 348 cal., 5 g total fat (1 g sat. fat), 67 mg chol., 648 mg sodium, 41 g carbo., 7 g fiber, 33 g pro.

Mushroom-and-Onion-Sauced Round Steak

Add a jar of beef gravy to a slow-cooker meat recipe and you get a smooth sauce that's the perfect consistency for topping mashed potatoes or noodles.

Prep: 20 minutes   *Cook:* 8 to 10 hours (low) or 4 to 5 hours (high)
Makes 8 servings

2	pounds boneless beef round steak, cut ¾ inch thick
1	tablespoon cooking oil
2	medium onions, sliced
3	cups sliced fresh mushrooms
1	12-ounce jar beef gravy
1	1.1-ounce package dry mushroom gravy mix
	Mashed potatoes or hot cooked noodles (optional)

1. Trim fat from steak. Cut steak into eight serving-size pieces. In a large skillet, brown meat, half at a time, in hot oil. Drain off fat. Place onions in a 3½- or 4-quart slow cooker. Place steak pieces and mushrooms on top of onions. Combine beef gravy and mushroom gravy mix; pour over all.

2. Cover and cook on low-heat setting for 8 to 10 hours or on high-heat setting for 4 to 5 hours. If desired, serve over mashed potatoes or noodles.

Per Serving: 194 cal., 7 g total fat (2 g sat. fat), 57 mg chol., 479 mg sodium, 7 g carbo., 1 g fiber, 24 g pro.

Mushroom-and-Onion-Sauced Round Steak

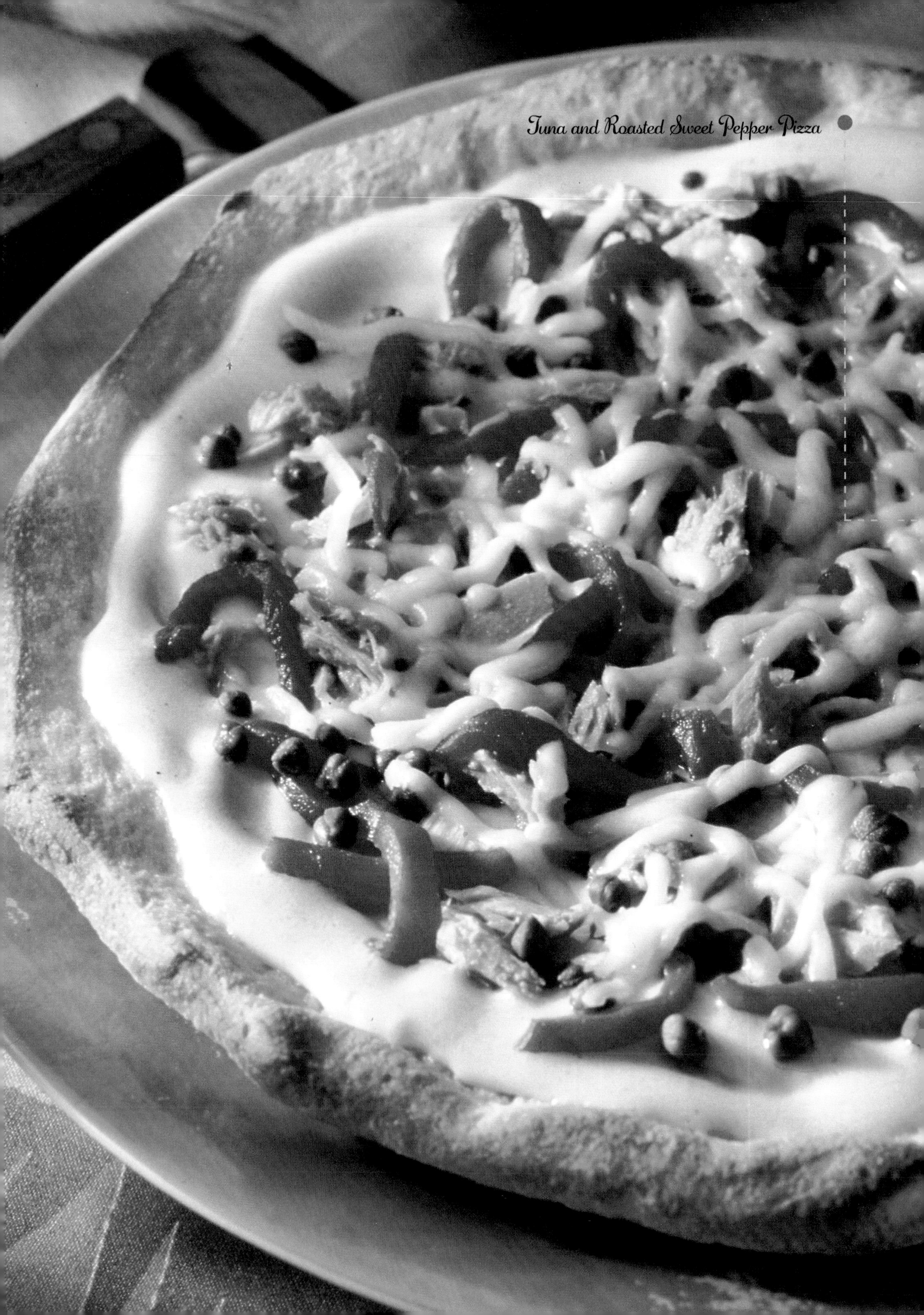

Tuna and Roasted Sweet Pepper Pizza

sandwiches & pizzas

For meals with big appeal, turn to hearty sandwiches and pizzas. The possible combinations for these layered favorites are almost endless, and you just pile on a new ingredient or try a different bread or spread to mix things up.

Tuna and Roasted Sweet Pepper Pizza

Alfredo sauce, refrigerated or canned, is on its way to becoming a kitchen staple. Add pizza topping to the list of terrific dishes the creamy sauce helps create.

Prep: 25 minutes   *Bake:* 17 minutes
Makes 4 servings

- 1   13.8-ounce package refrigerated pizza dough
- 1   10-ounce container refrigerated Alfredo pasta sauce
- 1   6- or 6.5-ounce can chunk white tuna (water pack), drained and broken into chunks
- 1   cup bottled roasted red sweet peppers, drained and cut into bite-size strips
- 1   tablespoon capers, drained (optional)
- 1   cup shredded mozzarella cheese (4 ounces)

1. Preheat oven to 425°F. Lightly grease a large baking sheet. Unroll pizza dough and transfer to prepared baking sheet. Press dough with your hands into a 15×11-inch rectangle; build up edges slightly. Prick generously with a fork. Bake for 7 to 10 minutes or until lightly browned.

2. Spread Alfredo sauce over the hot crust. Top with tuna, roasted peppers, and, if desired, capers. Sprinkle with mozzarella cheese.

3. Bake for 10 to 12 minutes more or until cheese melts and pizza is heated through.
Per Serving: 496 cal., 23 g fat (12 g sat. fat), 78 mg chol., 1,185 mg sodium, 45 g carbo., 3 g fiber, 26 g pro.

BBQ Chicken Sandwiches

Next time you fix chicken breast halves, cook a couple of extra ones and freeze them to use in these super supper sandwiches.

Start to Finish: 15 minutes
Makes 4 servings

- 2   cups cooked chicken or turkey breast, cut into strips
- ½   cup shredded carrot (1 medium)
- ½   cup bottled barbecue sauce
- 1   16-ounce loaf French bread, split and toasted, or 4 hamburger buns, split and toasted
- ½   cup shredded Monterey Jack cheese (2 ounces) (optional)
  Pickle slices (optional)

1. In a medium saucepan, heat the chicken, carrot, and barbecue sauce over medium heat until bubbly.

2. Spoon chicken mixture onto bottom half of bread loaf. If desired, top chicken mixture with cheese. Place on a baking sheet. Broil 3 to 4 inches from heat for 1 to 2 minutes or until cheese melts. If desired, top with pickle slices. Cover with bread top. Cut into serving-size pieces.
Per Serving: 269 cal., 6 g fat (2 g sat. fat), 53 mg chol., 520 mg sodium, 27 g carbo., 2 g fiber, 25 g pro.

Honey Chicken Sandwiches

Start to Finish: 20 minutes
Makes 4 servings

- 3 tablespoons honey
- 2 teaspoons snipped fresh thyme or
  ½ teaspoon dried thyme, crushed
- 1 small red onion, halved and thinly sliced
- 12 ounces thinly sliced cooked chicken,
  halved crosswise
- 4 croissants, halved horizontally and toasted

1. In a medium skillet, combine honey, thyme, and red onion. Cook and stir over medium-low heat just until hot (do not boil). Stir in chicken; heat through. Arrange chicken mixture in halved croissants.

Per Serving: 445 cal., 18 g fat (8 g sat. fat), 118 mg chol., 498 mg sodium, 40 g carbo., 2 g fiber, 29 g pro.

Roasted Vegetable and Pastrami Panini

A panini grill presses a sandwich as it cooks from both sides. You can get the same effect on an open griddle or in a skillet by using a foil-wrapped brick as a weight.
Start to Finish: 30 minutes
Makes 4 servings

- 4 thin slices provolone cheese (2 ounces)
- 8 ½-inch slices sourdough or Vienna bread
- 1 cup roasted or grilled vegetables from the deli or
  deli-marinated vegetables, coarsely chopped
- 4 thin slices pastrami (3 ounces)
- 1 tablespoon olive oil or basil-flavored olive oil

1. Place a cheese slice on each of four of the bread slices. Spread vegetables evenly over cheese. Top with pastrami and remaining four bread slices. Brush the outsides of the sandwiches with oil.

2. If desired, wrap a brick completely in foil. Heat a nonstick griddle or large skillet over medium heat. Place a sandwich on heated pan; place brick on top to flatten slightly.* Cook for 4 to 6 minutes or until sandwich is golden and cheese melts, turning once. Repeat for remaining sandwiches.
*Note: Or place sandwich on a covered indoor grill or panini grill. Close lid; grill for 4 to 5 minutes or until golden and cheese melts.

Per Serving: 314 cal., 16 g fat (6 g sat. fat), 29 mg chol., 689 mg sodium, 30 g carbo., 2 g fiber, 12 g pro

Open-Face Crab Ciabatta

Top crusty bread slices with dressed-up deli crab salad for this sophisticated sandwich.
Start to Finish: 15 minutes
Makes 6 servings

- 1 ½-pint container purchased deli
  crab salad
- ½ cup smoked almonds, chopped, or dried
  fruit-and-nut trail mix, chopped
- 1 teaspoon snipped fresh rosemary
- 6 ½-inch slices ciabatta or French bread,
  toasted

1. In a small bowl, combine crab salad, smoked almonds, and rosemary. To serve, spread on toasted bread.

Per Serving: 192 cal., 11 g fat (1 g sat. fat), 24 mg chol., 373 mg sodium, 15 g carbo., 2 g fiber, 9 g pro.

Mock Monte Cristo Sandwiches

Traditionally dipped in beaten egg and grilled, this sandwich is a true classic. You'll like our simple baked version.
Prep: 10 minutes   *Bake:* 15 minutes
Makes 3 servings

- 6 slices frozen French toast
- 2 tablespoons honey mustard
- 3 ounces thinly sliced cooked turkey breast
- 3 ounces thinly sliced cooked ham
- 3 ounces thinly sliced Swiss cheese

1. Preheat oven to 400°F. Lightly grease a baking sheet; set aside.

2. To assemble sandwiches, spread one side of each frozen French toast slice with honey mustard. Layer three of the toast slices, mustard sides up, with the turkey, ham, and cheese. Cover with remaining toast slices, mustard sides down. Place sandwiches on the prepared baking sheet.

3. Bake for 15 to 20 minutes or until sandwiches are heated through, turning sandwiches over once. Cut each sandwich in half diagonally.

Per Serving: 445 cal., 18 g fat (8 g sat. fat), 150 mg chol., 1,370 mg sodium, 43 g carbo., 1 g fiber, 27 g pro.

Mock Monte Cristo
Sandwiches

Shrimp
Avocado
Rolls

Peppy Pepperoni Pizza

Prep: 20 minutes   *Bake:* 18 minutes
Makes 6 servings

1	13.8-ounce package refrigerated pizza dough (for 1 crust)
1	8-ounce package shredded Monterey Jack cheese (2 cups)
1	cup bottled salsa
1	4-ounce can (drained weight) sliced mushrooms, drained
½	of a 3.5-ounce package sliced pepperoni

1. Preheat oven to 425°F. Grease a baking sheet; roll pizza dough into a 15×10-inch rectangle on prepared baking sheet. Build up edges of dough slightly. Sprinkle 1½ cups of the cheese over the dough. Spoon salsa evenly over cheese. Top with mushrooms and pepperoni. Sprinkle with remaining ½ cup cheese.

2. Bake for 18 to 20 minutes or until crust is golden and cheese melts.

Per Serving: 316 cal., 17 g fat (9 g sat. fat), 41 mg chol., 940 mg sodium, 26 g carbo., 2 g fiber, 16 g pro.

Shrimp Avocado Rolls

Start to Finish: 15 minutes
Makes 4 servings

1	10- to 12-ounce package frozen peeled, cooked shrimp, thawed and coarsely chopped
2	large avocados, pitted, peeled, and chopped
½	cup shredded carrot (1 medium)
⅓	cup bottled coleslaw salad dressing
4	6-inch ciabatta rolls or hoagie buns, split Lemon wedges (optional)

1. In a large bowl, combine shrimp, avocados, carrot, and salad dressing. Using a spoon, slightly hollow bottoms and tops of rolls, leaving ½-inch shells. Discard excess bread. Toast buns. Spoon shrimp mixture into rolls. If desired, serve with lemon wedges.

Per Serving: 560 cal., 24 g fat (4 g sat. fat), 144 mg chol., 825 mg sodium, 63 g carbo., 8 g fiber, 25 g pro.

Stock great breads (ciabatta, French loaves, country loaves) in your freezer. Add deli meats and cheeses and you can make grilled panini, Italian-sauced sandwiches, or subs.

Hot Sub Sandwich

With options for every ingredient, the possibilities for this sandwich are almost limitless. Check your refrigerator and create your own combinations.
Start to Finish: 30 minutes
Makes 6 to 8 servings

- 1 16-ounce loaf brown-and-serve French or Italian bread
- 6 ounces sliced American, cheddar, and/or Swiss cheese
- 12 ounces thinly sliced deli turkey, ham, roast beef, or chicken
  Ranch salad dressing or other creamy salad dressing

1. Bake the bread according to package directions. Cool slightly.

2. Using a long serrated knife, cut the baked loaf of bread in half horizontally. Arrange the cheese on the bottom half of the bread. Arrange the deli meat over the cheese.

3. Place the top half of the bread on the loaf. Return to oven; bake about 5 minutes more or until the cheese melts. Cool sandwich slightly.

4. Slice sandwich. Serve warm. Pass the salad dressing to use as a dipping sauce or to drizzle over the meat.
Per Serving: 433 cal., 16 g fat (7 g sat. fat), 52 mg chol., 1,648 mg sodium, 46 g carbo., 2 g fiber, 29 g pro.

DEPEND ON THE DELI
Deli foods can be the starting point for terrific dinners, especially if you add a few fresh touches. Add chopped tomato and dried Italian seasoning to three-bean salad, or stir in some cubed ham and cheese or cooked shell macaroni. Perk up macaroni salad with cubed ham and thawed frozen peas.

Ham and Pear Melt

Start to Finish: 10 minutes
Makes 2 servings

- 2 7- to 8-inch whole wheat flour tortillas
- 6 ounces very thinly sliced ham
- 2 small ripe pears, cored and thinly sliced
- 1 cup finely shredded Swiss, Colby-Monterey Jack, or mozzarella cheese (4 ounces)

1. Place tortillas on a cookie sheet or broiler pan. Broil tortillas 4 to 5 inches from the heat just until warm. Layer ham, pears, and cheese on warm tortillas. Broil about 2 minutes or until cheese is melted and bubbly. Fold tortillas in half or roll up into a spiral. Cut each in half.
Per Serving: 474 cal., 25 g fat (13 g sat. fat), 100 mg chol., 1,446 mg sodium, 29 g carbo., 11 g fiber, 33 g pro.

Fresh Tomato Pizza with Pesto

Prep: 20 minutes   Bake: 10 minutes
Makes 6 to 8 servings

- ½ cup purchased pesto
- 1 16-ounce Italian bread shell (Boboli) or one 12-inch purchased prebaked pizza crust
- 3 ripe medium tomatoes, thinly sliced
  Freshly ground black pepper
- 2 cups shredded Monterey Jack or mozzarella cheese (8 ounces)
- 1 2.25-ounce can sliced pitted ripe olives, drained (scant ⅔ cup)

1. Preheat oven to 425°F. Spread pesto evenly over bread shell. Place on a large pizza pan or baking sheet. Arrange tomato slices on top. Sprinkle with pepper. Top with cheese and olives.

2. Bake for 10 to 15 minutes or until cheese melts and tomatoes are warm. Cut into wedges.
Per Serving: 468 cal., 27 g fat (10 g sat. fat), 42 mg chol., 831 mg sodium, 38 g carbo., 2 g fiber, 22 g pro.

Ham and Cheese Calzones

The melted cheese gets mighty hot, so let these turnovers cool for a few minutes before serving them.

Prep: 15 minutes   *Bake:* 15 minutes   *Stand:* 5 minutes
Makes 4 servings

  1   13.8-ounce package refrigerated pizza dough
  ¼   cup coarse-grain mustard
  6   ounces sliced Swiss or provolone cheese
  1½ cups cubed cooked ham (8 ounces)
  ½   teaspoon caraway seeds

1. Preheat oven to 400°F. Line a baking sheet with foil; lightly grease foil. Set aside.

2. Unroll pizza dough. On a lightly floured surface, roll or pat dough into a 15×10-inch rectangle. Cut dough in half crosswise and lengthwise to make four rectangles. Spread mustard over rectangles. Divide half of the cheese among rectangles, placing cheese on half of each rectangle and cutting or tearing to fit as necessary. Top with ham and sprinkle with caraway seeds. Top with remaining cheese. Brush edges with water. For each calzone, fold dough over filling to opposite edge, stretching slightly if necessary. Seal edges with the tines of a fork. Place calzones on the prepared baking sheet. Prick tops to allow steam to escape.

3. Bake about 15 minutes or until golden. Let stand for 5 minutes before serving.

Per Serving: 421 cal., 21 g fat (10 g sat. fat), 72 mg chol., 1,390 mg sodium, 28 g carbo., 1 g fiber, 30 g pro.

Middle Eastern–Style Pitas

Start to Finish: 10 minutes
Makes 4 servings

  1   7- or 8-ounce container roasted garlic–flavor hummus
  4   pita rounds, halved crosswise
  12 ounces thinly sliced deli roast beef
  ½   cup plain yogurt
  ½   cup chopped cucumber

1. Spread hummus in the pita halves. Add beef to pita halves. In a small bowl, stir together yogurt and cucumber; spoon over beef in pita halves.

Per Serving: 463 cal., 18 g fat (5 g sat. fat), 70 mg chol., 735 mg sodium, 44 g carbo., 3 g fiber, 34 g pro.

Chicken Focaccia Sandwiches

Here's a simple solution for days you're extra rushed. These sandwiches are a fast meal in a package that every member of the family will like.

Start to Finish: 15 minutes
Makes 4 servings

  1   8- to 10-inch tomato or onion Italian flatbread (focaccia) or 1 loaf sourdough bread
  ⅓   cup light mayonnaise dressing or salad dressing
  1   cup lightly packed fresh basil
  1½ cups sliced or shredded deli-roasted chicken
  ½   cup bottled roasted red sweet peppers, drained and cut into strips

1. Using a long serrated knife, cut bread in half horizontally. Spread cut sides of bread halves with mayonnaise dressing. Layer basil leaves, chicken, and roasted sweet peppers between bread halves. Cut into quarters.

Per Serving: 314 cal., 10 g fat (1 g sat. fat), 40 mg chol., 597 mg sodium, 40 g carbo., 1 g fiber, 19 g pro.

Barbecue Beef Wrap

With this delicious wrap, there will be no noses turned up at leftovers.

Start to Finish: 10 minutes
Makes 2 servings

  4   ounces leftover roast beef, shredded (⅓ cup)
  2   7- to 8-inch flour tortillas
  2   tablespoons bottled barbecue sauce
  ¼   cup shredded Monterey Jack cheese
  ¼   cup packaged shredded broccoli (broccoli slaw mix)

1. Arrange beef on the tortilla. Drizzle with barbecue sauce and top with cheese and broccoli; roll up. Serve immediately or wrap tightly in plastic wrap and chill for up to 24 hours.

Per Serving: 280 cal., 13 g fat (6 g sat. fat), 57 mg chol., 367 mg sodium, 17 g carbo., 1 g fiber, 21 g pro.

Barbecue
Beef Wrap

Taco Pizza

Tell your teens that they're in charge of dinner, then hand them this recipe. It's fun to make, fun to eat.

Prep: 15 minutes   *Bake:* 20 minutes
Makes 6 servings

- 8 ounces lean ground beef and/or bulk pork sausage
- ¾ cup chopped red or green sweet pepper (1 medium)
- 1 11.5-ounce package refrigerated corn bread twists (8)
- ½ cup bottled salsa
- 3 cups shredded taco cheese (12 ounces)

1. Preheat oven to 400°F. Grease a 12-inch pizza pan; set aside. In a medium skillet, cook and stir beef and sweet pepper over medium heat until meat is brown; drain off fat. Set aside.

2. Unroll corn bread dough (do not separate into strips). Press dough into the bottom and up the edges of the prepared pan. Spread salsa on top of dough. Sprinkle with meat mixture and cheese.

3. Bake about 20 minutes or until bottom of crust is golden when lifted slightly with a spatula. Cut into wedges.

Per Serving: 465 cal., 30 g fat (15 g sat. fat), 73 mg chol., 870 mg sodium, 27 g carbo., 1 g fiber, 22 g pro.

Reuben Loaf

Hot roll mix combines with traditional Reuben fixings to make this sandwich in a loaf. Slice it to the thickness you desire.

Prep: 30 minutes   *Rise:* 30 minutes   *Bake:* 25 minutes
Makes 10 servings

- 1 16-ounce package hot roll mix
- 1 cup bottled Thousand Island salad dressing
- 1 pound sliced cooked corned beef
- 8 ounces Swiss cheese, thinly sliced or shredded
- 1 14- to 16-ounce jar or can sauerkraut, rinsed and drained

1. Prepare the hot roll mix according to package directions. Let rest for 5 minutes. Meanwhile, line an extra-large baking sheet with foil; grease foil. Set aside.

2. Divide dough in half; roll each half into a 12×8-inch rectangle. Spread each dough rectangle with ¼ cup of the Thousand Island salad dressing. On each rectangle, layer half of the corned beef, half of the cheese, and half of the sauerkraut, spreading to within 1 inch of the edges. Starting from a long side, roll up each rectangle to form a loaf. Brush edges with water and press to seal.

3. Place loaves, seam sides down, on the prepared baking sheet. Lightly cover; let rise in a warm place for 30 minutes.

4. Meanwhile, preheat oven to 375°F. Make four diagonal slits, ¼-inch deep, in the top of each loaf. Bake for 25 to 30 minutes or until golden. Serve with remaining salad dressing.

Per Serving: 495 cal., 27 g fat (8 g sat. fat), 92 mg chol., 1,338 mg sodium, 41 g carbo., 1 g fiber, 21 g pro.

Buffalo Chicken Pizzas

If the Southwest-flavor chicken breast strips aren't hot enough for you, add a few drops of bottled hot pepper sauce or buffalo wing sauce to your pizza.

Start to Finish: 20 minutes
Makes 4 servings

- 4 pita bread rounds
- ¼ cup bottled blue cheese salad dressing
- 1 9-ounce package refrigerated Southwest-flavor cooked chicken breast strips
- ¾ cup thinly sliced celery
    Blue cheese crumbles
    Bottled hot pepper sauce or buffalo wing sauce (optional)

1. Preheat oven to 450°F. Place pita rounds on a baking sheet. Brush with blue cheese dressing. Scatter chicken strips and celery on dressing.

2. Bake about 10 minutes or until heated through and pitas are crisp. Transfer to plates. Sprinkle with blue cheese crumbles. If desired, pass hot pepper sauce.

Per Serving: 353 cal., 14 g fat (3 g sat. fat), 45 mg chol., 1,084 mg sodium, 36 g carbo., 2 g fiber, 21 g pro.

Buffalo Chicken Pizzas

Just like buffalo wings, almost any of your *kids' favorite foods* can be adapted for pizza. How about BLT or PB&J? Sloppy Joes, tacos, or meatballs? *Be creative!*

Curried Tuna Sandwich

Make the tuna salad ahead and refrigerate until you're ready to assemble the sandwiches.
Start to Finish: 15 minutes
Makes 4 servings

1½ cups creamy deli coleslaw
1 small tomato, seeded and chopped
1 teaspoon curry powder
1 6-ounce can tuna, drained and flaked
¼ cup chopped peanuts
4 ciabatta rolls, sliced horizontally
4 large butterhead (Bibb or Boston) lettuce
   leaves

1. In a small bowl, stir together coleslaw, tomato, and curry powder. Fold in tuna and chopped peanuts. To serve, spoon the tuna mixture into rolls and top with lettuce leaves.

Per Serving: 254 cal., 9 g total fat (2 g sat. fat), 21 mg chol., 434 mg sodium, 28 g carbo., 3 g fiber, 17 g pro.

Parmesan Chicken Salad Sandwiches

Another time, serve this salad over mixed salad greens or wedges of cantaloupe.
Start to Finish: 10 minutes
Makes 6 servings

½ cup low-fat mayonnaise
1 tablespoon lemon juice
2 teaspoons snipped fresh basil
2½ cups chopped cooked chicken or turkey
¼ cup grated Parmesan cheese
¼ cup thinly sliced green onions
3 tablespoons finely chopped celery
   Salt and ground black pepper
6 croissants

1. In a small bowl, stir together mayonnaise, lemon juice and basil. Set aside.

2. In a medium bowl, combine chicken, Parmesan cheese, green onions and celery. Pour dressing over chicken mixture; toss to coat. Season to taste with salt and ground black pepper. Serve immediately or cover and chill in the refrigerator for 1 to 4 hours. Serve on croissants.

Per Serving: 424 cal., 24 g total fat (9 g sat. fat), 100 mg chol., 760 mg sodium, 29 g carbo., 2 g fiber, 23 g pro.

Brats with Onion-Pepper Relish

These slimmed-down brats are fast to fix, full of great flavor, and healthful too.
Start to Finish: 30 minutes
Makes 4 servings

4 uncooked turkey bratwurst
½ cup water
1 small onion, thinly sliced
1 small red or green sweet pepper, cut into thin
   strips
¼ teaspoon ground black pepper
⅛ teaspoon salt
2 teaspoons butter or margarine
4 bratwurst buns, split and toasted
3 tablespoons spicy brown mustard

1. In a large nonstick skillet, cook bratwurst over medium heat about 5 minutes or until brown, turning frequently. Carefully add the water. Bring to boiling; reduce heat. Cover and simmer for 15 to 20 minutes or until an instant-read meat thermometer inserted from the end of a bratwurst into the center registers 165°F. Drain on paper towels.

2. Meanwhile, in a covered medium saucepan, cook onion, sweet pepper, black pepper, and salt in hot butter for 3 minutes. Stir onion mixture. Cook, covered, for 3 to 4 minutes more or until onion is golden brown.

3. Spread cut sides of toasted buns with mustard. Serve bratwurst in buns topped with onion mixture.

Per Serving: 284 cal., 12 g total fat (4 g sat. fat), 43 mg chol., 1,100 mg sodium, 27 g carbo., 2 g fiber, 17 g pro.

PICK A PEPPER

While individual red, yellow, and orange sweet peppers can be pricey, look for those that are packaged in combinations along with green peppers. They're less perfect than those that are sold individually——small and not as nicely shaped—but more economically priced.

Brats with Onion-Pepper Relish

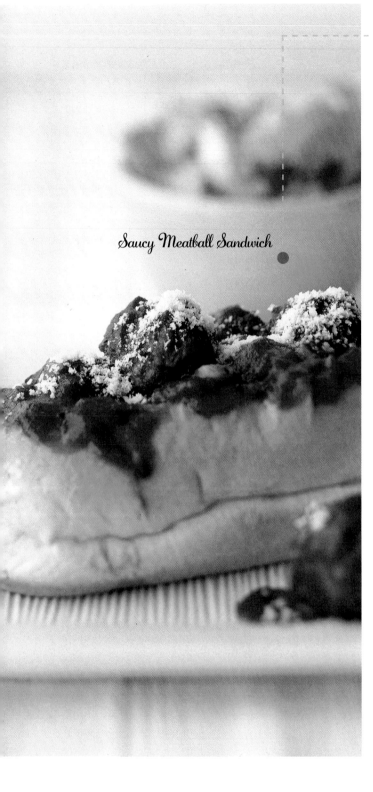

Saucy Meatball Sandwich

Saucy Meatball Sandwich

Hollowing out the tops of the hoagie buns keeps the sauce from oozing out the sides.
Start to Finish: 20 minutes
Makes 12 servings

2	eggs
1½	cups soft whole wheat bread crumbs
½	cup finely chopped onion
½	teaspoon salt
½	teaspoon dried Italian seasoning, crushed
2	pounds lean ground beef
2	26- to 28-ounce jars red pasta sauce
12	hoagie or bratwurst buns
½	cup grated Parmesan cheese

1. Preheat oven to 350°F. In a large mixing bowl, combine eggs, bread crumbs, finely chopped onion, salt, and Italian seasoning. Add ground beef; mix well. Shape into 48 meatballs. Arrange meatballs in a large roasting pan or 15x10x1-inch baking pan. Bake for 15 to 20 minutes or until done (160°). Drain well.

2. In a 4-quart Dutch, oven combine the pasta sauce and meatballs. Heat through. Split rolls or hollow out tops of unsplit rolls. Spoon hot meatball mixture into rolls. Spoon any remaining sauce over the meatballs. Sprinkle cheese over the meatballs. Top with bun halves, if rolls are split. Let stand 1 to 2 minutes before serving.

Per Serving: 599 cal., 18 g total fat (6 g sat. fat), 86 mg chol., 1,351 mg sodium, 83 g carbo., 6 g fiber, 29 g pro.

BUY IN BULK

Purchase ground beef in bulk, then package in 1-pound portions—or whatever size works best for your family. Label, date, and freeze in freezer wrap or bags.

Sandwiches made with ground meats make great money-saving meals. You can buy meat on sale and cook up a double batch. Use what you need for tonight's dinner, then freeze the rest.

Hot and Spicy Sloppy Joes

A coffee, vinegar, and ketchup sauce give this loose-meat sandwich a lively, interesting twist.

Prep: 30 minutes *Cook:* 50 minutes

Makes 7 to 8 servings

1	pound ground beef
2	medium green sweet peppers, chopped
1	medium red sweet pepper, chopped
2	medium onions, chopped (2 cups)
1	cup strong coffee
½	cup cider vinegar
¾	cup ketchup
1	teaspoon chili powder
1	teaspoon paprika
¼	teaspoon salt
¼	teaspoon ground black pepper
⅛	teaspoon cayenne pepper
7	to 8 hamburger or hot dog buns, split and toasted if desired

1. In a large skillet, oven cook ground beef, sweet peppers, and onions until meat is brown and vegetables are tender. Drain off fat. Stir in coffee and vinegar. Bring to boiling. Boil gently, uncovered, over medium heat for about 40 minutes or until most of the liquid evaporates, stirring occasionally.

2. Stir in ketchup, chili powder, paprika, salt, black pepper, and cayenne pepper. Cook and stir for 10 to 15 minutes more or until desired consistency. Serve meat in buns.

Per Serving: 283 cal., 9 g total fat (3 g sat. fat), 41 mg chol., 658 mg sodium, 36 g carbo., 3 g fiber, 17 g pro.

Spicy Pecan Pork Sandwiches

Chipotle chile–flavor mayonnaise adds the right amount of heat to these crispy pork loin sandwiches.

Start to Finish: 30 minutes

Makes 4 sandwiches

4	boneless pork loin chops, cut ½ inch thick (about 1 pound total)
¼	cup all-purpose flour
1	egg, lightly beaten
2	tablespoons Dijon–style mustard
¼	to ½ teaspoon cayenne pepper
½	cup fine dry bread crumbs
½	cup ground toasted pecans
2	tablespoons cooking oil
4	hoagie buns, kaiser rolls, or hamburger buns, split and toasted
	Chipotle chile-flavor light mayonnaise
	Lettuce leaves
	Tomato slices

1. Trim fat from chops. Place each chop between 2 pieces of plastic wrap. Working from center to edges, pound lightly with the flat side of a meat mallet to about ¼-inch thickness. Remove plastic wrap.

2. Place flour in a shallow dish. In another shallow dish combine egg, mustard, and cayenne pepper. In a third shallow dish, combine bread crumbs and pecans. Dip meat into flour, then dip into egg mixture and crumb mixture, turning to coat.

3. In a 12-inch skillet, heat oil over medium-high heat. Add meat. Cook for 6 to 8 minutes or until meat is slightly pink in center, turning once. If meat browns too quickly, reduce heat to medium.

4. Spread buns or bread with mayonnaise. Serve meat in buns with lettuce and tomato.

Per Sandwich: 634 cal., 31 g total fat (6 g sat. fat), 122 mg chol., 987 mg sodium, 51 g carbo., 4 g fiber, 38 g pro.

Honey and Poppy Seed Biscuits

tasty side dishes

The breads, vegetables, and salads that round out a meal usually draw less thought and attention than the main dish, but they're still important. Here are easy, creative recipes for side dishes that are both inexpensive and satisfying.

Honey and Poppy Seed Biscuits

Kids can help make these biscuits by brushing the tops with water and sprinkling on the poppy seeds.

Prep: 15 minutes   Bake: 10 minutes
Makes 10 to 12 servings

½	cup cream-style cottage cheese
¼	cup milk
2	tablespoons honey
2¼	cups packaged biscuit mix
	Water
	Poppy seeds

1. Preheat oven to 450°F. In a food processor or blender, combine cottage cheese, milk, and honey. Cover and process or blend until the mixture is nearly smooth.

2. Prepare biscuit mix according to package directions for rolled biscuits, except substitute the pureed cottage cheese mixture for the liquid called for on the package. Lightly brush with water and sprinkle with poppy seeds.

3. Bake for 10 to 12 minutes or until bottoms are lightly browned.

Per Serving: 143 cal., 5 g fat (1 g sat. fat), 3 mg chol., 393 mg sodium, 21 g carbo., 1 g fiber, 4 g pro.

Mixed Greens Salad with Pears

Start to Finish: 15 minutes
Makes 6 servings

1	10-ounce package spring salad mix
2	fresh pears, cored and sliced
2	ounces Gruyère cheese, cubed
¼	cup bottled white wine vinaigrette
2	teaspoons honey

1. In a large bowl, combine salad mix, pears, and cheese. For dressing, stir together vinaigrette and honey. Pour dressing over greens mixture; toss to coat. If desired, garnish each salad with a thin pear slice.

Per Serving: 148 cal., 10 g fat (3 g sat. fat), 10 mg chol., 85 mg sodium, 12 g carbo., 2 g fiber, 3 g pro.

Quick and Cheesy Veggies

Start to Finish: 10 minutes
Makes 4 servings

1	12-ounce package frozen broccoli and cauliflower in microwavable steaming bag
1	cup shredded American cheese (4 ounces)
2	tablespoons chopped walnuts, toasted

1. Steam vegetables in microwave according to package directions. Transfer vegetables to a serving bowl. Stir in cheese; let stand for 1 minute. Toss until cheese is melted and vegetables are coated. Sprinkle with nuts.

Per Serving: 158 cal., 11 g fat (6 g sat. fat), 27 mg chol., 445 mg sodium, 5 g carbo., 2 g fiber, 8 g pro.

Crumb-Topped Vegetables

Start to Finish: 10 minutes
Makes 4 to 6 servings

- 1 12-ounce package frozen cut green beans in microwavable steaming bag
- 1 cup cheese-flavored crackers, crushed
- ½ teaspoon dried thyme, crushed
- 2 tablespoons butter, melted
- ¼ cup finely shredded Parmesan cheese

1. Steam beans in microwave according to package directions.

2. Meanwhile, in a small resealable plastic bag, place the crackers and thyme. Release the air from the bag and seal the bag. With your hands, crush the crackers until they resemble fine crumbs. Add melted butter to the bag. Seal bag and toss to combine.

3. Place beans in a serving dish. Top with cracker mixture. Sprinkle Parmesan cheese over top.
Per Serving: 168 cal., 10 g fat (6 g sat. fat), 20 mg chol., 249 mg sodium, 13 g carbo., 2 g fiber, 4 g pro.

Penne with Snap Peas and Tomatoes

Cook the peas with the pasta to save washing another saucepan.
Start to Finish: 30 minutes
Makes 4 servings

- 8 ounces dried penne (4 cups)
- 8 ounces fresh sugar snap peas, trimmed and halved lengthwise (about 2 cups)
- 3 oil-packed dried tomatoes, drained and snipped, reserving 1 tablespoon drained oil
- 2 cloves garlic, minced, or 1 teaspoon bottled minced garlic
  Salt and ground black pepper

1. In a large saucepan, cook pasta according to package directions, adding the peas for the last 3 minutes of cooking time. Drain.

2. Return pasta and peas to pan. Add tomatoes, reserved oil, and garlic; toss to coat. Season to taste with salt and black pepper.
Per Serving: 270 cal., 5 g fat (1 g sat. fat), 0 mg chol., 157 mg sodium, 47 g carbo., 3 g fiber, 9 g pro.

Blueberry-Orange Scones

Fresh blueberries work better than frozen berries in these scones because their color doesn't bleed as much.
Prep: 20 minutes *Bake:* 12 minutes
Makes 6 servings

- 2¼ cups packaged biscuit mix
- ⅓ cup milk
- 1 egg, lightly beaten
- 1 teaspoon finely shredded orange peel
- ½ cup fresh blueberries
  Milk (optional)
  Sugar (optional)

1. Preheat oven to 400°F. In a large bowl, stir together biscuit mix, ⅓ cup milk, the egg, and orange peel until a soft dough forms. Carefully fold in blueberries.

2. Turn dough out onto a lightly floured surface. Lightly knead 10 times or until nearly smooth. Pat dough into a 6-inch circle. Cut into six wedges. Arrange wedges on an ungreased baking sheet. If desired, brush with milk and sprinkle with sugar. Bake for 12 to 14 minutes or until golden. Serve warm.
Per Serving: 230 cal., 8 g fat (2 g sat. fat), 37 mg chol., 598 mg sodium, 33 g carbo., 1 g fiber, 5 g pro.

Southern Succotash

Fresh green beans give a summertime spin to this old-fashioned classic of lima beans and corn.
Start to Finish: 25 minutes
Makes 12 servings

- 1 10-ounce package frozen lima beans
- 1 quart boiling water
- 2½ cups fresh green beans, trimmed
- 2 cups fresh or frozen yellow corn kernels
- 1 tablespoon butter
- ½ to 1 teaspoon cracked black pepper

1. In a Dutch oven, cook lima beans in the boiling water for 10 minutes. Add green beans; cook for 5 minutes. Add corn and cook for 5 minutes more; drain. Stir in butter and pepper; toss to mix.
Per Serving: 71 cal., 1 g fat (1 g sat. fat), 3 mg chol., 24 mg sodium, 13 g carbo., 3 g fiber, 3 g pro.

Southern Succotash

Creamy Lemon-Pepper Coleslaw

Cabbage holds its crispness overnight when chilled, so you can fix the salad while preparing dinner tonight and have it ready for a fast meal tomorrow.

Prep: 10 minutes   *Chill:* 2 hours
Makes 6 servings

- ½   cup mayonnaise or salad dressing
- 1   teaspoon lemon-pepper seasoning
- ½   teaspoon dried thyme, crushed
- 5   cups packaged shredded cabbage with carrot (coleslaw mix)
- ¼   cup shelled sunflower seeds

1. In a large salad bowl, combine mayonnaise, lemon-pepper seasoning, and thyme. Stir in shredded cabbage and sunflower seeds. Toss lightly to coat. Cover and chill for 2 to 24 hours.

Per Serving: 188 cal., 18 g fat (2 g sat. fat), 7 mg chol., 328 mg sodium, 5 g carbo., 2 g fiber, 2 g pro.

Fruit and Broccoli Salad

Fast to fix, easy to tote, and tempting to most everyone, this salad is a winner on the potluck table.

Prep: 15 minutes   *Chill:* 1 hour
Makes 12 to 16 servings

- 1   16-ounce package shredded broccoli (broccoli slaw mix)
- 2   cups seedless red and/or green grapes, halved
- 2   medium apples, cored and chopped
- ⅔   cup bottled citrus salad dressing (such as tangerine vinaigrette)
- 1   cup coarsely chopped pecans or walnuts, toasted,* if desired

1. In a very large bowl, combine shredded broccoli, grapes, and apples. Up to 1 hour before serving, pour salad dressing over broccoli mixture; toss to coat. Cover and chill. Transfer to a serving bowl. Sprinkle with nuts; toss again.

***To toast nuts:** Preheat oven to 350°F. Spread nuts in a single layer in a shallow baking pan. Bake for 5 to 10 minutes or until light golden brown, watching carefully and stirring once or twice.

Per Serving: 219 cal., 15 g fat (2 g sat. fat), 6 mg chol., 131 mg sodium, 21 g carbo., 2 g fiber, 3 g pro.

Hash Brown Potato Cakes

For smooth cakes that hold together, be sure to slice the onion very thinly. Don't turn the cakes until the first side is golden brown.

Prep: 20 minutes   *Cook:* 8 minutes per batch
Makes 8 (2-cake) servings

- 1   pound russet or round red potatoes
- ½   of a medium onion, very thinly sliced
- 1   tablespoon olive oil
- 2   teaspoons snipped fresh thyme or ¼ teaspoon dried thyme, crushed
- ¼   teaspoon salt
- ⅛   teaspoon ground black pepper
  Nonstick cooking spray

1. Preheat oven to 300°F. Peel and coarsely shred potatoes; immediately rinse with cold water in a colander. Drain well, pressing lightly, then pat dry with paper towels; place in a large bowl. Quarter the onion slices. Stir onion, oil, thyme, salt, and pepper into potatoes.

2. Lightly coat an unheated very large nonstick skillet or griddle with cooking spray. Heat skillet over medium heat.

3. For each cake, scoop a slightly rounded measuring tablespoon of potato mixture onto skillet. Using a spatula, press potato mixture to flatten evenly to 2½- to 3-inch diameter. Cook for 5 minutes. Using a wide spatula, carefully turn potato cakes (be sure not to turn cakes too soon or they will not hold together). Cook for 3 to 5 minutes more or until golden brown.

4. Remove cooked potato cakes from the skillet; keep warm, uncovered, in oven while cooking remaining potato cakes. Repeat with remaining potato mixture, stirring mixture frequently.

Per Serving: 59 cal., 2 g fat (0 g sat. fat), 0 mg chol., 75 mg sodium, 9 g carbo., 1 g fiber, 1 g pro.

Hash Brown
Potato Cakes

Volcano Potatoes

Use refrigerated potatoes to make rich, flavorful mashed potatoes with no need for gravy in a fraction of the time it would take from scratch.

Prep: 15 minutes   *Bake:* 65 minutes
Makes 10 servings

- 3   20-ounce packages refrigerated mashed potatoes
- ¾   cup whipping cream
- ¾   cup shredded Gruyère, Havarti, or American cheese (3 ounces)
      Freshly cracked black pepper

1. Preheat oven to 300°F. Spoon potatoes into a 2-quart casserole. Bake, covered, for 50 minutes.

2. Meanwhile, in a medium mixing bowl, beat cream with an electric mixer on medium speed until soft peaks form (tips curl); fold in cheese.

3. Remove casserole from oven. Increase oven temperature to 375°F. With a large spoon, make a hole in the center of the potatoes by pushing them from the center to the sides. Spoon the cream mixture into the hole. Sprinkle top with cracked black pepper.

4. Bake, uncovered, for 15 to 20 minutes more or until top is golden.
Per Serving: 243 cal., 13 g fat (6 g sat. fat), 37 mg chol., 300 mg sodium, 24 g carbo., 1 g fiber, 7 g pro.

Pesto Biscuits

Pesto made with dried tomatoes or another herb, such as cilantro, also adds intriguing flavor to hot biscuits.

Prep: 15 minutes   *Bake:* 10 minutes
Makes 10 to 12 servings

- 2¼   cups packaged biscuit mix
- ½   cup milk
- ¼   cup purchased basil pesto
- 2   teaspoons olive oil
- 2   tablespoons finely shredded Parmesan cheese

1. Preheat oven to 450°F. In a medium bowl, stir together the biscuit mix, milk, and pesto until a soft dough forms.

2. Turn dough out onto a lightly floured surface. Lightly knead 10 times or until nearly smooth.

Pat dough to ½-inch thickness. Using a 2½-inch round cookie cutter, cut dough into rounds. Place rounds on an ungreased baking sheet. Brush lightly with olive oil; sprinkle with cheese.

3. Bake about 10 minutes or until golden. Serve warm.
Per Serving: 165 cal., 8 g fat (2 g sat. fat), 4 mg chol., 426 mg sodium, 19 g carbo., 1 g fiber, 4 g pro.

Grilled Asparagus with Lemon

Partially precooking the asparagus ensures it is tender after grilling without burning, and it allows the asparagus to absorb more flavors from the marinade.

Prep: 15 minutes   *Marinate:* 30 minutes   *Grill:* 3 minutes
Makes 4 to 6 servings

- 1   to 1½ pounds fresh asparagus spears
- 2   tablespoons olive oil
- 2   tablespoons lemon juice
- ½   teaspoon salt
- ¼   teaspoon ground black pepper
      Lemon wedges

1. Snap off and discard woody bases from asparagus. If desired, scrape off scales. In a large skillet, cook the asparagus in a small amount of boiling water for 3 minutes; drain well.

2. Meanwhile, for marinade, in a 2-quart rectangular baking dish, stir together olive oil, lemon juice, salt, and pepper. Add asparagus, turning to coat. Cover and marinate at room temperature for 30 minutes.

3. Drain asparagus, discarding marinade. Place asparagus on a grill tray or in a grill basket. For a charcoal grill, grill asparagus on the rack of an uncovered grill directly over medium heat for 3 to 5 minutes or until asparagus is tender and beginning to brown, turning once halfway through grilling. (For a gas grill, preheat grill. Reduce heat to medium. Place asparagus on grill rack over heat. Cover and grill as above.)

4. To serve, arrange asparagus on a serving platter. Serve with lemon wedges.
Per Serving: 87 cal., 7 g fat (1 g sat. fat), 0 mg chol., 294 mg sodium, 7 g carbo., 3 g fiber, 3 g pro.

Grilled Asparagus with Lemon

Romaine with Creamy Garlic Dressing

You'll have some of the salad dressing left over; cover and chill it for up to 3 days. It makes a good topper for any combination of greens and vegetable.

Start to Finish: 5 minutes
Makes 4 servings

- ½ cup plain yogurt
- ⅓ cup bottled Italian salad dressing
- 1 clove garlic, minced, or ½ teaspoon bottled minced garlic
- 4 cups torn romaine
- ¼ cup finely shredded Parmesan cheese

1. For dressing, in a small bowl, stir together yogurt, salad dressing, and garlic.

2. Arrange romaine on four salad plates. Drizzle each salad with 1 tablespoon of the dressing. Sprinkle with Parmesan cheese.

Per Serving: 257 cal., 19 g fat (7 g sat. fat), 26 mg chol., 744 mg sodium, 7 g carbo., 1 g fiber, 15 g pro.

Green Beans and Tomatoes

Pair whole green beans and tiny tomatoes for a vegetable medley that's pleasing served at room temperature or chilled.

Start to Finish: 20 minutes
Makes 6 to 8 servings

- 1½ pounds fresh green beans, trimmed
- 1 pint small tomatoes (such as yellow pear, red grape, red and/or orange cherry), halved
- ¼ cup bottled basil vinaigrette salad dressing
    Salt and freshly ground black pepper

1. Cook beans, covered, in a small amount of boiling salted water for 10 to 15 minutes or until crisp-tender. Drain and rinse under cool water. Drain and pat dry with paper towels.

2. In a large bowl, combine green beans and tomatoes. Drizzle with vinaigrette salad dressing; toss to coat. Add more vinaigrette, if necessary. Season to taste with salt and pepper. Serve immediately or cover and chill for up to 8 hours.

Per Serving: 86 cal., 5 g fat (1 g sat. fat), 0 mg chol., 106 mg sodium, 10 g carbo., 4 g fiber, 4 g pro.

Orange-Asparagus Salad

Start to Finish: 20 minutes
Makes 2 servings

- 8 ounces fresh asparagus
- 1 medium orange, peeled and sliced crosswise
- 2 tablespoons orange juice
- 2 teaspoons olive oil
- ½ teaspoon Dijon-style mustard
- ⅛ teaspoon salt
    Dash ground black pepper

1. Snap off and discard woody bases from asparagus. If desired, scrape off scales. Cut stems into 2-inch pieces. In a covered small saucepan, cook asparagus in a small amount of boiling water for 1 minute; drain. Cool immediately in a bowl of ice water. Drain on paper towels.

2. Cut orange slices into two-section pieces; set aside.

3. For dressing, in a medium bowl, whisk together orange juice, oil, mustard, salt, and pepper. Add asparagus and orange sections; stir gently to coat. Serve immediately or cover and chill for up to 6 hours.

Per Serving: 94 cal., 5 g fat (1 g sat. fat), 0 mg chol., 177 mg sodium, 12 g carbo., 3 g fiber, 2 g pro.

Golden Green Bean Crunch

Prep: 15 minutes   *Bake:* 30 minutes
Makes 4 to 6 servings

- 1 16-ounce package frozen French-cut green beans
- 1 10.75-ounce can condensed golden mushroom soup
- 1 8-ounce can sliced water chestnuts, drained
- ½ of a 2.8-ounce can French fried onions (about ¾ cup) or 1 cup chow mein noodles

1. Preheat oven to 350°F. Cook frozen beans according to package directions; drain well. In a 1½-quart casserole, stir together the beans, soup, and water chestnuts.

2. Bake, uncovered, about 25 minutes or until bubbly around edges. Sprinkle with the onions. Bake about 5 minutes more or until heated through.

Per Serving: 188 cal., 6 g fat (1 g sat. fat), 3 mg chol., 719 mg sodium, 27 g carbo., 5 g fiber, 5 g pro.

Golden Green Bean Crunch

Pepper and Four-Bean Salad

Pepper and Four-Bean Salad

A tangy tarragon vinaigrette amps up the flavor of this simple make-ahead side.

Prep: 25 minutes *Chill:* 4 to 24 hours
Makes 14 servings

- 4 cups fresh green and/or wax beans, trimmed and cut into 1½-inch pieces, or one 16-ounce package frozen cut green beans
- 3 cups thin strips green, red, and/or yellow sweet pepper (3 medium)
- 1 15-ounce can red kidney beans, rinsed and drained
- 1 15-ounce can garbanzo beans (chickpeas), rinsed and drained
- 1 small red or white onion, thinly sliced and separated into rings
- ½ cup vinegar
- ¼ cup olive oil
- 1 tablespoon sugar
- 2 teaspoons snipped fresh tarragon or thyme or ½ teaspoon dried tarragon or thyme, crushed
- ½ teaspoon ground black pepper
  Lettuce leaves (optional)

1. In a covered large saucepan, cook fresh green and/or wax beans in a small amount of boiling water for 8 to 10 minutes or just until tender. (If using frozen green beans, cook according to package directions.) Drain beans. Immerse in a bowl of ice water to cool quickly; drain well.

2. In a large bowl, combine green and/or wax beans, sweet pepper, drained kidney beans, drained garbanzo beans, and onion.

3. For dressing, in a medium bowl, whisk together vinegar, oil, sugar, tarragon, and black pepper. Pour dressing over bean mixture; toss gently to coat. Cover and chill for 4 to 24 hours, stirring occasionally.

4. If desired, line a serving bowl with lettuce. Using a slotted spoon, spoon bean mixture into bowl.

Per Serving: 117 cal., 4 g total fat (0 g sat. fat), 0 mg chol., 146 mg sodium, 17 g carbo., 5 g fiber, 5 g pro.

A colorful salad or sweetly glazed hot vegetable dish can bring life to a simple main course such as a roast or broiled chops.

Corn Bread Salad

This layered salad is great any time of year.
Prep: 20 minutes Bake: 20 minutes Chill: 2 to 24 hours
Makes 10 to 12 servings

- 1   8.5-ounce package corn muffin mix
- 1   cup mayonnaise or salad dressing
- 1   8-ounce carton dairy sour cream
- 1   0.4-ounce envelope ranch dry salad dressing mix
- 2   15-ounce cans pinto beans, rinsed and drained
- 1   15.25-ounce can whole kernel corn, drained
- 1   cup chopped tomato (2 medium)
- ¾   cup chopped green sweet pepper (1 medium)
- ½   cup sliced green onions
- 8   slices bacon, crisp-cooked, drained, and crumbled
- 2   cups shredded cheddar cheese (8 ounces)

1. Preheat oven to 400°F. Grease an 8-inch oven-proof cast-iron skillet; set aside. Prepare muffin mix according to package directions. Spread batter in the prepared skillet. Bake, uncovered, for 20 to 25 minutes or until a toothpick inserted near the center comes out clean. Cool on a wire rack. Coarsely crumble corn bread; set aside.

2. For dressing, in a medium bowl, combine mayonnaise, sour cream, and salad dressing mix; set aside. In a large bowl, combine drained beans, drained corn, tomato, sweet pepper, green onion, and bacon.

3. In a 3-quart glass bowl, layer half of the corn bread, half of the bean mixture, and half of the cheese. Spread half of the dressing over layers in bowl. Repeat layers. Cover and chill for 2 to 24 hours.

4. To serve, toss gently to coat corn bread and vegetables with dressing.
Per Serving: 564 cal., 37 g total fat (13 g sat. fat), 68 mg chol., 1,126 mg sodium, 38 g carbo., 6 g fiber, 16 g pro.

Orange-Sauced Broccoli and Peppers

Choose a red or yellow pepper depending on price and how it complements the rest of your meal. Broccoli is widely available year-round and a good value.
Start to Finish: 35 minutes
Makes 6 servings

- 3½   cups broccoli florets
- 1   cup bite-size strips red or yellow sweet pepper (1 medium)
- 1   tablespoon butter or margarine
- 2   tablespoons finely chopped onion
- 1   clove garlic, minced
- 1½   teaspoons cornstarch
- ⅔   cup orange juice

1. In a covered medium saucepan, cook broccoli and sweet pepper in a small amount of boiling water about 8 minutes or until broccoli is crisp-tender; drain. Cover and keep warm.

2. For sauce, in a small saucepan, melt butter over medium heat. Add onion and garlic; cook about 5 minutes or until onion is tender. Stir in cornstarch. Slowly stir in orange juice. Cook and stir until thickened and bubbly. Cook and stir for 2 minutes more.

3. To serve, pour sauce over broccoli mixture; toss gently to coat.
Per Serving: 57 cal., 2 g total fat (1 g sat. fat), 5 mg chol., 32 mg sodium, 9 g carbo., 2 g fiber, 2 g pro.

Broccoli and Rice Bake

Rice, broccoli, and a savory soup-based sauce bake together for a true fix-and-forget favorite.

Prep: 15 minutes *Bake:* 65 minutes *Stand:* 5 minutes
Makes 6 servings

1	10.75-ounce can condensed cream of broccoli soup or cream of chicken soup
1¼	cups milk
1	8-ounce carton dairy sour cream
1	teaspoon dried basil, crushed
¼	teaspoon salt
⅛	teaspoon ground black pepper
1	16-ounce package frozen cut broccoli
1½	cups uncooked instant white rice
½	cup shredded Swiss cheese (2 ounces)

1. Preheat oven to 350°F. In a large bowl, whisk together soup, milk, sour cream, basil, salt, and pepper. Stir in frozen broccoli and rice. Transfer mixture to an ungreased 2-quart rectangular baking dish.

2. Bake, covered, about 65 minutes or until heated through. Sprinkle with cheese. Let stand, covered, for 5 minutes before serving.
Per Serving: 295 cal., 13 g total fat (8 g sat. fat), 31 mg chol., 511 mg sodium, 33 g carbo., 2 g fiber, 10 g pro.

Saucepan Baked Beans

Flavorful baked beans are an all-time-favorite side dish with an added bonus—they're economical.

Prep: 10 minutes *Cook:* 10 minutes
Makes 6 servings

1	15-ounce can pork and beans in tomato sauce, undrained
1	15-ounce can navy beans or Great Northern beans, rinsed and drained
¼	cup ketchup
2	tablespoons maple syrup or packed brown sugar
2	teaspoons dry mustard
2	slices bacon, crisp-cooked, drained, and crumbled

1. In a medium saucepan, combine undrained pork and beans, drained navy beans, ketchup, maple syrup, and dry mustard.

2. Bring mixture to boiling; reduce heat. Simmer, uncovered, about 10 minutes or until mixture reaches desired consistency, stirring frequently. Stir in bacon.
Per Serving: 191 cal., 2 g total fat (1 g sat. fat), 8 mg chol., 801 mg sodium, 35 g carbo., 6 g fiber, 10 g pro.

Creamed Corn Casserole

Canned soup and cream cheese create the flavorful sauce for this comfort dish.

Prep: 20 minutes *Bake:* 50 minutes
Makes 12 servings

	Nonstick cooking spray
2	16-ounce packages frozen whole kernel corn
2	cups chopped red and/or green sweet pepper
1	cup chopped onion (1 large)
1	tablespoon butter or margarine
¼	teaspoon ground black pepper
1	10.75-ounce can condensed cream of celery soup
1	8-ounce tub cream cheese spread with chive and onion or cream cheese spread with garden vegetables
¼	cup milk

1. Preheat oven to 375°F. Coat a 2-quart casserole with cooking spray; set aside. Place corn in a colander and thaw by running under cool water; drain. Set aside.

2. In a large saucepan, cook sweet pepper and onion in hot butter until tender. Stir in corn and black pepper. In a medium bowl, whisk together soup, cream cheese spread, and milk. Stir soup mixture into corn mixture. Transfer to the prepared casserole.

3. Bake, covered, for 50 to 55 minutes or until heated through, stirring once.
Per Serving: 176 cal., 9 g total fat (5 g sat. fat), 22 mg chol., 280 mg sodium, 22 g carbo., 3 g fiber, 4 g pro.

creamed corn casserole

Shortcut Malted
Chocolate Cake

sweet-tooth desserts

Not every menu requires a dessert, but we all know something sweet at the end makes a meal seem complete. Shortcut baking, ice cream and pudding fix-ups, and helpings of fruit are the keys to these economical treats.

Shortcut Malted Chocolate Cake

Malted milk powder adds flair to packaged cake mix and store-bought frosting.

Prep: 10 minutes   *Bake:* 30 minutes
Makes 20 servings

- 1   2-layer-size package dark chocolate fudge or devil's food cake mix
- ⅓   cup vanilla malted milk powder
- 1   12-ounce can whipped chocolate frosting
- ¼   cup vanilla malted milk powder
- 1½   cups coarsely chopped malted milk balls

1. Preheat oven to 350°F. Grease a 13×9×2-inch baking pan. Prepare cake mix according to package directions, adding the ⅓ cup malted milk powder to batter. Pour batter into prepared pan. Bake for 30 to 35 minutes or until a toothpick inserted near the center comes out clean. Place pan on a wire rack and cool completely.

2. In a medium bowl, stir together frosting and the ¼ cup malted milk powder. Spread evenly over cake. Top with chopped malted milk balls.

Per Serving: 231 cal., 7 g fat (2 g sat. fat), 2 mg chol., 281 mg sodium, 41 g carbo., 1 g fiber, 3 g pro.

Boston Cream Pie

Prep: 30 minutes   *Bake:* 30 minutes
Cool: 15 minutes   *Chill:* 2 hours
Makes 12 servings

- 1   2-layer-size package yellow cake mix
- ½   of a 4-serving-size package vanilla instant pudding mix (5 tablespoons)
- 1¼   cups milk
- 1   cup semisweet chocolate pieces

1. Preheat oven to 350°F. Grease and flour two 9×1½-inch round cake pans. Prepare cake mix according to package directions and spoon batter into prepared pans. Bake according to package directions. Cool in pans on a wire rack for 10 minutes. Remove cakes from pans; cool completely.

2. Meanwhile, in a small bowl, stir together the instant pudding and 1 cup of the milk. Whisk for 2 minutes or until it starts to set. Cover and chill until serving time.

3. For glaze, in a small saucepan, combine chocolate pieces and the remaining ¼ cup milk. Heat over low heat until chocolate is melted and smooth. Cool for 5 minutes.

4. To assemble, place one cake layer on a serving plate. Spoon pudding over layer on plate. Top with remaining cake layer. Spoon glaze over top, allowing it to drip down the sides. Cover and chill for 2 to 24 hours. Store leftovers in refrigerator.

Per Serving: 258 cal., 8 g fat (4 g sat. fat), 2 mg chol., 349 mg sodium, 49 g carbo., 1 g fiber, 3 g pro.

Peach-Blueberry Crisp

The cookies provide the "crisp" in this stove-top dessert. We like shortbread cookies, but you could use another favorite, such as gingersnaps or pecan sandies.

Start to Finish: 20 minutes

Makes 4 servings

- 2 cups frozen unsweetened peach slices
- 2 tablespoons packed brown sugar
- 1 tablespoon water
- ½ teaspoon pumpkin pie spice
- ¼ cup fresh or frozen blueberries
- 8 shortbread cookies or other crisp cookies, coarsely crushed

1. In a medium saucepan, stir together peaches, brown sugar, water, and pumpkin pie spice. Bring to boiling, stirring to combine; reduce heat. Simmer, uncovered, for 4 to 5 minutes or until thickened. Gently stir in blueberries. Remove from heat. Cover and let stand for 5 minutes. Spoon into dessert dishes. Sprinkle with cookies.

Per Serving: 208 cal., 8 g fat (0 g sat. fat), 10 mg chol., 133 mg sodium, 35 g carbo., 2 g fiber, 4 g pro.

Granola-Topped Pudding

Start to Finish: 15 minutes

Makes 4 servings

- 1 4-serving-size package chocolate instant pudding mix
- 2 cups milk
- ½ of an 8-ounce package reduced-fat cream cheese (Neufchâtel), softened
- ¼ cup peanut butter
- 1 cup granola cereal
  Milk chocolate curls* (optional)

1. In a large bowl, whisk together the pudding mix and 1¾ cups of the milk for 2 minutes or until thickened; set aside. In a medium bowl, whisk together the cream cheese, peanut butter, and the remaining ¼ cup milk until smooth.

2. Spoon pudding mixture into four dessert dishes. Top with cream cheese mixture. Sprinkle with granola. If desired, garnish with chocolate curls.

*To make milk chocolate curls: Draw a vegetable peeler across a thick bar of milk chocolate. It helps if the chocolate is at room temperature.

Per Serving: 428 cal., 19 g fat (8 g sat. fat), 31 mg chol., 661 mg sodium, 53 g carbo., 4 g fiber, 14 g pro.

Banana Split Trifles

Prep: 15 minutes   *Freeze:* Up to 1 hour

Makes 4 servings

- 4 soft-style chocolate chip or oatmeal cookies, crumbled
- 2 bananas, peeled and cut into chunks
- 1 quart tin roof sundae, chocolate chunk, or vanilla ice cream
- 1 12-ounce jar hot fudge sauce or strawberry preserves
  Whipped cream
  Chocolate chip or oatmeal cookies, crumbled

1. In each of four parfait glasses, layer cookies, bananas, scoops of ice cream, and sauce (you might not use all of the ice cream or sauce). Top with whipped cream and crumbled cookies. Cover and freeze for up to 1 hour.

Per Serving: 524 cal., 23 g fat (12 g sat. fat), 48 mg chol., 161 mg sodium, 73 g carbo., 3 g fiber, 6 g pro.

Cereal-Coated Ice Cream Sundaes

Start to Finish: 15 minutes

Makes 4 servings

- 1 10-ounce package frozen raspberries or strawberries in syrup
- 2 bananas, peeled
- 2 cups wheat cereal flakes, crushed
- ½ teaspoon ground cinnamon
- 1 pint ice cream (any flavor)

1. Thaw raspberries according to the quick-thaw directions on package; set aside. Meanwhile, cut bananas into ½-inch slices. Divide banana slices among four dessert dishes; set aside.

2. Place cereal in a shallow dish; stir in cinnamon. Using an ice cream scoop, place one scoop of ice cream in crumbs; roll the ice cream to coat with crumbs. Transfer to a dessert dish with bananas. Repeat with three more scoops of ice cream. Sprinkle any remaining cereal mixture over ice cream in dishes. Spoon raspberries in syrup over each serving.

Per Serving: 410 cal., 13 g fat (8 g sat. fat), 68 mg chol., 174 mg sodium, 71 g carbo., 5 g fiber, 5 g pro.

Cereal-Coated Ice Cream Sundaes

Use whatever *ice cream and fruit* you have on hand
for this dessert. Just be sure to use bananas as the base.
The cereal adds a *pleasing crunch*.

Berries and Brownies

Start to Finish: 15 minutes

Makes 6 servings

- 2 cups fresh red raspberries
- 3 tablespoons sugar
- 1 teaspoon finely shredded orange peel
- 2 cups whipped cream
- 2 to 3 three-inch squares bakery brownies, cut into irregular chunks

1. Set aside ⅓ cup of the berries. In a medium bowl, combine the remaining berries, the sugar, and the orange peel. Place the berry mixture into a 4- to 5-cup serving bowl or divide among six dessert dishes.

2. Spoon whipped cream over raspberry mixture. Top with the brownie chunks and reserved raspberries.

Per Serving: 327 cal., 27 g fat (15 g sat. fat), 95 mg chol., 85 mg sodium, 19 g carbo., 3 g fiber, 3 g pro.

Baked Fruit Ambrosia

Baked Fruit Ambrosia

Prep: 10 minutes   *Bake:* 15 minutes

Makes 4 servings

- 2 medium oranges
- 1 8-ounce can pineapple tidbits (juice pack), drained
- ¼ teaspoon ground cinnamon
- 2 tablespoons shredded coconut
  Fresh raspberries (optional)

1. Preheat oven to 350°F. Finely shred enough peel from one of the oranges to make ½ teaspoon peel; set aside. Peel and section the two oranges. Cut orange sections into bite-size pieces.

2. Divide orange pieces and pineapple among four 6-ounce custard cups. Sprinkle with orange peel and cinnamon. Top with coconut.

3. Bake about 15 minutes or until fruit is heated through and coconut is golden. If desired, garnish with fresh raspberries. Serve warm.

Per Serving: 66 cal., 1 g fat (1 g sat. fat), 0 mg chol., 12 mg sodium, 14 g carbo., 2 g fiber, 1 g pro.

Easy-as-Peach Pie

No pie-making experience necessary. Your secret to a great pie is refrigerated piecrust with a free-form, no-crimp edge.

Prep: 20 minutes   Bake: 60 minutes   Stand: 45 minutes
Makes 6 to 8 servings

½	of a 15-ounce package rolled refrigerated unbaked piecrust (1 crust)
1	cup sugar
3	tablespoons cornstarch
4	cups sliced, peeled peaches or one 16-ounce package frozen unsweetened peach slices
1	cup fresh or frozen red raspberries Whipped cream or vanilla ice cream (optional)

1. Bring piecrust to room temperature according to package directions. Preheat oven to 350°F. Meanwhile, in a large bowl, combine sugar and cornstarch. Add peaches and raspberries; toss to coat. (If using frozen fruit, let stand for 15 to 30 minutes or until partially thawed.)

2. Ease crust into a 9-inch foil disposable pie pan or pie plate, allowing edges of crust to hang over edges of pan. Spoon peach mixture into pastry-lined pan. Fold crust edges over filling (crust will not totally cover fruit mixture).

3. Place pie pan in a foil-lined shallow baking pan. Bake on the bottom rack of the oven for 60 to 70 minutes or until pastry is golden brown and filling is bubbly.

4. Remove pan from oven and let stand for 45 minutes before serving. Serve warm. If desired, top with whipped cream.
Per Serving: 401 cal., 11 g fat (2 g sat. fat), 0 mg chol., 205 mg sodium, 76 g carbo., 5 g fiber, 4 g pro.

Seared Nectarines with Angel Food Cake

Angel food cake turns toasty when grilled. Combine it with grilled fruit, a few fresh berries, and a drizzle of honey for a summer-fresh dessert.

Start to Finish: 20 minutes
Makes 4 servings

2	tablespoons orange juice
1	teaspoon ground cinnamon
2	ripe medium nectarines and/or peaches, quartered and pitted
1	7-inch purchased angel food cake Honey Fresh raspberries and/or blueberries (optional) Ground cinnamon

1. In a small bowl, stir together orange juice and the 1 teaspoon cinnamon. Brush the nectarines with the juice mixture and reserve excess liquid for the angel food cake. For a charcoal grill, cook nectarines directly over medium coals for 2 to 3 minutes on each side. (For a gas grill, preheat grill. Reduce heat to medium. Cover and grill as above.)

2. Cut four 2-inch slices of angel food cake (reserve remaining cake for another use). Brush one side of cake slices with orange juice mixture.

3. Grill cake slices on the rack of an uncovered grill directly over medium coals for 1 to 2 minutes or until lightly browned. Turn and grill for 1 to 2 minutes more. (Or cook cake on a griddle over medium heat for 1 to 2 minutes per side.)

4. To serve, place each cake slice on a plate or in a bowl. Spoon nectarines on top or alongside. Drizzle with honey. If desired, top with fresh berries. Sprinkle with additional cinnamon.
Per Serving: 106 cal., 0 g fat, 0 mg chol., 213 mg sodium, 24 g carbo., 2 g fiber, 2 g pro.

Simple Lemon-Sugar Snaps

Be sure to buy the kind of cake mix that boasts "pudding in the mix." Otherwise the mixture will be too dry to shape.

Prep: 25 minutes *Bake:* 9 minutes per batch
Makes about 42 cookies

- ¾ cup butter, softened
- 1   egg
- 1   2-layer-size package lemon cake mix
     (with pudding in the mix)
- 1   cup yellow cornmeal
- 2   tablespoons finely shredded lemon peel
     Granulated sugar or coarse sugar (optional)

1. Preheat oven to 375°F. In a large mixing bowl, beat butter and egg with an electric mixer on medium to high speed for 30 seconds. Gradually beat in cake mix until combined; stir in cornmeal and lemon peel. If necessary, knead dough until combined.

2. Using 1 tablespoon of dough for each cookie, roll into 1-inch balls. If desired, roll balls in sugar. Arrange balls 2 inches apart on ungreased cookie sheets.

3. Bake for 9 to 10 minutes or until bottoms are lightly browned. Let cool on cookie sheet for 1 minute. Transfer to a wire rack; cool completely.
Per Serving: 99 cal., 5 g fat (2 g sat. fat), 14 mg chol., 114 mg sodium, 14 g carbo., 0 g fiber, 1 g pro.

Fruit and Cereal Drops

Prep: 25 minutes *Stand:* 1 hour
Makes about 24 cookies

- 2   cups rice and wheat cereal flakes
- ¾ cup mixed dried fruit bits
- ½ cup whole almonds, toasted and coarsely
     chopped
- 6   ounces vanilla-flavor candy coating,
     chopped
- 1   tablespoon shortening

1. In a large bowl, stir together cereal flakes, fruit bits, and almonds; set aside.

2. In a medium saucepan, melt candy coating and shortening over low heat. Pour coating mixture over fruit mixture; toss gently to coat.

3. Working quickly, drop the cereal mixture from teaspoons onto a cookie sheet lined with waxed paper. Let stand about 1 hour or until set (or freeze for 5 minutes).
To Store: Place cookies in layers separated by waxed paper in an airtight container; cover. Store at room temperature for up to 3 days. Do not freeze.
Per Serving: 81 cal., 4 g fat (2 g sat. fat), 0 mg chol., 21 mg sodium, 10 g carbo., 0 g fiber, 1 g pro.

Praline Crunch Bars

Toffee bits and pecans give basic cookie dough a tasty twist. Let the chocolate pieces melt from the heat of the bars then spread them for an easy topping.

Prep: 10 minutes *Bake:* 12 minutes *Stand:* 5 minutes
Chill: 10 minutes
Makes 28 bars

- 1   18-ounce roll refrigerated sugar cookie dough
- ½ cup toffee pieces
- ½ cup finely chopped pecans
- 1   12-ounce package miniature semisweet
     chocolate pieces
- ⅓ cup toffee pieces

1. Preheat oven to 350°F. In a large resealable plastic bag, place cookie dough, the ½ cup toffee pieces, and the pecans; knead to combine. Press dough evenly in an ungreased 13×9×2-inch baking pan.

2. Bake for 12 to 15 minutes or until golden brown. Immediately sprinkle with semisweet chocolate pieces. Let stand for 5 to 10 minutes or until chocolate is softened, then spread evenly over the bars. Sprinkle with the ⅓ cup toffee bits.

3. Chill for 10 to 15 minutes to set chocolate. Cut into bars.
To Store: Cover and chill for up to 3 days or freeze for up to 1 month.
Per Serving: 191 cal., 11 g fat (4 g sat. fat), 8 mg chol., 105 mg sodium, 19 g carbo., 2 g fiber, 1 g pro.

Praline Crunch Bars

Chocolate Ricotta Mousse

Start to Finish: 8 minutes
Makes 10 servings

6   ounces dark chocolate, chopped
1   15-ounce container part-skim
      ricotta cheese
¼   cup fat-free half-and-half
½   teaspoon vanilla
      Raspberries or small strawberries (optional)
      Mint leaves (optional)

1. Place chopped chocolate in a 2-cup glass measure or small microwave-safe bowl. Microwave, uncovered, on 70% power (medium-high) for 1 minute; stir. Microwave on 70% power for 1 to 2 minutes more or until chocolate is melted, stirring every 15 seconds.

2. In a food processor, combine ricotta cheese, half-and-half, and vanilla. Cover and process until combined. Add melted chocolate while food processor is running. Process until well combined. Spoon into demitasse cups or small bowls. Serve immediately, or cover and chill for up to 24 hours. If desired, garnish with fresh berries and mint leaves.

Per Serving: 153 cal., 9 g fat (2 g sat. fat), 14 mg chol., 63 mg sodium, 13 g carbo., 1 g fiber, 6 g pro.

Black Forest Trifle

Prep: 40 minutes   *Chill:* 30 minutes
Makes 10 servings

1   1-layer-size package chocolate cake mix
1   4-serving-size package instant chocolate
      pudding mix
2   cups milk
1   pound fresh pitted dark sweet cherries or one
      16-ounce package frozen unsweetened
      pitted dark sweet cherries, thawed and
      well drained
2   cups frozen whipped dessert topping, thawed
      Unsweetened cocoa powder (optional)

1. Prepare cake mix according to package directions, using an 8-inch square or round cake pan. Cool cake in pan on a wire rack for 10 minutes; remove cake from pan. Cut cake into 1-inch pieces.

2. Meanwhile, prepare pudding mix according to package directions using the 2 cups milk; cover and chill about 30 minutes or until set.

3. Place half of the cake cubes in a 3-quart trifle bowl. Spoon half the cherries over cake; spread half the pudding over cherries and top with half the whipped topping. Repeat layers. If desired, sprinkle with cocoa powder.

Make-Ahead Directions: Prepare as directed. Cover and chill for up to 4 hours.

Per Serving: 281 cal., 10 g fat (5 g sat. fat), 25 mg chol., 331 mg sodium, 43 g carbo., 2 g fiber, 4 g pro.

Rocky Road Parfaits

Layer chocolate pudding into these dreamy duotone desserts topped with a rocky road trio of chocolate, peanuts, and marshmallows.
Start to Finish: 20 minutes
Makes 4 servings

1   4-serving-size package chocolate or
      chocolate fudge instant pudding mix
2   cups milk
½   cup frozen whipped dessert topping, thawed
¼   cup unsalted peanuts, coarsely chopped
¼   cup tiny marshmallows
      Chocolate curls (optional)

1. Prepare pudding mix according to package directions using the 2 cups milk. Remove ¾ cup of the pudding and place in a small bowl; fold in whipped topping until combined.

2. Divide remaining plain chocolate pudding among four 6-ounce glasses or dessert dishes. Top with dessert topping mixture. Let stand for 5 to 10 minutes or until set.

3. Sprinkle with peanuts and marshmallows. If desired, garnish with chocolate curls (see tip, page 178).

Make-Ahead Directions: Prepare as directed through Step 2. Cover and chill parfaits for up to 24 hours. Serve as directed in Step 3.

Per Serving: 246 cal., 9 g fat (4 g sat. fat), 10 mg chol., 412 mg sodium, 34 g carbo., 1 g fiber, 7 g pro.

Rocky Road Parfaits

Peanut Butter Swirl Ice Cream Cake

Peanut Butter Swirl Ice Cream Cake

Use a generic, less expensive brand of cream-filled sandwich cookies for the crumb crust. No one will be able to taste the difference.

Prep: 45 minutes   Freeze: 6 to 24 hours
Makes 16 servings

½	gallon vanilla ice cream
24	chocolate sandwich cookies with white filling
5	tablespoons butter or margarine, melted
30	chocolate-covered wafer cookies or your favorite chocolate-covered stick-shape candy bar
⅔	cup peanut butter (not reduced-fat)
¼	cup honey
2	tablespoons cooking oil
½	of an 8-ounce container frozen whipped dessert topping, thawed
½	cup bottled hot fudge sauce

1. Remove ice cream from freezer 30 minutes before using. Place sandwich cookies in a food processor. Cover and process into fine crumbs. Add melted butter; cover and process until combined.

2. Line the sides of a 9-inch springform pan with wafer cookies. Reserve ¾ cup of the chocolate crumb mixture. Press the remaining crumb mixture evenly onto the bottom of the pan.

3. In a small bowl, stir together peanut butter, honey, and oil until combined. Spoon half of the ice cream into the pan; spread evenly. Spoon half of the peanut butter mixture over ice cream and spread to edges. Sprinkle evenly with the remaining chocolate crumb mixture, pressing mixture down with the back of a spoon.

4. Top with the remaining ice cream; spread evenly. Top with the remaining peanut butter mixture, spreading to edges. Pipe whipped topping over cake. Place the cake on a baking sheet, cover loosely, and freeze for 6 to 24 hours.

5. To serve, in a small saucepan, heat fudge sauce until warm. Drizzle over cake. Slice cake into wedges.

Per Serving: 539 cal., 33 g total fat (17 g sat. fat), 78 mg chol., 269 mg sodium, 54 g carbo., 1 g fiber, 7 g pro.

Black Forest Bread Pudding

Chocolate and cherries are an unbeatable combo in this crowd-pleasing dessert.

Prep: 25 minutes *Bake:* 70 minutes *Cool:* 45 minutes
Chill: 2 to 24 hours
Makes 16 to 20 servings

12	ounces black rye bread, cut into ½-inch slices
⅓	cup butter, softened
1	12- or 16-ounce package frozen pitted dark sweet cherries
2	12-ounce packages semisweet chocolate pieces
½	teaspoon ground cinnamon
3¼	cups whipping cream
¾	cup sugar
8	eggs, lightly beaten
½	teaspoon almond extract
	Whipped cream or vanilla ice cream (optional)
	Sliced almonds, toasted (optional)

1. Lightly butter a 3-quart rectangular baking dish. Spread bread slices with the ⅓ cup butter. Place bread slices in the prepared baking dish, overlapping as necessary to fit. Sprinkle with frozen cherries, half of the chocolate, and the cinnamon. Set aside.

2. In a medium saucepan, combine the remaining chocolate, 1 cup of the cream, and the sugar. Cook and stir just until chocolate melts. Gradually stir in the remaining 2¼ cups cream. In a very large bowl, combine eggs and almond extract; stir in melted chocolate mixture. Gradually pour over bread in dish (dish will be very full). Cover and chill for 2 to 24 hours.

3. Preheat oven to 325°F. Uncover bread pudding and place dish on a foil-lined baking sheet. Bake for 70 to 80 minutes or until the temperature in the center reaches 160°F. Cool on a wire rack for at least 45 minutes. Serve warm. If desired, top with whipped cream and almonds.

Per Serving: 546 cal., 38 g total fat (22 g sat. fat), 183 mg chol., 229 mg sodium, 51 g carbo., 4 g fiber, 8 g pro.

Baked Rice Pudding

Smooth and custardy, this Indian-style rice pudding makes the ideal ending for almost any meal.

Prep: 25 minutes *Bake:* 40 minutes
Makes 5 servings

3	egg whites
1	egg
1½	cups fat-free milk
¼	cup sugar
1	teaspoon vanilla
⅔	cup cooked rice
2	tablespoons snipped dried apricots and/or golden raisins
¼	teaspoon ground cardamom
¼	teaspoon finely shredded orange peel (optional)

1. Preheat oven to 325°F. In medium bowl, combine egg whites, egg, milk, sugar, and vanilla. Beat with whisk until combined but not foamy. Stir in rice, apricots and/or raisins, cardamom, and, if desired, orange peel.

2. Place five 6-ounce custard cups or souffl dishes in large shallow baking dish. Divide rice mixture among custard cups. Place baking dish on oven rack. Pour enough boiling water into baking dish around custard cups to a depth of 1 inch.

3. Bake about 40 minutes or just until set, stirring after 20 minutes. Serve warm or chilled.

Per Serving: 126 cal., 1 g total fat (0 g sat. fat), 44 mg chol., 84 mg sodium, 22 g carbo., 0 g fiber, 7 g pro.

DRIED FRUIT FACTS

Just because you don't have a specific dried fruit called for in a recipe doesn't mean you have to run out and buy it. Substitute equal amounts of dried cranberries, cherries, or blueberries for raisins; or an equal amount of snipped dates or apricots.

Golden Cake with Apricot-Nut Topping

Golden Cake with Apricot-Nut Topping

Another time, serve the tempting nut-and-apricot topper over purchased angel food cake.

Prep: 15 minutes *Bake:* 40 minutes *Cool:* 10 minutes
Makes 16 servings

- 1   2-layer-size yellow cake mix
- 1   15-ounce can unpeeled apricot halves in light syrup
- ⅔   cup unsweetened pineapple juice
- 2   teaspoons cornstarch
- ½   cup coarsely chopped blanched almonds
- 2   tablespoons shredded coconut, toasted

1. Preheat oven to 350°F. Prepare cake mix according to package directions. Bake in a greased and floured 10-inch tube pan for 40 to 45 minutes or until a toothpick inserted near the center comes out clean. Cool on wire rack 10 minutes. Remove cake from pan. Serve warm or cool completely on a wire rack.

2. While cake cools, rinse and drain apricot halves. Cut apricot halves into strips; set aside. In a small saucepan, combine ⅔ cup pineapple juice and cornstarch. Cook and stir until thickened and bubbly; cook and stir for 2 minutes more. Stir in nuts and apricot strips.

3. Place cake on a serving plate. Top with warm apricot mixture. Sprinkle with coconut. Serve immediately.

Per Serving: 240 cal., 11 g total fat (2 g sat. fat), 41 mg chol., 220 mg sodium, 34 g carbo., 1 g fiber, 3 g pro.

CAKE MIX
Purchase boxed cake and brownie mixes when they are on sale. They are handy to have in the pantry for a last-minute dessert when you have to bring something sweet to a potluck—and they cost less than bakery products.

When cooking apples instead of eating them out of hand, use a crisp variety, such as tart Granny Smith or sweet Golden Delicious so that the apples will keep their shape.

Apple Dumpling Roll-Ups

Prep: 15 minutes *Bake:* 25 minutes *Cool:* 30 minutes
Makes 8 servings

½	cup apple juice or apple cider
⅓	cup packed brown sugar
2	tablespoons butter
2	tablespoons granulated sugar
1	teaspoon ground cinnamon
1	large cooking apple, peeled (if desired), cored, and cut into 8 wedges
1	8-ounce package (8) refrigerated crescent rolls
1	teaspoon white coarse decorating sugar or granulated sugar
	Vanilla or cinnamon ice cream (optional)

1. Preheat oven to 375°F. Lightly grease a 2-quart square baking dish; set aside. In a small saucepan, combine apple juice, brown sugar, and butter. Cook over medium-low heat until butter is melted, stirring to dissolve brown sugar.

2. Meanwhile, in a medium bowl, stir together granulated sugar and cinnamon. Add apple wedges; toss gently to coat. Unroll crescent rolls; separate at perforations. Place a coated apple wedge along the wide edge of each roll. Roll up dough around apple wedges. Place in the prepared baking dish. Slowly drizzle apple juice mixture over filled rolls. Sprinkle with coarse sugar.

3. Bake, uncovered, for 25 to 30 minutes or until rolls are golden brown and apples are tender. Cool about 30 minutes before serving. Serve warm. If desired, serve with ice cream.

Per Serving: 201 cal., 9 g total fat (4 g sat. fat), 8 mg chol., 245 mg sodium, 28 g carbo., 1 g fiber, 2 g pro.

Pumpkin Pear Cake

Skip the frosting! When you invert the pan, a delicious caramel topping oozes over the fruit-studded cake.

Prep: 25 minutes *Bake:* 35 minutes *Cool:* 35 minutes
Makes 16 servings

1	cup packed brown sugar
⅓	cup butter, melted
1½	teaspoons cornstarch
2	15-ounce cans pear halves in light syrup, undrained
½	cup coarsely chopped pecans
1	package 2-layer-size spice cake mix
1	cup canned pumpkin

1. Preheat oven to 350°F. In a small bowl, combine brown sugar, melted butter, and cornstarch. Drain pears, reserving 3 tablespoons of the syrup. Stir the reserved 3 tablespoons syrup into brown sugar mixture. Pour mixture into an ungreased 13×9×2-inch baking pan. If desired, cut each pear half into a fan by making 3 or 4 lengthwise cuts ¼ inch from the stem end to the bottom. Arrange whole or fanned pear halves, cored sides down, on brown sugar mixture. Sprinkle with pecans.

2. Prepare cake mix according to package directions, except decrease the oil to 2 tablespoons and add the pumpkin. Slowly pour cake batter over pear halves, spreading evenly.

3. Bake, uncovered, for 35 to 40 minutes or until a toothpick inserted near the center comes out clean. Cool in pan on a wire rack for 5 minutes.

4. Run a thin metal spatula around edges of cake. Carefully invert cake into a 15×10×1-inch baking pan or onto a very large serving platter with slightly raised edges. Cool about 30 minutes before serving. Serve warm.

Per Serving: 337 cal., 15 g total fat (4 g sat. fat), 51 mg chol., 254 mg sodium, 51 g carbo., 2 g fiber, 3 g pro.

Ginger Peach Freeze

Prep: 10 minutes *Stand:* 30 minutes *Freeze:* 3 hours
Makes 8 servings

- 1 cup water
- 1 cup sugar
- 3 tablespoons lemon juice
- ¼ teaspoon ground ginger
- 1 16-ounce package frozen unsweetened peach slices
  Fresh peach slices (optional)

1. In a medium saucepan, combine water, sugar, lemon juice, and ginger. Bring to boiling. Remove from heat and add frozen peaches. Let stand about 30 minutes or until peaches are thawed and mixture has cooled.

2. Transfer peach mixture, half at a time, to a blender. Cover and blend until smooth. Pour mixture into a 2-quart rectangular baking dish. Cover and freeze for 3 to 4 hours. Break up mixture with a fork and serve. If desired, garnish with fresh peach slices.

Per Serving: 119 cal., 0 g fat, 0 mg chol., 1 mg sodium, 31 g carbo., 1 g fiber, 0 g pro.

Tropical Angel Cake

Start to Finish: 15 minutes
Makes 12 servings

- 1 8- to 9-inch purchased angel food cake
- 3 cups desired fruit-flavored sherbet
- ¼ cup unsweetened pineapple juice
- 1 8-ounce container frozen whipped dessert topping or frozen light whipped dessert topping, thawed
  Fresh raspberries (optional)

1. Slice cake in half horizontally. Hollow out insides, leaving two 1-inch-thick shells. Spoon sherbet into bottom shell. Set top half, hollow side down, over bottom. Poke holes in top using a long wooden skewer or the tines of a long fork. Drizzle pineapple juice over top of cake.

2. Frost top and sides of cake with whipped topping. Serve immediately or cover loosely with plastic wrap and freeze for up to 1 week. If desired, garnish with fresh raspberries.

Per Serving: 222 cal., 4 g fat (4 g sat. fat), 0 mg chol., 305 mg sodium, 41 g carbo., 2 g fiber, 3 g pro.

Easy Apple Crisp

Prep: 5 minutes *Bake:* 20 minutes
Makes 6 servings

- 2 21-ounce cans apple pie filling
- ¼ cup dried cherries, cranberries, or mixed dried fruit bits
- 1½ cups granola
  Vanilla ice cream (optional)

1. Preheat oven to 375°F. In a 2-quart square baking dish, stir together the pie filling and dried cherries; sprinkle with granola.

2. Bake, uncovered, for 20 to 25 minutes or until heated through. Serve warm. If desired, top with ice cream.

Per Serving: 326 cal., 2 g fat (0 g sat. fat), 0 mg chol., 155 mg sodium, 79 g carbo., 4 g fiber, 3 g pro.

Angel Food Cake with Lemon Cream and Berries

Blueberries not in season? Substitute another seasonal berry for them in this simple, light dessert.

Start to Finish: 15 minutes
Makes 16 servings

- 3 6-ounce cartons lemon yogurt
- 1 4-serving-size package instant vanilla pudding mix
- 1 8-ounce container frozen light whipped dessert topping, thawed
  Fresh blueberries
- 1 8- to 9-inch purchased angel food cake, cubed
  Fresh mint sprigs (optional)

1. For lemon cream, in a medium bowl, whisk together yogurt and one-fourth of the pudding mix until smooth. Gradually add remaining pudding mix to yogurt, whisking until smooth after each addition. Fold in whipped topping, half at a time.

2. Serve lemon cream and berries over cubed cake. If desired, garnish with mint sprigs.

Per Serving: 172 cal., 2 g fat (2 g sat. fat), 2 mg chol., 269 mg sodium, 34 g carbo., 4 g fiber, 3 g pro.

index

index